Legal Capacity & Gender

Anna Arstein-Kerslake

Legal Capacity & Gender

Realising the Human Right to Legal Personhood and Agency of Women, Disabled Women, and Gender Minorities

Springer

Anna Arstein-Kerslake
Melbourne Law School
University of Melbourne
Melbourne, VIC, Australia

ISBN 978-3-030-63492-6 ISBN 978-3-030-63493-3 (eBook)
https://doi.org/10.1007/978-3-030-63493-3

This Springer imprint is published by the registered company Springer Nature Switzerland AG.
The registered company address is: Gewerbestrasse 11, 6330 Cham, Switzerland

Foreword

The concept of legal capacity has long mystified ethicists, lawyers, and policymakers. Legal capacity may have an abstruse and technical quality, but it is in fact central to the way we engage in society. It regulates, for example, who can vote, enter contracts, inherit, marry or form intimate relationships, and make decisions about their own medical treatment. This path-breaking book addresses a long-hidden problem—the way that legal capacity is bestowed and denied according to a person's status and power. Scholars have paid little attention to the reality that some marginalised groups of people are restricted in how they can participate in political and social communities via denials of legal capacity. Gender plays a critical role in these restrictions.

Here, Anna Arstein-Kerslake builds on her impressive work in the field of human rights and disabilities to investigate a broader field of enquiry. She deftly marshals an extraordinary range of literature in her journey—including philosophical, legal, sociological, and psychological writing—as well as drawing on her own experiences working with civil society and the United Nations. Dr Arstein-Kerslake offers a historical exploration of the allocation and denial of legal capacity and charts the engrained patterns of discrimination that developed. But restrictions on legal capacity are not just a historical relic and Dr Arstein-Kerslake highlights the continuing oppressive treatment of gendered categories of people: women, disabled women, and gender minorities (especially those who resist binary identities).

The book gives a finely grained account of the international jurisprudence on legal capacity. It shows how a right to legal capacity emerged from the right to recognition as a person before the law, first set out in Article 6 of the 1948 Universal Declaration of Human Rights. This right, often overlooked or misunderstood, was elaborated in increasing detail in a series of United Nations treaties, culminating in Article 12 of the 2006 Convention on the Rights of Persons with Disabilities. This provision presents legal capacity as involving both personhood and agency. It guarantees the right to legal capacity 'on an equal basis with others in all aspects of life' and obliges states to support persons with disabilities so that they can actually exercise legal capacity. It also details the need for safeguards to allow the right to be effectively realised.

Dr Arstein-Kerslake guides the reader through the complex debates around, and the politics of, Article 12. Some states have resisted giving the provision its full force, whittling back its scope through 'interpretative declarations' made at the time of ratification. Others have struggled to implement the right because of lack of experience or deep-seated beliefs about disability.

Dr Arstein-Kerslake skilfully deploys critical social theory along with legal analysis to illuminate the concept of gender, drawing from feminist, queer, and disability studies literatures. She shows the power of an intersectional analysis to uncover the linkages between legal capacity and privilege. The book traverses images of women's irrationality, incapacity of persons with disabilities, and the deviance of gender minorities and tracks the tenacity of these views in modern legal systems.

Despite the disturbing picture of gender oppression that emerges from Dr Arstein-Kerslake's careful research, this book is infused with optimism about the possibility of change. Dr Arstein-Kerslake argues that legal capacity must be available for everyone on the basis of equality. She proposes the notion of a 'continuum of support' to respond to people's differing abilities for decision-making.

This book juggles three significant tasks with aplomb. First, it presents a contextual history of the development of the right to legal capacity. Second, it forges new ground in scholarly terms, highlighting the role that gender plays in the construction of personhood and agency. Third, its clear identification of the paths to secure and sustain the right to legal capacity will be a valuable companion in campaigns for law reform, and for states that wish to deliver on the promise of the CRPD. Dr Arstein-Kerslake identifies striking examples of the right in action from Peru, Ireland, the United Kingdom, and Australia.

Written with clarity and spirit, the book is no dry legal tome. It is engaging and passionate and makes clear the urgency of addressing legal capacity. This rich book will guide, challenge, and inspire in equal measure.

Melbourne Law School, Carlton, VIC, Australia
October 2020

Hilary Charlesworth

Preface

The right to legal capacity is a new line of scholarly inquiry. It had been largely ignored by academics until the 2006 Convention on the Rights of Persons with Disabilities (CRPD), which provided new detail to the right to legal capacity (Dhanda 2006; Minkowitz 2006; Dinerstein 2011). The author's 2017 book, *Restoring Voice to People with Cognitive Disabilities* (Cambridge University Press), was the first book published on the topic. She has also published numerous journal articles on the subject and has been invited to consult with international and domestic government bodies across the globe (Flynn and Arstein-Kerslake 2014; Arstein-Kerslake 2015, 2019; Arstein-Kerslake and Flynn 2016, 2017; Arstein-Kerslake and Black 2020). Over and over again, she has uncovered denials of the right to legal capacity that are uniquely experienced by women, disabled women, or gender minorities (Arstein-Kerslake 2015, 2019). To date, there has been no significant scholarly work in this area. This book fills that gap.

This book examines this new line of scholarly inquiry, the right to legal capacity, with a focus on the role of gender. It uses human rights law, critical social theory, and selected domestic law and policy to provide an analysis of how gender influences denials of the right to legal capacity and what protections are needed to secure the right. The aim is that the book is both a scholarly analysis and a useful tool for law reform.

The book draws on the research and knowledge the author has gained as a leader in the field of legal capacity rights. It builds on her 2017 book and explores the far-reaching implications of Article 12 of the CRPD. Most jurisdictions are struggling to understand the meaning of Article 12 and to bring their laws into compliance. The author's 2017 book laid out the history, theoretical underpinnings, and legal meaning of the right to legal capacity. This book begins to explore the multitude of practical implications of Article 12 in order to provide guidance for those struggling jurisdictions. It will focus on gender because some of the most significant oppression as a result of denials of legal capacity occur on the basis of gender (Arstein-Kerslake 2019; Cannoot 2019). Women, disabled women, and gender minorities are suffering from historical and modern denials of their legal agency and personhood—the two components of legal capacity (Devereux 2014). This book reveals these denials and the resulting oppression. It also presents a way forward. Steps towards the realisation of the right to legal capacity can be achieved through law, policy, and practice reform. This book presents examples of good practice in such reform and makes recommendations for further reform to secure the right to legal capacity for women, disabled women, and gender minorities.

Melbourne, VIC, Australia Anna Arstein-Kerslake

References

Arstein-Kerslake, Anna. 2015. Understanding Sex: The Right to Legal Capacity to Consent to Sex. *Disability & Society* 30: 1459–1473. https://doi.org/10.1080/09687599.2015.1116059.

———. 2019. Gendered Denials: Vulnerability Created by Barriers to Legal Capacity for Women and Disabled Women. *International Journal of Law and Psychiatry* 66: 101501. https://doi.org/10.1016/j.ijlp.2019.101501.

Arstein-Kerslake, Anna, and Jennifer Black. 2020. Right to Legal Capacity in Therapeutic Jurisprudence: Insights from Critical Disability Theory and the Convention on the Rights of Persons with Disabilities. *International Journal of Law and Psychiatry* 68: 101535. https://doi.org/10.1016/j.ijlp.2019.101535.

Arstein-Kerslake, Anna, and Eilionóir Flynn. 2016. The General Comment on Article 12 of the Convention on the Rights of Persons with Disabilities: A Roadmap for Equality Before the Law. *The International Journal of Human Rights* 20: 471–490. https://doi.org/10.1080/13642987.2015.1107052.

———. 2017. The Right to Legal Agency: Domination, Disability and the Protections of Article 12 of the Convention on the Rights of Persons with Disabilities. *International Journal of Law in Context* 13: 22–38. https://doi.org/10.1017/S1744552316000458.

Cannoot, Pieter. 2019. '#WontBeErased': The Effects of (De)pathologisation and (De)medicalisation on the Legal Capacity of Trans* Persons. *International Journal of Law and Psychiatry* 66: 101478. https://doi.org/10.1016/j.ijlp.2019.101478.

Devereux, Cecily. 2014. Hysteria, Feminism, and Gender Revisited: The Case of the Second Wave. *English Studies in Canada* 40: 19–45. https://doi.org/10.1353/esc.2014.0004.

Dhanda, Amita. 2006. Legal Capacity in the Disability Rights Convention: Stranglehold of the Past or Lodestar for the Future Symposium: The United Nations Convention on the Rights of Persons with Disabilities. *Syracuse Journal of International Law and Commerce*: 429–462.

Dinerstein, Robert D. 2011. Implementing Legal Capacity Under Article 12 of the UN Convention on the Rights of Persons with Disabilities: The Difficult Road from Guardianship to Supported Decision-Making Human Rights and the Protection of Persons with Disabilities. *Human Rights Brief*: 8–74.

Flynn, Eilionoir, and Anna Arstein-Kerslake. 2014. Legislating Personhood: Realising the Right to Support in Exercising Legal Capacity. *International Journal of Law in Context* 10: 81–104. https://doi.org/10.1017/S1744552313000384.

Minkowitz, Tina. 2006. The United Nations Convention on the Rights of Persons with Disabilities and the Right to Be Free from Nonconsensual Psychiatric Interventions Symposium: The United Nations Convention on the Rights of Persons with Disabilities. *Syracuse Journal of International Law and Commerce*: 405–428.

Acknowledgements

I would first and foremost like to thank my daughter, Freya. I began writing this book when she was 6 months old. She graciously allowed me to write between nursing, pram naps, and tummy time. I hope that this book will contribute, in some small way, to making the world a more equitable place for her to live in.

I would also like to thank my partner, Matthias, for his consistent support—and, in particular for cooking, baking, and cleaning. Not only is the food delicious, but without his efforts, I would not have had the time to write this book, nor the nourishment necessary to do so.

I would also like to thank Professor Eilionoir Flynn for ongoing inspiration, in many ways, but specifically in securing the right to legal capacity for women and disabled women. Her work is continually inspiring—as is her friendship.

I would also like to thank Professor Mary Donnelly and Dr Claire Murray at University College Cork, Ireland for inviting me to be part of the special issue of the International Journal of Law and Psychiatry entitled 'Gendering Mental Health and Capacity Law'. In particular, I would like to thank them and the rest of the workshop participants for their invaluable feedback and comments on early drafts of portions of this book.

I would also like to thank Professor Hilary Charlesworth for writing the forward to this book. Her work on international law has influenced me significantly and I believe all international law students should engage with her work.

I would also like to thank Tina Minkowitz and Professor Gerard Quinn who inspired me to work on the right to legal capacity. Their work is a guiding light for me.

I would also like to thank Melbourne Law School for creating a rich and collegiate environment which facilitated the development and creation of this book.

Finally, I would like to thank the team at Springer Law—in particular, I would like to thank Anke Seyfried and Julia Bieler for their prompt and thorough work—without their wonderful assistance, this book would not have been possible.

Contents

1 Right to Legal Capacity: Debates and Legal Argument 1
1.1 Introduction 1
1.1.1 Women, Disabled Women, and Gender Minorities as Minority Groups 1
1.1.2 Social Model and the Term 'Disabled Women' 2
1.1.3 Neo-liberal Capitalism, Individual Rights, and the Importance of Legal Capacity 4
1.1.4 Right to Legal Capacity of Women, Disabled Women, and Gender Minorities 4
1.1.5 Focus on 'Global North' 6
1.1.6 Overview of Chap. 1 6
1.2 History of the Right: UDHR to CRPD 7
1.3 Debates in the Drafting of Article 12 CRPD 10
1.4 General Comment No. 1: UN CRPD Committee's Interpretation of Legal Capacity 13
1.4.1 Solidification of Legal Capacity as Including Personhood and Agency 14
1.4.2 Legal Capacity Should Not Be Denied on the Basis of Mental Capacity 14
1.4.3 Definition of Substituted Decision-Making 15
1.4.4 Elements of Support for the Exercise of Legal Capacity . . . 15
1.5 Resistance to Article 12 CRPD 19
1.6 Argument for Legal Capacity on an Equal Basis for All 22
1.7 Conclusion 23
References 25

2 Personhood: Perspectives from Critical Feminist, Disability and Queer Studies 29
2.1 Introduction 29
2.2 Moral and Legal Personhood 30

2.3 Personhood and Critical Social Theory . . . 33
2.3.1 Critical Feminist Theory and Personhood . . . 37
2.3.2 Critical Disability Theory and Personhood . . . 48
2.3.3 Critical Queer Theory and Personhood . . . 54
2.3.4 Conclusion on Personhood and Critical Feminist, Disability, and Queer Theory . . . 59
2.4 Power and Privilege: Importance of Legal Personhood . . . 59
2.5 Conclusion . . . 61
References . . . 61

3 Gender, Disability and Decision-Making: Historical Discrimination . . . 67
3.1 Introduction . . . 67
3.2 Women and Decision-Making: Myth of Hysteria . . . 68
3.3 Disability and Decision-Making: Myth of Incapacity . . . 72
3.4 Gender Minorities and Decision-Making: Myth of Illness . . . 75
3.5 Conclusion . . . 79
References . . . 80

4 Gendered Denials: Law, Policy and Practice . . . 83
4.1 Introduction . . . 83
4.2 Historical Denials . . . 84
4.2.1 Women: Voting, Contracting and Marriage . . . 84
4.2.2 Disabled Women: Institutionalisation, Eugenics, and Reproductive Choice . . . 87
4.2.3 Gender Minorities: Forced Treatment and Criminalisation . . . 91
4.3 Modern Denials . . . 95
4.3.1 Women: Immigration, Inheritance, Contracting, Reproductive Choice, and Consent to Sex . . . 95
4.3.2 Disabled Women: Guardianship, Forced Sterilisation and Consent to Sex . . . 99
4.3.3 Gender Minorities: Gender Recognition, Marriage, and Reproductive Choice . . . 105
4.4 Conclusion . . . 107
References . . . 108

5 Vulnerability Created by Legal Capacity Denials . . . 117
5.1 Introduction . . . 117
5.2 Vulnerability . . . 117
5.3 Vulnerability as a Social Construct . . . 119
5.4 Creating Vulnerability: Gender, Legal Capacity Barriers, Autonomy, and Vulnerability . . . 122
5.4.1 Creating Vulnerability by Denying Reproductive and Sexual Choice of Women, Disabled Women, and Gender Minorities . . . 122

5.4.2 Creating Vulnerability in Women, Disabled Women, and Gender Minorities Under Guardianship with Limited Decision-Making Control Over Their Own Lives 126
5.4.3 Creating Vulnerability Through Forced Psychiatric Treatment of Women, Disabled Women, and Gender Minorities 127
5.4.4 Creating Vulnerability in Gender Minorities Through the Exclusionary Effect of Gender Binary Requirements . . . 128
5.5 Conclusion 129
References 130

6 Creating Change: Examples of Modern Reform and Recommendations 135
6.1 Introduction 135
6.2 Case Studies: Examples to Learn From 135
6.2.1 Peru: Guardianship Abolished 136
6.2.2 Ireland: Capacity to Consent to Sex 138
6.2.3 Malta: Gender Recognition 146
6.3 Conclusion 149
6.4 Reform Recommendations 149
References 151

Chapter 1
Right to Legal Capacity: Debates and Legal Argument

1.1 Introduction

The recognition of an individual's legal capacity is the recognition of an individual as a decision-maker. It elevates the individual in the social order. They are recognised as a legal person and a legal actor and they possess the ability to leverage legal relationships and change the legal landscape that they are existing within. Equality requires not only the absence of discrimination but also such means to navigate our complex social world. In this way, the freedom to make decisions and to have those decisions respected is core to equality. Women, disabled women, and gender minorities experience denials of the right to legal capacity at higher rates and in unique ways. These denials are often due to discrimination and they can result in women, disabled women, and gender minorities lacking the tools necessary to wield power and inhabit positions of privilege.

1.1.1 Women, Disabled Women, and Gender Minorities as Minority Groups

Women, disabled women, and gender minorities are discussed, at times, in this book as three separate minority groups. They are minority groups because they experience social marginalisation in various ways as a result of their membership in these groups. These groups are discussed as separate intentionally in order to acknowledge that there are unique experiences of decision-making restrictions that individuals within these groups have experienced that are directly due to their membership in one of these groups. It is also important to acknowledge that many people may be a member of more than one of these groups—as well as other additional groups, such as ethnic or religious minorities. Where possible, I will try to shed light on experiences of people that are subjected to decision-making restrictions and have

A. Arstein-Kerslake, *Legal Capacity & Gender*,
https://doi.org/10.1007/978-3-030-63493-3_1

intersectional identities across multiple groups, because these experiences are also unique from the experiences of people that only hold membership in one minority group.

Disabled women, in particular, are always both women and disabled women. However, I believe it is important to recognise and discuss the distinction between disabled women and the larger group of women. Disabled women experience marginalisation in a unique way and at a higher rate than non-disabled women. Separating the groups may seem to imply that disabled women are a distinct group from women. However, I discuss the two groups separately to identify the unique experiences that disabled women have, not to signal that disabled women are not an integral and inherent part of the larger minority group of women.

Terminology related to sexual and gender minorities is not consistent in academic literature or elsewhere (Eliason 2014). The term 'gender minorities' is used in this book to refer to individuals who experience and/or express gender as non-binary. I have chosen this term and other related terms in an effort to use terminology that is consistent with the queer scholarship and the queer rights movement (Wojcik 1994; Butler 2004; Spade 2009; Rahman 2014; Spade 2015; Altman and Symons 2016; Langlois 2017). As used in this book, the term 'gender minorities' includes transgender, intersex, transsexual, and other non-binary people. The term 'transgender' is used to refer to people who identify as a different gender from their sex at birth—and those that are gender nonconforming (Currah 2006; Eliason 2014). The term 'intersex' is used to refer to individuals who have sex organs that are gender indeterminate (Blizzard 2002; Preves 2003; Harper 2007; Karkazis 2008). The term 'cisgender' is used to refer to non-transgender people or individuals who identify with the same gender as their sex at birth (Cava 2016, p. 1). In this book, 'gender minorities' is differentiated from 'sexual minorities.' Sexual minorities is used, in this book, to refer to those whose sexual preference is other than heterosexual. This book primarily discusses gender minorities, as opposed to sexual minorities, because it focuses on commonalities in experiences of legal capacity barriers and denials on the basis of gender, not sexual preference—although research in this area is also needed.

1.1.2 Social Model and the Term 'Disabled Women'

I have chosen to use the terms 'disabled women' and 'disabled people' to acknowledge the social model of disability. The social model of disability theorises that disability is created by an individual's social environment. As such, many scholars and activists adhering to the social model, prefer the use of terminology that places the word 'disabled' first, in acknowledgement that the individual is disabled by the environment (Mallett and Slater 2014; Andrews et al. 2019). According to the social model, an individual with an impairment only becomes disabled when social barriers are erected that prevent the individual from engaging, on an equal basis, in the social and physical world (Oliver 2013; Shakespeare 2016). For example, a woman becomes disabled when she is prevented from attending sexual education courses because she has a cognitive impairment. That lack of information—or accessible information—can disable the women to the point of placing her in sexually abusive situations because she has not been given the same education as others on the management of sexual relationships. According to the social model, it is this social barrier—the lack of accessible information related to sexual education—that disables the women, not her cognitive impairment. If the woman were to receive the same sexual education information available to others in a format that was accessible to her, she may have the tools necessary to prevent sexual abuse—or, at least, be able to prevent sexual abuse in the same way or to the same capability level as those without cognitive impairment. In this way, it is the social environment that is disabling the individual, not her impairment.

This book uses the social model of disability throughout its analyses (Oliver 2013). It considers an individual as disabled when they are not able to participate in the social and physical world on an equal basis with others. In line with the social model of disability, the discussions within this book assume that social barriers are disabling individuals—as opposed to assuming that an individual is disabled due to their actual or perceived impairment alone (Hughes and Paterson 1997; Traustadóttir 2009). In other words, I place the burden of disabling on an unaccommodating social environment instead of on the individual or their impairment. However, I do not want to give the impression that the embodied experience of the individual is not critical to the experience of disability (Shakespeare 2013). For some, it may be solely the social environment that interacts with their actual or perceived impairment to create barriers to participation, citizenship, and other areas that cause the individual to be disabled. For others, they may have bodily experiences of pain, discomfort, or other physical manifestations of impairment that create barriers to participation, citizenship, and other areas that cause the individual to be disabled—and changes in the social environment may not alleviate the situation. This book does not engage with a full debate or theoretical discussion of the social model—however, I do utilise the social model as a lens through which to examine law, policy, and practice that create barriers to legal capacity for women, disabled women, and gender minorities. In line with the social model, I assume that most of the barriers to legal capacity that women, disabled women, and gender minorities face are due to unaccommodating and prejudicial law, policy, and practice. I also assume that where these aspects of the social environment are reformed appropriately—sometimes necessitating extra measures to support the unique socio-political position of women, disabled women, and gender minorities—these groups would be able to enjoy legal capacity on an equal basis with others.

1.1.3 Neo-liberal Capitalism, Individual Rights, and the Importance of Legal Capacity

Many of our neo-liberal capitalist systems have evolved to increasingly incorporate welfare models and socialist goals which include values of equality and efforts towards achieving some level of wealth distribution. Nonetheless, the position of the individual is primary and the individual's ability to navigate social and legal relationships plays a significant role in determining that individual's position in the social order. For these reasons, the individual's recognition as a decision-maker and their freedom and ability to engage in legal decision-making is core to the individual's success in our neoliberal capitalist systems. It is the recognition of an individual's legal capacity that gives them recognition as a decision-maker and the ability to have their legal decisions respected and enforced.

There are multitudes of critiques of the neo-liberal capitalist system—however, it remains the prevailing social structure that we live within in much of the world. As such, in this book, I am not challenging the neo-liberal capitalist model—instead, I acknowledge the prevalence of the model and the values that it espouses that permeate so much of civilization. One of those values is the importance of the individual in the social order and the importance of individual autonomy and decision-making power in order to achieve success in such a model. It is this importance of the individual that has played a prominent role in the development of individual rights—including human rights law. While I would question many aspects of neo-liberal capitalist theory, the rights of the individual is one aspect of neo-liberal capitalist theory that I believe has—perhaps paradoxically—brought about many positive advances, including the human rights framework. It is important to acknowledge, however, that it is likely that human rights law itself will never have the power to eliminate the inequalities that capitalism creates and perpetuates. What it may do, is create a framework for establishing a bare minimum level of equality that is achievable. This would include equality in the right to decision-making—the right to legal capacity—which, as discussed above, is essential for the individual to have the tools necessary to navigate the neo-liberal capitalist social order and to have a chance at elevating their position within that social order.

1.1.4 Right to Legal Capacity of Women, Disabled Women, and Gender Minorities

Women, disabled women, and gender minorities have suffered denials of their ability to be decision-makers as well as denials of the recognition and enforcement of their decisions. This may be one of the most significant contributory factors in the inequality of individuals within these groups—because, as mentioned above, without the power to make decisions, an individual is significantly disadvantaged in our current neo-liberal capitalist social order. For this reason, this book delves into the history of the denial of decision-making power to these groups. It discusses the human right to decision-making—the right to legal capacity—and what impact the realisation of such a right may have on the inequalities experienced by these groups.

Many of the decision-making barriers that women, disabled women, and gender minorities experience are denials of legal capacity. They experience these denials at high rates. Historically, women have been denied legal capacity to vote, inherit, contract and many other areas—many of which continue today. Disabled women have their legal capacity denied in various ways, including through laws that deny decision-making on the basis of disability, such as guardianship, mental health laws and capacity to consent laws. Gender minorities also experience legal capacity denials in various ways, for example situations where government issued identification, such as passports, are required for the exercise of legal capacity but require gender binary identification. In these situations, it may be impossible or very dangerous for some gender minorities to acquire or use such identification—resulting in an inability to exercise legal capacity. In these ways and many others, disability, gender, and the intersection between the two can result in marginalisation through legal capacity denial.

One commonality between these groups is that the denial of decision-making and legal capacity has often resulted from the prejudicial notion that individuals in these groups lack the appropriate level of rationality or cognitive skills to engage in legal decision-making. Women have been burdened with the assumption that their bodies—and their reproductive systems, in particular—render them irrational or 'hysterical.' Disabled women are burdened with the vastly overinclusive notion that disability renders an individual deficient in decision-making skills. Gender minorities are often thought of as suffering from a mental illness that causes their non-binary gender expression and experiences and may be perceived to be unable to make rational choices for themselves. In this book, I explore these historical prejudices against the decision-making skills of individuals in these groups. I also explore the new interpretation of the human right to legal capacity in the United Nations Convention on the Rights of Persons with Disabilities (CRPD) that articulates that even if an individual does have difficulty with decision-making, it is not a justification for the denial of legal capacity (Committee on the Rights of Persons with Disabilities 2014, p. 3). In this way, I argue that the historical notion of irrationality of women, disabled women, and gender minorities is inaccurate and discriminatory. In addition, I argue that it has been incorrectly used as a justification for the denial of legal capacity.

This book identifies patterns of oppression through legal capacity barriers and denial in various jurisdictions. It discusses modern law that continues to maintain such barriers and execute such denials. It also identifies good practice in the protection of the right to legal capacity from various jurisdictions around the world. Finally, it begins to explore the ways in which existing law, policy and practice can be reformed.

1.1.5 *Focus on 'Global North'*

In this book, I will be primarily discussing social and legal structures in the 'global north'—including, in particular, the United Kingdom, Ireland, the United States, Canada, and Australia. However, in places, I will draw on examples from elsewhere around the world. The focus on the global north is due to my own interest in legal and political theory in this region—it is also due to the availability of research in English on legal systems in this area. A deeper examination of the denial of decision-making and legal capacity to women, disabled women, and gender minorities in other regions is also much needed—and I hope it is undertaken at some point in the near future.

1.1.6 *Overview of Chap. 1*

In order to begin exploring the role of decision-making denial in the development and perpetuation of inequality for women, disabled women, and gender minorities, it is important to first establish how the human right to legal capacity protects decision-making, where the right comes from, and what exactly it may have the power to protect. The first chapter of this book explores this—it discusses the origins of the right to legal capacity through the development of the right to equality before the law and it then goes on to interpret the right to legal capacity based on human rights jurisprudence.

The right to legal capacity is not unique to one group. All people have the same right to legal capacity, regardless of group membership—men, women, disabled women, refugees, gender minorities, and all other individuals have a right to legal capacity on an equal basis. This universality is true for all human rights—in general, no right applies more or differently to one individual or one group of people (Donnelly 2013). However, the means to achieve realisation of a particular right can vary greatly between individuals and groups. This variation is due to a number of factors, including a need to break historical patterns of denial of the right as well as social marginalisation that may lead to a unique social position for an individual or group and may require correspondingly unique efforts to ensure that particular rights can be realised for that person or group.

This chapter explores the foundations of the right to legal capacity and provides an argument for the modern interpretation of this right in human rights law. This interpretation is applicable for all peoples right to legal capacity—not only women, disabled women, or gender minorities. This book begins with this discussion in order to establish what the right to legal capacity is so that the following chapters of the book can discuss how that right has been denied to women, disabled women, and gender minorities as well as the unique solutions that are necessary for the realisation of the right for these groups.

This chapter introduces the right to legal capacity found in Article 12 of the CRPD. It discusses the history of the right, beginning with Article 6 of the Universal Declaration of Human Rights (UDHR) and Article 16 of the 1966 International Covenant of Civil and Political Rights (ICCPR) and continuing to Article 12 of the 2006 Convention on the Rights of Persons with Disabilities (CRPD). It draws on the *travaux préparatoires* of the CRPD, the documentation of the treaty negotiation, to discuss the debates during the drafting of Article 12—including the contentious inclusion of both personhood and agency with the definition of legal capacity (Dhanda 2006). It then discusses the 2014 General Comment on Article 12 adopted by the Committee on the Rights of Persons with Disabilities, the United Nations monitoring body for the CRPD. I draw on my experience drafting the General Comment in Geneva with the Committee (Arstein-Kerslake and Flynn 2016). The chapter then explores the resistance to Article 12 (Freeman et al. 2015). It illuminates the legal arguments as well the ethical debates. The chapter concludes with an argument supporting the right to legal capacity on an equal basis for all people—an argument for universal legal capacity (Dhanda 2006). It describes both the practical and legal basis for this argument and a way forward towards its realisation.

1.2 History of the Right: UDHR to CRPD

The right to legal capacity, at its core, is the right of an individual to make choices for themselves and for those choices to be recognised by the law and by other legal entities. It is also the right of the individual to be recognised as a legal entity. It is the right to be a legal person and a legal agent (McSherry 2012). I will discuss these concepts more in the following two sections—first, I will lay out the history of this right within United Nations human rights law.

The right to legal capacity in the CRPD is guaranteed in a provision of the broader right to equal recognition before the law. It is relevant to note that the CRPD did not create any new rights—the international bill of human rights contains the negotiated and agreed upon gamut of universal human rights and all proceeding United Nations human rights treaties are merely re-enumerations of those core rights in relation to particular groups or particular circumstances (Kayess and French 2008). The international bill of human rights includes the non-binding Universal Declaration of Human Rights (UDHR) as well as the binding International Covenant of Civil and Political Rights (ICCPR) and the International Covenant of Economic, Social, and Cultural Rights (ICESCR). Therefore, all rights within the CRPD, including the right to legal capacity, have ‘parent’ rights within these documents—in other words, they are all rights that are a part of the rights in those core UN treaties. The parent right of the right to legal capacity is the right to equal recognition before the law.

Not all scholars agree that the CRPD, in particular, has not created new rights. Some argue that, although the intention was that the CRPD not create any new rights—in actuality, it has enumerated some rights in such a way that new rights with new state obligations have emerged (Kayess and French 2008). The counter argument is that these seemingly new rights and state obligations have always existed—under the ICCPR or ICESCR—they were just never fully explained or understood until they were included in the CRPD. Regardless, the right to legal capacity, as enumerated in Article 12 of the CRPD, emanates from the right to equal recognition before the law, which can be found in the UDHR and the ICCPR.

As I have discussed elsewhere, while the right to legal capacity in Article 12 of the CRPD, has some novel components, the broader right to equal recognition before the law has a much longer history (Arstein-Kerslake 2017). The UDHR itself includes the right to "recognition everywhere as a person before the law" in Article 6. As the UDHR is a non-binding document, the ICCPR and the ICESCR were adopted—about two decades later—to create binding documents that enshrine the rights with the UDHR as part of the emerging legally binding international human rights law. Two documents were created, instead of one, in part due to the political climate at the time—the 1960s were rife with tension between capitalist and communist systems. In particular, the cold war tensions between the United States and the Soviet Union led to a desire to separate civil and political rights from economic, social, and cultural rights. Capitalist countries in Europe and North America advocated strongly for the prominence of civil and political rights. Their political cultures dictated that civil and political rights are individual rights that must take precedence over economic, social, and cultural rights, which are perceived as more community centred rights. As a result, the ICCPR was created and includes the requirement that state parties to the covenant take immediate steps to realise the rights with the document. The right to equal recognition before the law was made legally binding by Article 16 of the ICCPR, which states, "Everyone shall have the right to recognition everywhere as a person before the law." The right to equal recognition before the law is a civil and political right and has the accompanying weight and privileges granted this group of rights.

Civil and political rights are viewed as rights that immediately attach to the individual upon a state's ratification of the ICCPR or any other treaty that includes civil and political rights. As such, they are immediately adjudicable. Conversely, the rights within the ICESCR are only subject to progressive implementation and they are not viewed as immediately adjudicable—they do not attach to the individual upon a state's ratification of a relevant treat. This separation between civil and political and social, economic, and cultural rights is controversial in modern human rights law. Many argue that it is a false distinction and that the rights are all interwoven and interdependent (Whelan 2006). Nonetheless, civil and political rights continue to have more strength in international human rights law and are often given greater consideration by domestic governments (Alston and Quinn 1987, pp. 158–160).

Legal capacity is also a civil and political right, in part, because its parent right is the right to equal recognition before the law in the ICCPR. This gives the right to legal capacity the strength of immediate realisation. It attaches immediately to the individual upon ratification of a relevant treaty, the individual can—in theory—seek adjudication immediately if they feel the right is being denied, and the state party to the treaty must take immediate steps to realise the right for all individuals under its jurisdiction.

Legal capacity did not emerge for the first time in the CRPD. It first appeared explicitly in a United Nations human rights instrument in the Convention Against the Elimination of Discrimination Against Women (CEDAW). The right to legal capacity was first included as part of the right to equal recognition before the law in Article 15(1 & 2) of CEDAW, which states, "1. States Parties shall accord to women equality with men before the law. 2. States Parties shall accord to women ... a legal capacity identical to that of men and the same opportunities to exercise that capacity." The CRPD then solidified the right to legal capacity as an element of the right to equal recognition before the law in Article 12, which is titled "Equal recognition before the law," and the first two provisions state, "1. States Parties reaffirm that persons with disabilities have the right to recognition everywhere as persons before the law. 2. States Parties shall recognize that persons with disabilities enjoy legal capacity on an equal basis with others in all aspects of life." Therefore, this book argues that although the right to legal capacity was not mentioned in the UDHR, further iterations of the right to equal recognition before the law in CEDAW and the CRPD establish the right to legal capacity as falling within the right to equal recognition before the law.

While there are separate instruments that discuss human rights in relation to particular groups—such as CEDAW and the CRPD—these instruments are not discussing rights that only apply to those groups. Instead, they are discussing rights that are universal and they are applying those rights to the particular situations of the relevant groups in an effort to create clarity in how those rights can be realised for these unique groups. On this basis, this book analyses the right to legal capacity and the right to equal recognition before the law as universal human rights that apply to all people.

Article 12 of the CRPD goes into more detail than any prior United Nations human rights instrument. It explicitly lists legal capacity as a right underneath the heading of the right to equal recognition before the law. Building on Article 16 of CEDAW, it solidifies that the right to legal capacity includes both static (personhood) and active (legal agency) elements because paragraph 5 of Article 12 explicitly lists actions that require legal agency as actions that states parties must ensure on an equal basis for disabled people—for example: inheriting property, controlling financial affairs, access to bank loans and credit, as well as the right to not be arbitrarily deprived of property.

In addition, paragraph 3 requires that states parties provide access to support for the exercise of legal capacity. This requirement establishes that the right to legal capacity includes an active element of exercising legal capacity. It is also the first time that a United Nations human rights instrument explicitly stated that states have an obligation to not merely recognise legal capacity but also ensure that support is provided for the exercise of legal capacity—this is significant because it recognises that autonomy—including legal autonomy—does not necessarily need to be exercised independently. Instead, it opens the door for an individual to have their legal capacity recognised—to be recognised as a legal person and legal agent—even when they require assistance to exercise their legal capacity. The significance of this will be explored later in this book.

Essentially, Article 12 fosters individual autonomy while also recognising the inherent interconnectedness of all individuals and the possibility that an individual may exercise their legal personhood and legal agency in collaboration with other individuals. It is a direct challenge to liberal political theory that advocates for individual liberty and freedom for autonomous decision-making. It embraces the importance of individual liberty—however, it revolutionises the concept by opening the door to the possibility of exercising individual liberty and autonomy via a collective—multiple people supporting an individual to express her will and preference, make legal decisions, and have those decisions enforced by law.

These revolutions in Article 12 evolved from CEDAW and the previous history of the right to equal recognition before the law that had been developing since the Universal Declaration of Human Rights in 1948. However, Article 12 has elucidated the right to legal capacity in a manner that challenges many aspects of modern legal systems and provides a revolutionary new perspective on what a legal person is and how their legal agency must be protected. These advances were not easily come by for the CRPD. In fact, Article 12 was one of the most contentious articles of the CRPD and its drafting engendered significant debate.

1.3 Debates in the Drafting of Article 12 CRPD

Amongst legal capacity scholars, the debates during the drafting of Article 12 have taken on a legendary status. During the drafting there was significant contention regarding the meaning of 'legal capacity' (Dhanda 2006). Some argued that the right to legal capacity includes only the right to be a person before the law. Others argued that the right to legal capacity is virtually meaningless if it only includes the right to be a person before the law. They argued that the right to legal capacity must include both the right to be a person before the law and the right to be a legal agent—to take actions that have legal consequences and will be enforced as such. They argued that if the right to legal capacity only includes the right to be a person before the law, then individuals with disability could be formerly recognised as persons before the law, but may have no power to act because their legal agency is not recognised. For example, in some systems, a person can have their legal personhood fully recognised, yet may have their legal agency removed from them and placed in the hand of another person or a court by virtue of a guardianship or other type of interdiction. If the right to legal capacity only includes the right to legal personhood, then such laws would be permitted and disabled people could have their legal capacity to act removed without it implicating the human rights regime—without it amounting to a human rights violation.

These debates took on legendary status because they are a microcosm of the larger debates around the rights of disabled people—are disabled people due the same rights and responsibilities as others, or are they due a different, limited, gamut of rights? Are there times that disabled people do not hold the same responsibilities as others specifically due to the existence of disability? Disability rights activists and human rights scholars, like myself, argue that disabled people must be entitled to the full gamut of human rights and they must enjoy those rights on an equal basis with others. In other words, disabled people are entitled to the same rights and responsibilities as others. On the other side of the argument, are those that argue that disabled people are not entitled to the same rights and responsibilities as others. The argument is that there are times that a person with disability should not be held responsible for their actions because the existence of disability excuses an individual from responsibility for certain actions. In addition, they argue that disabled people must be protected more than people without disability. As such, disabled people are not entitled to rights in relation to autonomy, in particular, on an equal basis with others. Instead, where a person with disability would like to exercise autonomy in such a way that would jeopardise their health or life—or possibly other rights—then they should be protected from themselves and they should be prevented from exercising such autonomy—the right to health or other right should take precedence.

Interestingly, it is rare that the debates are explicitly framed in this way. Instead, there are often activists and human rights scholars arguing for equal rights and responsibilities for disabled people and those on the other side of the argument are much less explicit. Instead, they often, seemingly innocuously, argue—using 'hard case' scenarios—that there is a moral responsibility to not leave disabled people to be harmed or disadvantaged by their own decisions or those of others. Yet, those without disabilities are free to make good or bad decisions and are much more commonly perceived to have the right to do so free from intervention. The common—almost generalised and popular—belief is that disabled people need to be protected to a higher degree than others.

The emphasis on protection over autonomy becomes particularly poignant when gender is added to the equation. Women have, similarly, historically been perceived as lacking decision-making skills equivalent to that of men. They have also been perceived as needing more protection than others—men, in particular. Historically, fathers or husbands were given decision-making power over women's lives—often with the argument that it was for their own good. In addition, women did not have the same rights and responsibilities in public life as men. For example, they were—and in some cases still are—treated differently in criminal law (Feinman 1994; Naffine 2019); they did not have the right to vote or the responsibility to be politically active (Rokkan 1961; Firebaugh and Chen 1995; Coffé and Bolzendahl 2010); and they didn't—and in some places still don't—have the same right to inheritance as male heirs (Richardson 2004; Bennett et al. 2006; Ezer 2006; Htun and Weldon 2011; Demirguc-Kunt et al. 2013). Gender minorities, similarly, have been perceived as lacking sufficient decision-making skills to make decisions for themselves—such as their own gender identity. Many gender minorities—transgender people, in particular—have been pathologized as having a mental health problem and have had their right to make decisions—particularly medical decisions—removed from them (Butler 2004; Spade 2015). Where disability intersects with gender—for example, women with disability and gender minorities with disability—

there are multiple layers of historical denials of autonomy. It is, perhaps, not surprising then that CEDAW and the CRPD are the two international human rights instruments in which activists fought hard to get the right to legal capacity included.

In the CRPD debates, these underlying beliefs regarding the need for disabled people, in particular, to be protected led to protracted arguments against legal capacity including the right to act—legal agency. The argument was that disabled people could be respected as legal persons on an equal basis, but there were times in which disabled people needed to have their legal agency denied in order to protect them from their own decisions or from the influence of others. There was a desire to ensure that regimes that remove decision-making power from disabled people could be maintained—for example, guardianship, interdiction, conservatorship, and others (Dhanda 2006). To achieve this, during the drafting of Article 12, certain state delegations argued to include a footnote to the text of Article 12 that specified that legal capacity only included the right to be a person before the law and it did not include a right to be an actor before the law.

Fortunately, the debates did not result in a footnote being added to Article 12. However, the text of Article 12 does also not explicitly include the definition of the right to legal capacity as including the right to be a person before the law and an actor before the law. It does include multiple mentions of protections that require the right to legal capacity to include the right to legal agency. For example, Article 12 (5) includes "the equal right of persons with disability to own or inherit property, to control their own financial affairs and to have equal access to bank loans, mortgages and other forms of financial credit, and shall ensure that persons with disabilities are not arbitrarily deprived of their property." These all require a recognition of legal agency—not just legal personhood.

In this way, it can be implied from the text of Article 12 that the right to legal capacity includes both personhood and agency. This can also be implied from the text of Article 16 of CEDAW because it states that women must be accorded "a legal capacity identical to that of men and the same opportunities to exercise that capacity. In particular, they shall give women equal rights to conclude contracts and to administer property and shall treat them equally in all stages of procedure in courts and tribunals." In this way, the text of Article 12 of the CRPD and Article 16 of CEDAW can be viewed as providing revolutionary clarity in ensuring that the right to legal agency is protected within the right to legal capacity for disabled people and women. This is in recognition of—and an effort to provide a tool to combat—the historical and ongoing denial of decision-making to these groups—often under the argument of providing protection to these groups, as was argued by some during the drafting of Article 12 of the CRPD (Dhanda 2006, pp. 442–443).

These areas of contention have been, in some parts, further clarified by the first general comment adopted by the UN CRPD Committee. I was fortunate to work with the Committee in interpreting Article 12 and drafting the general comment to reflect that interpretation (Arstein-Kerslake and Flynn 2016).

1.4 General Comment No. 1: UN CRPD Committee's Interpretation of Legal Capacity

A general comment is an interpretation of international human rights law provided by a United Nations body. The procedure for the creation and adoption of general comments varies—however, it generally is a document created by a member or working group of a human rights body that is then presented to that body with an opportunity for amendments and additions. If there is sufficient support for the general comment within the human rights body, the body will adopt the general comment and it will become a part of the jurisprudence of that human rights body. General comments are regarded as an authoritative interpretation of international human rights law. They are not binding on states parties because they are not negotiated and agreed upon by states parties. The nature of international human rights law is such that—in general—states are only bound by instruments that they agree to be bound by and whose text they have had the opportunity to negotiate.

In 2013, myself and Professor Eilionóir Flynn were invited to be involved in the drafting of a general comment on the right to equal recognition before the law. Professor Theresia Degener, the German Member and Vice Chair of the CRPD Committee at the time, was chairing the working group on the general comment and she invited us to come to Geneva when the Committee was in session. She invited us to bring a draft general comment and to support the working group to develop the comment and ultimately, to support the entire Committee in the adoption of the comment (Arstein-Kerslake and Flynn 2016).

Key elements of the general comment are: that it solidifies legal capacity as including personhood and agency; it states that legal capacity should not be denied on the basis of mental capacity; it establishes substituted decision-making as impermissible under Article 12 and provides a definition of what qualifies as substituted decision-making; it also provides a list of necessary elements for systems of support for the exercise of legal capacity (Committee on the Rights of Persons with Disabilities 2014). The general comment has been met with some resistance from scholars and practitioners (Freeman et al. 2015). Most of the resistance comes from those working in the field of psychiatry—either as a scholar or practitioner. The concepts in the general comment were not new—they had all been written about elsewhere before they were included in the general comment (Dhanda 2006; Minkowitz 2006; McSherry 2012; Flynn and Arstein-Kerslake 2014b). However, the general comment gave these concepts a new standing and a new level of influence. Those that are resistant to these ideas have been resistant to the new higher level of influence that the general comment gave these ideas. This resistance is discussed more below—the reason that I have raised it here is that I want to be upfront about critiques of the general comment. I also want to highlight the source of the resistance and provide an explanation that will hopefully provide a greater depth of understanding for these key elements of the general comment, which are also some of the most controversial elements.

1.4.1 Solidification of Legal Capacity as Including Personhood and Agency

As discussed previously, there was debate during the drafting of Article 12 regarding whether legal capacity includes both legal personhood and legal agency or whether it only includes legal personhood. As discussed above, disability activists were strongly opposed to legal capacity only including legal personhood and they lobbied strongly for the inclusion of both legal personhood and legal agency (Dhanda 2006). Although the negotiated text does not explicitly state that legal capacity includes both legal personhood and legal agency, it does include elements—such as equality in financial affairs, which are guaranteed in Article 12(5)—that implicitly indicate that legal agency is included as part of legal capacity because legal agency is required for equality in such areas. The General Comment explicitly states that "Legal capacity is the ability to hold rights and duties (legal standing) and to exercise those rights and duties (legal agency)" (Committee on the Rights of Persons with Disabilities 2014, p. 3).

1.4.2 Legal Capacity Should Not Be Denied on the Basis of Mental Capacity

Legal capacity is often conflated with mental capacity. Legal capacity is often denied to individuals that are not deemed to have sufficient mental capacity (Committee on the Rights of Persons with Disabilities 2014; Arstein-Kerslake 2017). However, the interpretation of Article 12 in the General Comment solidifies that legal capacity is a distinct concept from mental capacity in the context of international human rights law (Committee on the Rights of Persons with Disabilities 2014, p. 3; Arstein-Kerslake and Flynn 2016; Arstein-Kerslake 2017). This definition of legal capacity refers only to the recognition of legal personhood and agency. It does not refer to an individual's decision-making skills in relation to the exercise of legal capacity—it does not refer to an individual's mental capacity. This definition of legal capacity is commonly utilised across legal disciplines and is particularly evident when legal capacity is discussed in the context of non-human entities, such as corporations, animals, and the environment (Epstein 2002; Blair 2013; O'Donnell and Talbot-Jones 2018). These entities may have their legal capacity recognised but may not have the ability to independently engage in decision-making to exercise such legal capacity. In this way, mental capacity only relates to legal capacity in that where mental capacity is lacking there may be a need for additional support in the exercise of legal capacity or a third party to exercise legal capacity on behalf of the individual or entity (Flynn and Arstein-Kerslake 2014a, b).

1.4.3 *Definition of Substituted Decision-Making*

The General Comment defines substituted decision-making as any system in which the individual's legal capacity is denied, an outside decision-maker is appointed against the will of the individual, and that decision-maker makes decisions in the 'best interests' of the individual without an obligation to uphold the will and preference of the individual (Committee on the Rights of Persons with Disabilities 2014, p. 6). A denial of legal capacity occurs when an individual is either not respected as a person before the law or is not permitted to exercise legal agency. An outside decision-maker is anyone that is not the individual themselves. An appointment occurs against the will of the individual when the individual is expressing that they do not want an outside decision-maker and such an appointment is made regardless. Best interests decision-making occurs where the outside decision-maker is empowered to make whatever decision she or he believes would be in the best interests of the individual. A system is incompliant with Article 12 if it denies legal capacity and appoints an outside decision-maker against the will of the individual and permits that decision-maker to use a best interest paradigm (Committee on the Rights of Persons with Disabilities 2014, p. 6).

There has been continued misinterpretation of what constitutes impermissible substituted decision-making under Article 12. There are situations in which someone else needs to make a legal decision on behalf of another person, for example where the will and preference of the individual cannot be ascertained. The demand to replace substituted decision-making regimes with support paradigms leaves room for such decisions. If it did not, it would be unworkable and impractical. The need for such decision-making may occur in anyone's life and the law must provide a response for when that situation arises. According to the General Comment, Article 12 merely requires that when the situation arises, the law's response does not amount to 'substituted decision-making,' as defined by the General Comment (Committee on the Rights of Persons with Disabilities 2014, p. 6). This disallows many pieces of legislation and practices that currently exist, including much of mental health law. However, it does not disallow all decisions that are made on behalf of another person. Instead, it demands that the law responds differently to such situations. It demands that the law respect the right to legal capacity of all on and equal basis and implement a paradigm of support.

1.4.4 *Elements of Support for the Exercise of Legal Capacity*

The guidelines provided in the General Comment on the implementation of a support paradigm for the exercise of legal capacity are as follows:

(a) Supported decision-making must be available to all. A person's level of support needs, especially where these are high, should not be a barrier to obtaining support in decision-making;

(b) All forms of support in the exercise of legal capacity, including more intensive forms of support, must be based on the will and preference of the person, not on what is perceived as being in his or her objective best interests;
(c) A person's mode of communication must not be a barrier to obtaining support in decision-making, even where this communication is non-conventional, or understood by very few people;
(d) Legal recognition of the support person(s) formally chosen by a person must be available and accessible, and States have an obligation to facilitate the creation of support, particularly for people who are isolated and may not have access to naturally occurring support in the community. This must include a mechanism for third parties to verify the identity of a support person as well as a mechanism for third parties to challenge the action of a support person if they believe that the support person is not acting in accordance with the will and preferences of the person concerned;
(e) In order to comply with the requirement, set out in article 12, paragraph 3, of the Convention, for States parties to take measures to "provide access" to the support required, States parties must ensure that support is available at nominal or no cost to persons with disabilities and that lack of financial resources is not a barrier to accessing support in the exercise of legal capacity;
(f) Support in decision-making must not be used as justification for limiting other fundamental rights of persons with disabilities, especially the right to vote, the right to marry, or establish a civil partnership, and found a family, reproductive rights, parental rights, the right to give consent for intimate relationships and medical treatment, and the right to liberty;
(g) The person must have the right to refuse support and terminate or change the support relationship at any time;
(h) Safeguards must be set up for all processes relating to legal capacity and support in exercising legal capacity. The goal of safeguards is to ensure that the person's will and preferences are respected.
(i) The provision of support to exercise legal capacity should not hinge on mental capacity assessments; new, non-discriminatory indicators of support needs are required in the provision of support to exercise legal capacity (Committee on the Rights of Persons with Disabilities 2014, p. 7).

The primary goal of these guidelines is to ensure that the rights, will and preferences of individuals using support for the exercise of legal capacity are protected. This means that the will and preferences of the individual must be central to any system related to the exercise of legal capacity. It also means that such a system must include safeguards to protect the full gamut of rights, including rights to autonomy—for example, Articles 12 and 19(a) (choice of residence) of the CRPD—and rights to health and physical integrity—for example, Articles 17 (bodily integrity) and 25 (health) of the CRPD.

1.4.4.1 Application of the Guidelines for Support Beyond Disabled People

The General Comment gave these new guidelines on support for the exercise of legal capacity because the denial of decision-making power to disabled people is a pervasive and harmful form of discrimination. This also may be significant for people beyond disabled people—because there are many forms of marginalization that have resulted in a need for support for the exercise of legal capacity either because individuals may be newly free to exercise legal agency and may need assistance in doing so or because our socio-legal systems are often ill suited for the needs of minority group members such as women, disabled women, and gender minorities.

This interpretation of Article 12 recognizes that every person has a will, desires, and needs and that every person is capable of making choices accordingly. Any arguments—historical or modern—that women, disabled women, or gender minorities are not sufficiently cognitively developed or stable to hold and exercise legal capacity become meaningless because, even if there was an element of truth of those arguments, this interpretation of Article 12 indicates that the appropriate response is to provide support for the exercise of legal capacity—not to deny legal capacity.

Not every person is able to express their choices in ways that are conventionally accepted communication. Some people communicate through words, others through signs, others through writing, and others through simple smiles. Conventional communication—legal communication in particular—is dominated by white, able-bodied, cisgender male notions of communication. It favors one independent individual speaking—in written or verbal form—to one or more other independent individuals. For women, disabled women, and gender minorities, communication—including legal communication—may look different. Some studies show that women are more likely to use nonverbal communication—such as smiling and nodding their heads (Helweg-Larsen et al. 2004). There is also evidence that they are more likely to listen rather than interrupt another speaker (Nohara 1992; Briton and Hall 1995). They are also more frequently interrupted, in some studies, than their male counterparts (Patton and Smith 2017). Still other studies show that differential intonation in female speech has an impact on communication (Hancock et al. 2014). Feminist theory also posits that women make decisions collectively and in relation to others—and research has supported this claim (Kirtley and Weaver 1999; Mackenzie and Stoljar 2000). Disabled women may have additional differences in communication styles—due either to an impairment that affects communication or to intersecting forms of marginalization that impact the individual's patterns of communication. Gender minorities may be impacted in similar ways and their communication methods may be similarly impacted by ongoing marginalization. In addition, gender expression can have a significant on a person's communication—for example, seeking to take on female intonation may mean that the individual also takes on the potential for social bias and prejudice against female intonation (Hancock et al. 2014). When a person communicates with the world in unconventional ways—or ways that do not fit with the dominant, white, able-bodied, cisgender male social and legal systems—others may not recognize their communication or may not give as much weight to their communicated decisions.

In the interpretation of Article 12 in the General Comment, whichever way an individual communicates, conventional or not, Article 12 requires that their legal decisions not be ignored. As can be seen in the guidelines listed above, the support paradigm is a system in which people work together to understand an individual's desires and choices and then provide the means for that person to exercise legal capacity and live life in the way they choose as opposed to a way imposed by someone else's decision made on her or his behalf (Arstein-Kerslake and Flynn 2016). It was written in the context of disability—where communication can be uniquely impacted. However, I believe that principle applies across minority groups, including women and gender minorities. Similar to disabled people, it would require that the state provide access to support for women and gender minorities to ensure that they have access to accessible and tailored information regarding their legal decisions. It would also require that support is provided for the communication of legal decisions for women and gender minorities. This may look very similar to support provide for disabled people—independent individuals that are tasked with assisting women and gender minorities in understanding their rights and legal issues and weighing the relevant choices to the extent that they desire in order to arrive at a decision.

The guidelines for the support paradigm in Article 12 articulated in the General Comment also require that, in any support system, the individual is the core decision-maker. The support persons or people are there to explain details, when necessary, and interpret the signs and desires of the individual when it is needed. The onus is on the supporter to ensure that he or she is accurately and completely comprehending and interpreting the will and preferences of the individual. This applies to all people, including individuals experiencing significant disability that may greatly affect cognitive process and communication (Watson 2016). Supporters may play a more significant role in decision-making. However, their primary purpose is discovering the will and preference of the individual and supporting the individual to realize that will and preference. Disabled people may experience decision-making denial to a great and more profound extent than women and gender minorities. However, women and gender minorities have also experienced systemic and interpersonal denial of decision-making—as will be discussed in the coming chapters. As such, support for the exercise of legal capacity that is centered on empowering and amplifying the decisions of women and gender minorities is likely similarly important for these groups.

1.4.4.2 Positive Effects of the Support Paradigm

The legal recognition of an individual as a decision-maker has significant effects. It fosters equality across many areas of life such as employment and personal relationships. It also affirms the power of choice thereby enabling individual development (Winick 1995; Deci and Ryan 2012a). When the law permits support for individuals when making decisions, there are also significant effects. The support paradigm fosters social solidarity without sacrificing the recognition of equal legal capacity. By offering the choice of assistance, the support paradigm removes the illusion that legal capacity can only be exercised through self-sufficiency. This opens the door for a societal dialogue about the interdependence of all individuals (Quinn and Arstein-Kerslake 2012).

The support paradigm's humanistic approach—adapting to the needs of all individuals and not allowing the law to sanction one person taking control of the decisions of another person—has the potential to provide a much lower risk of exploitation for marginalized groups such as women, disabled women, and gender minorities. Studies have shown that where autonomy is fostered and where individuals are given meaningful choices, intrinsic motivation is increased and the overall well-being of the individual is enhanced (Deci and Ryan 2012a, b; Ryan and Deci 2017). It can be argued that when every individual is recognized as a decision-maker, it may serve to foster autonomy and create stronger individuals who are better able to protect themselves from abuse and exploitation. This increased resilience combined with the potential for increased power and privileged due to the ability to better maneuver the socio-legal world when one has their legal personhood and legal agency recognized may be provide greater equality and great power and privileged for women, disabled women, and gender minorities.

1.5 Resistance to Article 12 CRPD

The resistance to Article 12 has been palpable. The General Comment also engendered significant resistance. Much of the resistance has come from practitioners—especially psychiatrists. The underlying theme of such critiques is that there will be times that legal capacity should be denied on the basis of disability—in particular, cognitive disability. The argument is that there are times that the right to health or the right to life supersedes the right to legal capacity or equality before the law. For example, when a person makes a decision that would lead to the endangering of their life or health—as when a person with anorexia chooses not to eat. Those that critique Article 12 and the General Comment believe that in such circumstances, the right to legal capacity should be denied and the individual should be forced to take the action that others would determine to be in their best interests and would—in theory—lead to optimal health outcomes.

I believe that these critiques are problematic in several ways. First and foremost, they assume that disabled people are entitled to a different balance of rights than others. They assume that the right to legal capacity can be superseded by the right to health or life for disabled people in instances that it would not be superseded for people without disability. This assumption is problematic from an equality perspective, but also from an international human rights perspective. International human rights law does not apply to certain privileged groups in unique ways—people without disability should not have a greater entitlement to the right to legal capacity than disabled people. If all people—regardless of disability—were subject to denial of legal capacity when the right to health and/or life are at risk, then equality would be satisfied. However, I have significant doubts that it would be acceptable to many people to have their right to make medical and other decisions removed from them because others believe that they are making decisions that are not in the best interests of their health or life. In particular, I believe that white men would be outraged at such a suggestion. When white men—and able bodied, privileged individuals, more broadly—make choices, such and the cessation of life sustaining treatment, that would lead to the deterioration of their health or life—these decisions are largely respected—if not by everyone around them, then at least by the law.

This desire to balance the rights of disabled people differently to that of non-disabled people is problematic for several reasons. It undermines the integrity of international human rights law by attempting to circumvent the element of universality that is a fundamental aspect of international human rights law. It also fosters a charity model of disability that perpetuates a notion that disabled people survive by the grace of others and they are not bearers of rights and responsibilities on an equal basis with others. It also marginalises disabled people and the experience of disability by asserting that disabled people inherently have diminished decision making skills. These are significant problems that I believe are sufficient to demonstrate that there cannot be a different balance of rights for disabled people than there is for non-disabled people—and, by extension, that disabled people are entitled to equal recognition before the law and legal capacity on and equal basis with others—as it guaranteed to disabled people in Article 12 of the CRPD.

The critiques of Article 12 and the General Comment are also problematic because they are often aimed at situations that disproportionately affect women and gender minorities. For example, several times, I have heard anorexia be given as an illustration of why disabled people cannot be entitled to the same right to legal capacity as others. While anorexia is not exclusively experienced by women and gender minorities, there is a much higher proportion of women that are diagnosed with anorexia (Smolak and Murnen 2001; Till 2011). It has also been theorised that anorexia may be disproportionately experienced by gender minorities or those who have non-binary gender expressions or experience—especially expressions and experiences that they are forced to repress because of societal expectations (Mahowald 1992). It is an inherently gendered disease in that it was historically associated with hysteria—which is a gendered pathologization of the female body and female characteristics and is discussed in depth in Chap. 3 (Mahowald 1992; Malson 1998; Gremillion 2003, p. 2). It is likely that this gendering of anorexia has led, in part, to the perception that people with anorexia are largely incapable of making decisions related to their health and nutrition (Tan et al. 2008).

Because anorexia is a 'woman's disease'—like hysteria—it carries the assumption that an individual experiencing anorexia is also deficient in decision-making skills and cannot be allowed to make decisions for themselves. I have heard critics of Article 12 and the General Comment maintain that people (mostly women) with anorexia are an example of disabled people whose right to legal capacity—including their right to make medical decisions for themselves—should be denied where the individual's life or health are at risk. To the contrary, I find that the case of anorexia is a good example of where it is particularly important for the right to legal capacity to be respected. There is evidence that experiences of anorexia are tied to experiences of a loss of control and the individual seeking to regain control (Corrington 1986). It is possible that respect for the individual's autonomy—via the right to legal capacity—may be a critical aspect of addressing an underlying need of an individual experiencing anorexia to gain control in their lives. It is also possible that the support required in Article 12 CRPD for the exercise of legal capacity—such as legal decision-making—may be particularly empowering for those experiencing anorexia because they would be able to maintain control while receiving support for their decision-making. In addition, there is very little empirical evidence that forced treatment is effective for anorexia (Tan et al. 2008, p. 2). However, I would also posit this argument as a purely human rights argument—people with anorexia are due the same balance between the right to life or health and the right to legal capacity as those without anorexia.

This equality in the balance of rights is important for the integrity of international human rights law—as discussed above—but it is also an issue of morality. Discussing morality in legal scholarship is controversial. However, I believe that to not discuss my views on morality would simply be disingenuous. When we are arguing a particular legal position—particularly in the case of human right law—we are frequently making our arguments based on our own moral convictions—which arise from our individual socio-cultural positions, as well as, potentially, a deeper ingrained and inborn sense of right and wrong. Without taking the time to debate the existence of a higher law—I merely want to acknowledge here that I, like many if not all legal scholars, am inspired to make some of these arguments on the basis that I believe that it is the morally correct path to take. I believe that the moral compass points us not to a world in which people who have a disability, such as anorexia, are relegated to non-decision-makers whose will and preference may be considered but may also be disregarded—instead, I believe that the moral compass points us to a world where, regardless of what label an individual has been given or what medical or health issues an individual may be facing, they are entitled to treatment as a full legal person with rights and responsibilities. I believe that the same moral compass dictates that there may be situations—and anorexia is likely one of these situations—where an individual may need additional assistance to exercise their decision-making skills and their legal personhood.

Because there is not significant evidence to indicate the forced treatment is effective in addressing anorexia, it is a prime example where there is an additional argument for efficacy that can be made in favour of recognising legal capacity of people with anorexia on an equal basis with others (Tan et al. 2008, p. 2). In other words, allowing people with anorexia to make legal and medical treatments for themselves. When they are not permitted to do so—when their legal capacity and legal personhood is removed from them, there is often no positive effect or, at least, no therapeutic effect. This suggests that the instinct to remove their legal capacity and their ability to make medical and other decisions for themselves is rooted not in therapeutic effectiveness, but elsewhere. Potentially, such removal of legal capacity is rooted in deep seated prejudice against the decision-making capabilities of disabled people as well as women—because, as discussed above, anorexia is often gendered by the medical profession for various reasons and in various ways (Mahowald 1992; Malson 1998; Gremillion 2003).

Such resistance to Article 12, I imagine, will not dissipate completely any time soon. I believe that this is due to this resistance being so deeply rooted in these preconceived notions of disability—and disabled people—necessitating a higher degree of protection than others. Similarly, I suspect that denials of legal capacity have been—and continue to be—disproportionately experienced by women and gender minorities because of deep seated notions of women and gender minorities as having diminished decision-making skills due to various historical and modern prejudices. In this book, I am attempting to highlight those historical prejudices; examine the denials of legal capacity that have arisen from those prejudices; present a human rights argument for why disabled people, women, and gender minorities must have their legal capacity respected on an equal basis with others; and present a way forward towards ameliorating the impact of those prejudices and realising the right to legal capacity for these groups.

1.6 Argument for Legal Capacity on an Equal Basis for All

I have provided the history of the rights to equal recognition before the law and legal capacity and the debates surrounding these rights in order to give depth to arguments around the interpretation of the content of these rights, but also to demonstrate that they are not rights that are only applicable in the context of disability. Instead, they are rights that, in fact, originated in a much broader context in the UDHR and then momentum for their importance and realisation was created with Article 16 of CEDAW. This highlights both the importance of the rights as well as the relevance of gender in the realisations of the rights. The right to legal capacity first appears in CEDAW because it is women who have suffered significantly throughout history and who are continuing to suffer under legal regimes that either explicitly deny their rights to legal personhood and agency or provide avenues, in practice, for those rights to be ignored.

It may be important at this point to re-trace the origins of the right to legal capacity and the argument for why it applies to all people—and, for the purposes of this book, why, I believe, it applies, in particular, not only to disabled people but also to women and gender minorities. The UDHR was intended as a document that set out the full gamut of rights for all people—hence the term 'universal' in its title (Donnelly 2013). The United Nations human rights instruments that have followed the UDHR are legally binding documents that secure the rights already set out in the UDHR. The right to equal recognition before the law can be found in Article 6 of the UDHR, which states, "Everyone has the right to recognition everywhere as a person before the law." This right was made legally binding by Article 16 of the ICCPR, which states, "Everyone shall have the right to recognition everywhere as a person before the law." The right to legal capacity was first included as part-in-parcel of the right to equal recognition before the law in Article 15(1 & 2), which state, "1. States Parties shall accord to women equality with men before the law. 2. States Parties shall accord to women . . . a legal capacity identical to that of men and the same opportunities to exercise that capacity." The CRPD then solidified the right to legal capacity as an element of the right to equality before the law in Article 12, which is titled "Equal recognition before the law," and the first two provisions state, "1. States Parties reaffirm that persons with disabilities have the right to recognition everywhere as persons before the law. 2. States Parties shall recognize that persons with disabilities enjoy legal capacity on an equal basis with others in all aspects of life." In this way, while the right to legal capacity was not mentioned in the UDHR, CEDAW and the CRPD solidified the right to legal capacity as falling within the right to equal recognition before the law, which can be traced to the UDHR and then the ICCPR and, as such, is a right that is applicable to all. Furthermore, there is no intention in international human rights law that certain rights apply to certain groups but not to others. While there are separate instruments that discuss human rights in relation to particular groups—such as CEDAW and the CRPD—they are not discussing rights that only apply to those groups. Instead, they are discussing rights that are universal and they are applying those rights to the particular situations of the relevant group in an effort to create clarity in how those rights can be realised for these unique groups.

The concept of 'universal legal capacity,' which was introduced by legal scholar and disability rights activist, Amita Dhanda, provides additional fuel to the need for an exploration of how the right to legal capacity applies to various minority groups (Dhanda 2012). Universal legal capacity is the demand for the recognition of legal capacity on an equal basis for all, regardless of group membership. Dhanda discusses universal legal capacity primarily in relation to disabled people—although, she draws on the history of the right to equal recognition before the law (outlined above) to support her argument that all people, including disabled people, are entitled to legal capacity on an equal basis. This book explores the other side to that coin—the concept that universal legal capacity necessitates not only an examination of where disabled people are disproportionately denied legal capacity, but also where other minority groups are disproportionately denied legal capacity—such as women and gender minorities. Dhanda argues, very eloquently, that universal legal capacity should be recognised for disabled people because they are humans and are entitled to the protections of the human rights regime on an equal basis with other groups (Dhanda 2012). I agree with that proposition and, in this book, I am extending it to women and gender minorities. If there is an international human right to legal capacity (as is evident from the history of the right to equal recognition before the law outlined above) then there is a human rights imperative to recognise universal legal capacity—and there is also a need to examine how other groups, such as women and gender minorities, are disproportionately denied legal capacity and what the human rights implications are of those denials.

1.7 Conclusion

It is important to fully explain these concepts in order to have a solid foundation from which to begin to apply these concepts to denials of legal capacity on the basis of gender—and, specifically, to women, disabled women, and gender minorities. In particular, it is significant for women, disabled women, and gender minorities, that the General Comment makes it clear that legal capacity cannot be denied on the basis of mental capacity. As will be explored later, women, disabled women, and gender minorities have all experienced historical prejudice that has disregarded and devalued their decision-making. They have been perceived to lack rationality—for various different reasons, which are explored further later in this book. This prejudice, coupled with the liberal political emphasis on cognition for a granting of personhood and agency, has resulted in the denial of legal capacity, in various forms, to women, disabled women, and gender minorities on the basis that they lack cognition or rationality (Flynn and Arstein-Kerslake 2014b). Although much of the perception of deficiencies in cognition for women, disabled women, and gender minorities is false—it has, nonetheless, been a powerful roadblock to the enjoyment of legal capacity by these groups. The general comment's clear statement that legal capacity cannot be denied on the basis of mental capacity disallows this powerful roadblock—this is significant, even though the premise of these groups lacking sufficient cognition to hold legal capacity is also erroneous.

It is also significant for women, disabled women, and gender minorities that the General Comment solidified the definition of legal capacity as including personhood and agency. For women and disabled women, in particular, many arguments have been put forth throughout history that essentially propose that women and disabled women can be granted personhood on an equal basis with others—but that there agency should be allow to be restricted for various reasons—often because they lack the cognition or rationality to successfully hold legal agency. The solidification of the definition of legal capacity including both personhood and agency disallows this—it means that the right to legal capacity is only realised where both personhood and agency are respected. Therefore, if women, disabled women, or gender minorities have their legal personhood respected but not their legal agency, then their right to legal capacity is violated.

It is also significant for women, disabled women, and gender minorities that the General Comment has identified elements that are essential for systems of support for the exercise of legal capacity. As discussed elsewhere (Arstein-Kerslake 2017) and in later chapters of this book, feminist, disability and queer theories of personhood have identified that women, disabled women, and gender minorities often do not exercise or enjoy their personhood in line with the dominant liberal political notion of the isolated individual male operating in his own interest to seek what he deems to be the 'good life' (West 1988). Instead, they often operate as entities intertwined with those around them—dependent upon others, but also allowing others to be dependent upon them. They even may exercise their autonomy in relation to others and the needs of others (Mackenzie and Stoljar 2000). They may make decisions collaboratively with others; make decisions based on what is best for others, not necessarily what is best for themselves; or allow others to make decision for them or to communicate their decisions for them.

It can be queried whether anyone—including white, able-bodied, cisgender men—actually operate as isolated atomistic individuals. It is likely that most people actually exercise autonomy in relation to others and not as an isolated individual. However, women, disabled women, and gender minorities, may exercise such relational autonomy to a higher degree than others. This may be because of the long history of oppression that all three groups have experienced and the resulting need and desire to band together against domination and oppression. It may also be because the pressure to compete and succeed as an individual is much more ever-present for those in the dominant class—such as white, able-bodied, cisgender men. Without this pressure, women, disabled women, and gender minorities are free to exists intertwined with each other and exercise their autonomy to better their own positions, but also to attempt to better the positions of those around them. With the reality and the recognition that women, disabled women, and gender minorities exercise their autonomy in relation to others, the state obligation in Article 12 CRPD to provide support for the exercise of legal capacity is particularly important for these groups. To explore these concepts further, the next chapter will examine feminist, disability and queer critical social theory in order to discover how scholarship related to these groups can elucidate further the role of legal capacity—legal personhood and legal agency—in overcoming inequality and increasing power and privilege for these groups.

References

Alston, Philip, and Gerard Quinn. 1987. The Nature and Scope of States Parties' Obligations under the International Covenant on Economic, Social and Cultural Rights Symposium: The Implementation of the International Covenant on Economic, Social and Cultural Rights. *Human Rights Quarterly* 9: 156–229.

Altman, Dennis, and Jonathan Symons. 2016. *Queer Wars*. John Wiley & Sons.

Andrews, Erin E., Anjali J. Forber-Pratt, Linda R. Mona, Emily M. Lund, Carrie R. Pilarski, and Rochelle Balter. 2019. #SaytheWord: A Disability Culture Commentary on the Erasure of "Disability". *Rehabilitation Psychology* 64: 111–118. https://doi.org/10.1037/rep0000258.

Arstein-Kerslake, Anna. 2017. *Restoring Voice to People with Cognitive Disabilities*. Cambridge University Press.

Arstein-Kerslake, Anna, and Eilionóir Flynn. 2016. The General Comment on Article 12 of the Convention on the Rights of Persons with Disabilities: A Roadmap for Equality Before the Law. *The International Journal of Human Rights* 20: 471–490. https://doi.org/10.1080/13642987.2015.1107052.

Bennett, Valerie, Ginger Faulk, Anna Kovina, and Tatjana Eres. 2006. Inheritance Law in Uganda: The Plight of Widows and Children International Women's Human Rights Clinic Special Issue - Report. *Georgetown Journal of Gender and the Law* 7: 451–530.

Blair, Margaret M. 2013. Corporate Personhood and the Corporate Persona Symposium: In the Boardroom. *University of Illinois Law Review*: 785–820.

Blizzard, Robert M. 2002. Intersex Issues: A Series of Continuing Conundrums. *Pediatrics* 110: 616–621. https://doi.org/10.1542/peds.110.3.616.

Briton, Nancy J., and Judith A. Hall. 1995. Beliefs About Female and Male Nonverbal Communication. *Sex Roles* 32: 79–90. https://doi.org/10.1007/BF01544758.

Butler, Judith. 2004. *Undoing Gender*. Routledge. https://doi.org/10.4324/9780203499627.

Cava, Peter. 2016. Cisgender and Cissexual. In *The Wiley Blackwell Encyclopedia of Gender and Sexuality Studies*, 1–4. American Cancer Society. https://doi.org/10.1002/9781118663219.wbegss131.

Coffé, Hilde, and Catherine Bolzendahl. 2010. Same Game, Different Rules? Gender Differences in Political Participation. *Sex Roles* 62: 318–333. https://doi.org/10.1007/s11199-009-9729-y.

Committee on the Rights of Persons with Disabilities. 2014. General Comment No. 1 – Article 12: Equal Recognition Before the Law. UN Doc. No. CRPD/C/GC/1.

Corrington, Gail. 1986. Anorexia, Asceticism, and Autonomy: Self-Control as Liberation and Transcendence. *Journal of Feminist Studies in Religion* 2: 51–61. JSTOR.

Currah, Paisley. 2006. Gender Pluralisms under the Transgender Umbrella. In *Transgender Rights*, ed. Paisley Currah, Richard M. Juang, and Shannon Price Minter, 3–31. University of Minnesot Press.

Deci, Edward L., and Richard M. Ryan. 2012a. Self-determination Theory. In *Handbook of Theories of Social Psychology*, vol. 1, 416–436. Thousand Oaks, CA: Sage Publications Ltd. https://doi.org/10.4135/9781446249215.n21.

———. 2012b. Motivation, Personality, and Development Within Embedded Social Contexts: An Overview of Self-determination Theory. In *The Oxford Handbook of Human Motivation*, 85–107. Oxford Library of Psychology. New York, NY, US: Oxford University Press.

Demirguc-Kunt, Asli, Leora Klapper, and Dorothe Singer. 2013. *Financial Inclusion and Legal Discrimination Against Women: Evidence from Developing Countries. Policy Research Working Papers*. The World Bank. https://doi.org/10.1596/1813-9450-6416.

Dhanda, Amita. 2006. Legal Capacity in the Disability Rights Convention: Stranglehold of the Past or Lodestar for the Future Symposium: The United Nations Convention on the Rights of Persons with Disabilities. *Syracuse Journal of International Law and Commerce*: 429–462.

———. 2012. Universal Legal Capacity as a Universal Human Right. In *Mental Health and Human Rights: Vision, Praxis, and Courage*, ed. Michael Dudley, Derrick Silove, and Fran Gale. Oxford University Press.

Donnelly, Jack. 2013. *Universal Human Rights in Theory and Practice*. Ithaca; London: Cornell University Press.

Eliason, Michele J. 2014. An Exploration of Terminology Related to Sexuality and Gender: Arguments for Standardizing the Language. *Social Work in Public Health* 29: 162–175. https://doi.org/10.1080/19371918.2013.775887.

Epstein, Richard A. 2002. *Animals as Objects, or Subjects, of Rights. SSRN Scholarly Paper ID 359240*. Rochester, NY: Social Science Research Network.

Ezer, Tamar. 2006. Inheritance Law in Tanzania: The Impoverishment of Widows and Daughters International Women's Human Rights Clinic Special Issue - Report. *Georgetown Journal of Gender and the Law* 7: 599–662.

Feinman, Clarice. 1994. *Women in the Criminal Justice System*. ABC-CLIO.

Firebaugh, Glenn, and Kevin Chen. 1995. Vote Turnout of Nineteenth Amendment Women: The Enduring Effect of Disenfranchisement. *American Journal of Sociology* 100: 972–996. https://doi.org/10.1086/230606.

Flynn, Eilionoir, and Anna Arstein-Kerslake. 2014a. The Support Model of Legal Capacity: Fact, Fiction, or Fantasy. *Berkeley Journal of International Law*: 124–143.

———. 2014b. Legislating Personhood: Realising the Right to Support in Exercising Legal Capacity. *International Journal of Law in Context* 10: 81–104. https://doi.org/10.1017/S1744552313000384.

Freeman, Melvyn Colin, Kavitha Kolappa, Jose Miguel Caldas de Almeida, Arthur Kleinman, Nino Makhashvili, Sifiso Phakathi, Benedetto Saraceno, and Graham Thornicroft. 2015. Reversing Hard Won Victories in the Name of Human Rights: A Critique of the General Comment on Article 12 of the UN Convention on the Rights of Persons with Disabilities. *The Lancet Psychiatry* 2: 844–850. https://doi.org/10.1016/S2215-0366(15)00218-7.

Gremillion, Helen. 2003. *Feeding Anorexia: Gender and Power at a Treatment Center*. Duke University Press.

Hancock, Adrienne, Lindsey Colton, and Fiacre Douglas. 2014. Intonation and Gender Perception: Applications for Transgender Speakers. *Journal of Voice* 28: 203–209. https://doi.org/10.1016/j.jvoice.2013.08.009.

Harper, Catherine. 2007. *Intersex*. Berg.

Helweg-Larsen, Marie, Stephanie J. Cunningham, Amanda Carrico, and Alison M. Pergram. 2004. To Nod or Not to Nod: An Observational Study of Nonverbal Communication and Status in Female and Male College Students. *Psychology of Women Quarterly* 28: 358–361. https://doi.org/10.1111/j.1471-6402.2004.00152.x.

Htun, Mala, and S. Laurel Weldon. 2011. State Power, Religion, and Women's Rights: A Comparative Analysis of Family Law. *Indiana Journal of Global Legal Studies* 18: 145–165. JSTOR. https://doi.org/10.2979/indjglolegstu.18.1.145.

Hughes, Bill, and Kevin Paterson. 1997. The Social Model of Disability and the Disappearing Body: Towards a Sociology of Impairment. *Disability & Society* 12: 325–340. https://doi.org/10.1080/09687599727209.

Karkazis, Katrina Alicia. 2008. *Fixing Sex: Intersex, Medical Authority, and Lived Experience. E-Duke Books Scholarly Collection*. Duke University Press.

Kayess, Rosemary, and Phillip French. 2008. Out of Darkness into Light - Introducing the Convention on the Rights of Persons with Disabilities. *Human Rights Law Review* 8: 1–34.

Kirtley, Michelle D., and James B. Weaver. 1999. Exploring the Impact of Gender Role Self-Perception on Communication Style. *Women's Studies in Communication* 22: 190–209. https://doi.org/10.1080/07491409.1999.10162420.

Langlois, Anthony J. 2017. Queer Rights? *Australian Journal of International Affairs* 71: 241–246. https://doi.org/10.1080/10357718.2017.1290047.

Mackenzie, Catriona, and Natalie Stoljar. 2000. *Relational Autonomy: Feminist Perspectives on Autonomy, Agency, and the Social Self*. Oxford University Press.

Mahowald, Mary Briody. 1992. To Be or Not Be a Woman: Anorexia Nervosa, Normative Gender Roles, and Feminism. *The Journal of Medicine and Philosophy: A Forum for Bioethics and Philosophy of Medicine* 17: 233–251. https://doi.org/10.1093/jmp/17.2.233.

Mallett, Rebecca, and Jenny Slater. 2014. Language. In *Disability Studies: A Student's Guide*, ed. Colin Cameron, 91–94. Sage.

Malson, Helen. 1998. *The Thin Woman: Feminism, Post-structuralism, and the Social Psychology of Anorexia Nervosa*. Psychology Press.

McSherry, Bernadette. 2012. Legal Capacity under the Convention on the Rights of Persons with Disabilities. *Journal of Law and Medicine* 20: 22–27.

Minkowitz, Tina. 2006. The United Nations Convention on the Rights of Persons with Disabilities and the Right to Be Free from Nonconsensual Psychiatric Interventions Symposium: The United Nations Convention on the Rights of Persons with Disabilities. *Syracuse Journal of International Law and Commerce*: 405–428.

Naffine, Ngaire. 2019. *Criminal Law and the Man Problem*. Bloomsbury Publishing.

Nohara, Michiko. 1992. Sex Differences in Interruption: An Experimental Reevaluation. *Journal of Psycholinguistic Research* 21: 127–146. https://doi.org/10.1007/BF01067991.

O'Donnell, Erin, and Julia Talbot-Jones. 2018. Creating Legal Rights for Rivers: Lessons from Australia, New Zealand, and India. *Ecology and Society* 23. https://doi.org/10.5751/ES-09854-230107.

Oliver, Mike. 2013. The Social Model of Disability: Thirty Years on. *Disability & Society* 28: 1024–1026. https://doi.org/10.1080/09687599.2013.818773.

Patton, Dana, and Joseph L. Smith. 2017. Lawyer, Interrupted: Gender Bias in Oral Arguments at the US Supreme Court. *Journal of Law and Courts* 5: 337–361. https://doi.org/10.1086/692611.

Preves, Sharon E. 2003. *Intersex and Identity: The Contested Self*. Rutgers University Press.

Quinn, Gerard, and Anna Arstein-Kerslake. 2012. Restoring the 'Human' in "Human Rights": Personhood and Doctrinal Innovation in the UN Disability Convention. In *The Cambridge Companion to Human Rights Law*, ed. Connor Gearty and Costas Douzinas, 36–55. Cambridge University Press.

Rahman, Momin. 2014. Queer Rights and the Triangulation of Western Exceptionalism. *Journal of Human Rights* 13: 274–289. https://doi.org/10.1080/14754835.2014.919214.

Richardson, Abby Morrow. 2004. Women's Inheritance Rights in Africa: The Need to Integrate Cultural Understanding and Legal Reform. *Human Rights Brief* 11: 19–22.

Rokkan, Stein. 1961. Mass Suffrage, Secret Voting and Political Participation. *European Journal of Sociology / Archives Européennes de Sociologie* 2: 132–152. https://doi.org/10.1017/S0003975600000333.

Ryan, Richard M., and Edward L. Deci. 2017. *Self-Determination Theory: Basic Psychological Needs in Motivation, Development, and Wellness*. Guilford Publications.

Shakespeare, Tom. 2013. *Disability Rights and Wrongs Revisited*. Routledge.

———. 2016. The Social Model of Disability. In *The Disability Studies Reader*, ed. Lennard J. Davis, 195–203. Taylor & Francis.

Smolak, Linda, and Sarah K. Murnen. 2001. Gender and Eating Problems. In *Eating Disorders: Innovative Directions in Research and Practice*, 91–110. Washington, DC, US: American Psychological Association. https://doi.org/10.1037/10403-005.

Spade, Dean. 2009. Documenting Gender. *Dukeminier Awards - Best Sexual Orientation and Gender Identity Law Review* 8: 137–248.

———. 2015. *Normal Life: Administrative Violence, Critical Trans Politics, and the Limits of Law*. Duke University Press.

Tan, Jacinta O.A., Helen A. Doll, Raymond Fitzpatrick, Anne Stewart, and Tony Hope. 2008. Psychiatrists' Attitudes Towards Autonomy, Best Interests and Compulsory Treatment in Anorexia Nervosa: A Questionnaire Survey. *Child and Adolescent Psychiatry and Mental Health* 2: 40. https://doi.org/10.1186/1753-2000-2-40.

Till, Chris. 2011. The Quantification of Gender: Anorexia Nervosa and Femininity. *Health Sociology Review* 20: 437–449. https://doi.org/10.5172/hesr.2011.20.4.437.

Traustadóttir, Rannveig. 2009. Disability Studies, the Social Model and Legal Developments. In *The UN Convention on the Rights of Persons with Disabilities: European and Scandinavian Perspectives*, ed. Gerard Quinn and Oddný Mjöll Arnardóttir, 1–16. Brill.

Watson, Joanne. 2016. Assumptions of Decision-Making Capacity: The Role Supporter Attitudes Play in the Realisation of Article 12 for People with Severe or Profound Intellectual Disability. *Laws* 5: 6. https://doi.org/10.3390/laws5010006.

West, Robin. 1988. Jurisprudence and Gender. *The University of Chicago Law Review* 55: 1–72. JSTOR. https://doi.org/10.2307/1599769.

Whelan, Daniel J. 2006. *Interdependent, Indivisible and Interrelated Human Rights: A Political and Historical Investigation*. University of Denver.

Winick, Bruce J. 1995. The Side Effects of Incompetency Labeling and the Implications for Mental Health Law. *Psychology, Public Policy, and Law* 1: 6–42. https://doi.org/10.1037/1076-8971.1.1.6.

Wojcik, Mark E. 1994. Using International Human Rights Law to Advance Queer Rights: A Case Study for the American Declaration of the Rights and Duties of Man Symposium: The Constitutionality of Anti-Gay Ballot Initiatives. *Ohio State Law Journal* 55: 649–664.

Chapter 2
Personhood: Perspectives from Critical Feminist, Disability and Queer Studies

2.1 Introduction

This chapter will explore personhood—one of the two components of legal capacity—through the lens of critical social theory. It will draw on feminist, disability and queer studies to examine historical and modern structures that deny personhood to these groups. I am focusing on personhood because recognition of personhood is the prerequisite for an individual being entitled to rights—including the right to legal agency, the second component of the right to legal capacity. There is also much less scholarship available on the right to legal agency (Arstein-Kerslake and Flynn 2017), so I have chosen to explore personhood here in order to be able to draw on a breadth of literature. I use critical social theory because it is focused on unearthing systemic domination and oppression—which, as I will explore throughout this book, is particularly pertinent to how women, disabled women, and gender minorities experience the right to legal capacity because they have, in different ways, been systemically excluded from personhood throughout history and into the present. The aim of this chapter is to bring together these different discussions of personhood from these various areas of scholarship in order to inform how the right to legal personhood—as part of the right to legal capacity—can best be realised for these groups.

The chapter begins with a discussion of the theoretical underpinnings of legal personhood and moral personhood in order to establish a working definition of personhood as well as insight into the exclusion of certain groups—including, in some cases, women, disabled women, and gender minorities. I then provide a comparative analysis as well as an intersectional analysis of theories from critical feminist, disability, and queer studies in order to discuss both individual group marginalisation and overlapping group marginalisation. For each, I provide an analysis in light of the right to legal capacity—as defined in Article 12 of the Convention on the Rights of Persons with Disabilities (CRPD) and discussed in

A. Arstein-Kerslake, *Legal Capacity & Gender*,
https://doi.org/10.1007/978-3-030-63493-3_2

Chap. 1. The intention of this is to explore how personhood is discussed by critical social theorists in this area—who are particularly focused on addressing marginalisation of these groups—and to explore whether and how Article 12 CRPD can provide a framework for ameliorating exclusions from personhood and potentially reimagining personhood to ensure universal inclusion for these groups. Building on these analyses, it will conclude with a discussion of the importance of legal personhood as a predictor of power and privilege.

I am not endeavouring to undertake a philosophical analysis of what it means to be a person—moral or legal. I am interested in reviewing different models of personhood, has they have been developed by scholars in critical social theory, in particular, in order to explore the meaning of personhood from the perspective of the experiences of women, disabled women, and gender minorities. These models will then be used to discuss what legal personhood can—or should—mean for individuals in these groups within the context of the right to legal capacity, which includes (as discussed above) the right to legal personhood and legal agency. Personhood has been thoroughly discussed by scholars in the context of moral and legal personhood and these theories have been influential in subsequent scholarship on personhood (Macklin 1983, p. 36). For this reason, it is necessary to identify some of the main theories related to moral and legal personhood, in order to then go on to discuss them in relation to critical feminist, disability, and queer studies. Although the right to legal capacity includes legal personhood, it is pertinent to discuss moral personhood as well because there are significant parallels in why certain groups are excluded from moral and legal personhood—which will be discussed below.

2.2 Moral and Legal Personhood

Moral philosophers have long grappled with the concept of personhood and have discussed the exclusion of certain groups (Maitland 1905). Moral personhood is ascribed when an entity or individual is recognised as a moral agent. Moral agents are those who take actions that can be determined to be moral or immoral—right or wrong. They can be held morally responsible for their intentional actions (Scott 1990; Warren 2000; Kittay 2005; Jaworska and Tannenbaum 2018).

Legal personhood has a slightly different perspective. It endeavours to assign personhood to those who are deemed able to be recognised by the law as legal persons with some degree of rights and/or responsibilities (Smith 1928). However, an individual or entity can be recognised as a legal person to varying degrees—they do not have to have full rights and responsibilities ascribed to them in order to be recognised as a legal person. Instead, the recognition of legal personhood provides the designation that a person or entity has the possibility for rights and responsibilities to be ascribed to them. This entitlement has not been restricted to humans—on the contrary, it has included other entities, such as corporations, rivers, and animals (Green 1945; Epstein 2002; O'Donnell and Talbot-Jones 2018).

The concepts of moral personhood and legal personhood intersect, or are related to each other, in that much of the same discussion occurs regarding theories of who and/or what should be included or excluded from personhood. For example, women have been excluded from both at different points in history under the argument that they lack the necessary rationality to be granted full personhood—they lack the rationality to be held morally responsible for their actions; and they lack the rationality to be recognised as holders of rights and responsibilities (Kittay 2005; Assassi 2009; Naffine 2011). Disabled people have been subjected to similar arguments (Kittay 2005; Wong 2010; Flynn and Arstein-Kerslake 2014b). Gender minorities have been under-theorised in scholarship on moral personhood—however, they have their legal personhood denied in various ways due to prejudicial notions of their mental health and rationality (Wahlert and Fiester 2012; Cannoot 2019).[1] Although the theories of moral and legal perosnhood exclude these groups on similar bases, they have notably different meanings.

It is possible for an individual or entity to be recognised as a legal person—but not a moral person (Kramer 2008; Naffine 2009). For example, rivers have been found to hold legal personhood—meaning that they are holders of some degree of rights and responsibilities. Rivers are, however, generally not considered moral persons—they cannot be held morally responsible for their actions. This example also highlights the interaction between the concepts of moral personhood and legal capacity.

Legal capacity, as discussed above, encompasses an individual's or entity's legal personhood and legal agency. In the example above, a river can be recognised as having legal personhood—because it can be recognised as a holder of rights (O'Donnell and Talbot-Jones 2018). In order for a rivers' full legal capacity to be recognised, it would also need to be recognised as a legal agent—an entity able to enter into, alter, and extinguish legal relationships. Although rivers are generally not considered sentient beings and they are generally not considered to be capable of cognition or decision-making—those are not necessarily required for the recognition of legal agency. For example, corporations are also not sentient beings and they have had some degree of legal agency recognised (Green 1945; Fisse 1995; Frenkel and Lurie 2001; Blair 2013). This shows how legal capacity (and, by extension, legal personhood) can be recognised in an entity and yet moral personhood can be denied. Table 2.1 depicts the distinction between moral and legal personhood.

It is interesting to note that while the concepts of legal personhood and moral personhood are quite distinct and do not overlap in many circumstances, such as the example above, the rationales for excluding certain groups are often quite similar for both theories of moral personhood and legal personhood (as well as legal capacity, more broadly)—such as a lack of rationality or cognition.

---

[1]The history of women, disabled women, and gender minorities being excluded from legal capacity—including legal personhood and legal agency—due to prejudicial notions of insufficient capacity is explored more in Chap. 3.

Table 2.1 Relationship between moral personhood and legal capacity

	Recognition (static)	Responsibility (active)
Moral personhood	Moral personhood = recognition as a person (static) who can understand right from wrong and can be held responsible for their actions (active)	
Legal capacity Legal personhood + Legal agency	Legal personhood = recognition as a legal person who holds rights (static)	Legal agency = holds legal responsibility and actions are recognised in law (active)

As is perhaps evident, the concept of personhood is fraught—there is not one clear definition of what a person is or when personhood should be denied or granted (Macklin 1983, p. 36). This may not be problematic. This lack of clarity may provide the flexibility that is necessary for a concept that is so critical to an individual's or entity's participation in the moral and/or legal order. The lack of clarity allows for changes and adaptation—for the evolution of the concept of personhood. In light of this inevitable and ongoing evolution of personhood—and because it is a core component of legal capacity—it is critical to examine existing theories related to personhood and explore how they may be relevant for the realisation of the right to legal capacity.

The original concept of personhood in our legal systems, as well as in theories of moral personhood, largely did not envision women as holding personhood (Naffine 2009, 2011, 2019). Instead, in Western legal systems, it was generally white men, often upper class and land holding, that were granted personhood. This is important because it reminds us that the foundations of personhood often excluded the three groups that we are addressing—women, disabled women, and gender minorities. Many of the legal and social structures surrounding a granting of personhood were largely not created with these groups in mind. Instead, they were primarily created with a very different group in mind—white, able-bodied, cisgender, heterosexual, upper class men. As such, many of these structures were created to meet the needs of white, able-bodied, cisgender, heterosexual, upper class men. Many of these structures have yet to adapt to address the needs of the wider population, including women, disabled women, and gender minorities (Naffine 2011). This highlights the importance of an examination of critical social theory in the areas of feminism, disability theory, and queer theory.

Critical social theory provides a lens through which to expose domination and oppression—including those forms of domination and oppression that are based on histories of marginalisation and structural inequality (Agger 2006; Bohman 2019; Campbell 2020). Therefore, theories of personhood in critical feminist, disability, and queer theory may be able to highlight the many areas of our socio-legal structures that construct or recognise personhood in such a way that excludes women, disabled women, and gender minorities. They may also be able to highlight how personhood could be constructed in order to better include these groups. In the section below, I explore theories of personhood—legal and moral—in critical social theory and draw conclusions about what these theories may mean for the right to legal personhood within the right to legal capacity.

2.3 Personhood and Critical Social Theory

Critical social theory has a narrow and a broad meaning. Both meanings provide a descriptive or normative foundation for social inquiry that is aimed at decreasing domination and increasing freedom (Bohman 2019). The narrow sense refers to the school of thought developed by German-American social theorists in the first half of the twentieth Century, which is described further below. The broader sense refers to the wide array of social theories that have emerged as offshoots of that original school of thought. They are theories that aim to explain and transform circumstances that enslave individuals. They have emerged in connection with social movements—such as the women's rights movement, the disability rights movement, and the queer rights movement—that identify the domination of certain groups in modern societies (Bohman 2019). In this book, some of the theories that I will be examining specifically refer to themselves as 'critical social theory,' others do not, however, they are theories that are aimed at decreasing domination and increasing freedom and equality—as such, I am referring to them as critical social theory.

Critical social theory aims to shed light on social conditions in order to create an awareness that may encourage and enable change (Campbell 2020). Critical social theory arose in the early twentieth century, with the Frankfurt School of thought. It was a group of German-American social theorists who sought to build upon Marxist theory to not only explain and understand social phenomenon; but also, to critique, and ultimately change society (Horkheimer 1972; Calhoun 1995). The Frankfurt School's core goals were: the transformation of capitalism into meaningful democracy; human emancipation; and the decrease of social hierarchies of dominance (Horkheimer 1972). Today, critical social theory has developed into a widely used social theory that takes an interdisciplinary perspective across the social sciences to critique modern bastions of power and create social change to emancipate the oppressed. Many fields have developed out of critical social theory, including: feminist theory, critical race theory, queer theory, and critical disability theory, among others (Agger 2006).

Critical social theory is relevant to personhood in so far as personhood is essential for individual interaction with our legal and social world. As I will explore further at the end of this chapter, personhood is a predictor of power and privilege. For better or for worse, we exist in a neo-liberal world which largely centres around the individual—the rights of the individual as well as the economic capital of the individual and her ability to engage, as an individual, with economic markets. As such, the recognition of the personhood of the individual is essential in order for her to be able to engage with economic markets and to seek both resources for basic living conditions as well as a higher socio-economic status. In addition, the recognition of her personhood is essential because rights and responsibilities only attach, for the most part, to individuals who are recognised as full persons.

Ironically, as mentioned above, critical social theory arose out of Marxist theory that critiques the capitalist prioritisation of the individual. However, it has developed into a tool, which I am using in this book, to identify and examine marginalisation and oppression more broadly. Here, I am accepting the reality of our neo-liberal world that places high value on the individual—and in order for an individual to take advantage of their power as an individual, they must be recognised as a legal (and moral person). Because of this importance of personhood in our socio-legal world—and its role as a predictor of power and privilege—I am using the lens of critical social theory in order to shed light on the social conditions created by the granting or denying of personhood. I hope to create an awareness that may encourage and enable change, in line with the goals of critical social theory. I aim to identify and examine how women, disabled women, and gender minorities experience personhood—including where and how it is denied and, ultimately, the impact that has on the social capital of the individual.

As I have written elsewhere (Flynn and Arstein-Kerslake 2014b; Arstein-Kerslake 2017), the neo-liberal concept of the person dominates most of the global north. This is derived from liberal political theory which views the individual as the centre of society (Rawls 2005). It prioritises individual rights above all else—including community rights and family rights (Minow and Shanley 1996). It largely sees the individual as an atomistic able-bodied male free to navigate the socio-legal world and to take advantage of economic opportunities; compete with other individuals; and maximise profit, productivity, and efficiency for himself (Mackenzie and Stoljar 2000; Kittay 2005). For various reasons, women, disabled people, gender minorities, and other minority groups are excluded, in many ways from this view of the individual—and thereby, the granting of personhood to such individuals. It is only individuals that are recognised as capable of these activities that are recognised as persons.

Women are often not capable of these activities because they are charged with care for others. The care of others often makes it impossible to navigate the socio-legal world independently, serving your own interests and seeking profit for yourself. This often requires significant time demands that caregivers often do not have—it also requires a mentality that prioritises the self over others, which caregivers often lack (Kittay 1999; Whitney 2011). As will be discussed later, women are also excluded from these activities because of a perception that they lack the necessary rationality and logic skills to undertake such tasks (Naffine 2011). There is a perception that they would be overwhelmed with the responsibility to navigate the socio-legal world, compete with others, and wrestle profit and power for themselves. Of course, as gender equality measures become more effective and women are granted such personhood on an equal basis with men—it is more and more apparent that in many ways they are very well suited for such activities—or, at least, as well suited to them as men are when they are given the same advantages as men such as the benefits of cronyism, others to support their health and home life, etc. It is, of course, another matter altogether whether we—as women—and as humans—want to live in the neo-liberal world that men have created. And whether we want to possess and use personhood to undertake liberal political activities such as navigating the socio-legal world and taking advantage of economic opportunities; competing with other individuals; and maximising profit, productivity, and efficiency for ourselves.

Perhaps most obviously, women are also perceived by the neo-liberal world as less than full persons because of the notion that they lack the strength necessary to take on the activities of a 'person' in the liberal world order. They are too weak to compete—to seek profit for themselves by pushing away, or down, others. Again, as a feminist, we are faced with the question of whether we want to be the person that neo-liberal theory prizes—do we want to compete and seek self-serving profit above most other things? Regardless of the answer to that question—the reality is that we live in a world where, in many circumstances, you must be the individual who can and will compete and seek self-serving profit over most other things. Otherwise, you will be disadvantaged. As such, desirable to you personally, or not, if you are not recognised as a person in the neo-liberal landscape, then you are marginalised—you are no longer able to take on a dominate role—you are the oppressed.

Disabled people—including disabled women—are often excluded from these neo-liberal definitions of the person. They are perceived to lack the cognitive ability to engage with activities such as navigating the socio-legal world and taking advantage of economic opportunities; competing with other individuals; and maximising profit, productivity, and efficiency for themselves (Wong 2010; Flynn and Arstein-Kerslake 2014b; Quinn and Rekas-Rosalbo 2016). They are often also perceived as generally lacking the necessary capabilities to be economically productive and therefore, they are excluded from the category of person in a neo-liberal landscape that only identifies those with economic value as being worthy of full rights and responsibilities—full personhood. Intersectionally, the oppressive assumptions about both women and disabled people are foisted upon disabled women (Collins 2019). This leaves disabled women oppressed on multiple fronts and denied personhood from multiple angles with varying justifications—not sufficient rationality and not sufficient strength.

Gender minorities are often excluded from personhood in moral philosophy and liberal political theory not because, like disabled people, they are activity considered and deemed unfit for full personhood (Wong 2010). On the contrary, gender minorities have rarely even been given consideration by moral philosophers and liberal political theorists (Phelan 2000). This speaks to the depth of the marginalisation that this group experiences—they are oppressed not only by ideology that actively excludes them—but also by their lack of consideration by most dominant moral, legal and political theorists. If a group has never been considered by a school of thought, their needs and abilities are most likely missing from the models and theories developed.

Although they were largely not considered by theorists—there are very specific ways in which gender minorities are excluded from legal personhood. One significant barrier is that some gender minorities experience social and legal barriers to the recognition of their gender—in various forms. Some gender minorities do not identify in line with the dominant gender binary models and there is often no option for the identification of gender outside the male/female binary. If gender identification was not required at all for legal documentation, then this would not be an issue. However, it remains a requirement for many forms of legal identification. Other gender minorities would like to identify with the gender binary of male/female—however, the gender that they would like to identify with is different from the gender that was ascribed to them at birth. There is often not bureaucratic channels for appropriately making the necessary change in their identity documents. In other cases, the bureaucratic channels may exist, however they may not be safe for individuals to pursue for various reasons, which I will explore further below. These barriers to the identification of gender do not inherently exclude gender minorities from personhood—however, without the necessary documentation an individual is effectively excluded from personhood because they do not have a means to effectively and accurately access personhood.

In liberal political systems, such as those that dominate much of the world, the need for flexibility in legal identification of gender has largely been overlooked. Again, this is likely due to the fact that liberal political theory was developed by white, able-bodied, cisgender, heterosexual, upper class men who were never faced with barriers in relation to gender identity and could not conceive of the need for personhood to be divorced from gender identity. It may be that the reality is that in order to achieve equality in designation of personhood, there is a need to not only provide recognition beyond the gender binary of male/female. It may be that there is a need to divorce the recognition of personhood from gender identity entirely (Cannoot 2019).

It may be no surprise that the vast majority of the economic and political theorists that write about and have developed liberal political theory were, and are, white, able-bodied, cisgender, heterosexual men (Hudson 2006). They created a theory of the world that suited them best. A world where a person is someone who has significant personal capital at his disposal. Who has others—mostly women—successfully managing their home lives and tending to their health needs—things that, in their absence, would likely render the individual unable to function, let alone compete in a marketplace. However, recognition of this is largely missing from liberal political theory (Shaver 1996).

Male legal and social theorists have often—inadvertently or intentionally—constructed their theories of justice, law, and the social order with the male as the central figure (Minow 1987; Naffine 2019). The male entity holds personhood and much of the theoretical frameworks stem from assumptions that are inherently male—such as a legal person being an individual that seeks power, autonomy, and resources. It assumes that individuals have support behind them that provide for their nutrition, health, and care needs. It assumes that they are able-bodied and lithely manoeuvring legal and social relationships to seek the good life for themselves. In essence, it assumes that a person is a man (McConnell 1996).

This is an over-simplification of the construction and meeting of personhood—although, I would argue that even though it is an over-simplification, there are important truths here that have the potential to transform our socio-legal world if they are better incorporated into reform efforts. Those core truths are that our socio-legal systems were not constructed with women, disabled women, or gender minorities in mind as persons—at least not as persons wielding power or as full legal persons. As such, they are not constructed in a way that always meets the needs of these groups or fosters the development of these groups. This sometimes manifests itself in explicit denials of legal personhood to these groups—discussed in Chaps. 3 and 4. However, it doesn't always manifest itself in the explicit denial of the legal or moral personhood of these groups. Sometimes the socio-legal world is simply constructed in such a way that doesn't take the perspectives, needs, and desires of that group into consideration and this can result in insidious barriers to the recognition and enjoyment of legal and/or moral personhood. In the following section, critical feminist, disability, and queer theory is explored to discover their various perspectives on personhood and where personhood is and is not realised for these groups.

2.3.1 *Critical Feminist Theory and Personhood*

Critical feminist theory has many different scholars that have engaged with the meaning and boundaries of personhood. Liberal and relational feminist scholars, in particular, have unique perspectives on personhood. Individual scholars have also explored the person from a critical feminist perspective.

2.3.1.1 Liberal Feminism and Personhood

Liberal feminism largely embraces liberal political theory and inserts a feminist perspective (McConnell 1996). As discussed above, traditional liberal political theory supports a legal system based on discrete, atomistic individuals who compete with one another. The role of the law is to protect them from intrusions of other individuals or entities, including the state, on their freedom to exercise their individual rights (Locke 1794; Dunn 1982; Smith 1987). Liberal feminism largely adheres to this theory and, in particular, it adopts one of the strongest threads of liberalism, which is equality—or equal treatment under the law. These ideologies were a large part of the second wave of feminism—which included the Equal Rights Amendment in the United States and the women's rights movement of the 1970s and 1980s. In addition, it adopts liberal political theory's emphasis on autonomy. For example, much of the reproductive justice movement is based on the concept of women's equal right to autonomy and privacy (McConnell 1996; Ross and Solinger 2017). There is a debate within liberal feminism as to whether equality—and equal rights to autonomy—requires merely equal treatment or also differential preferential treatment to account for oppression (McConnell 1996). This relates to the liberal feminist view of personhood, in that it essentially embraces the traditional liberal view of personhood—but asks that women be included within this view—with some debate about whether this can be done purely by breaking down discriminatory barriers to personhood or whether active steps to counteract historical oppression must be taken.

This liberal feminist view of the person relates to the right to legal capacity—as it is articulated in Article 12 CRPD and Article 15 CEDAW—in that the right to legal capacity inherently embraces the liberal view of individual rights—as the right to legal capacity is an individual human right. It also embraces the importance of autonomy and equality that are espoused in liberal political theory and embraced by liberal feminists. It embraces autonomy by demanding legal capacity—which is, in essence, as described in Chap. 1, a right to autonomy (Article 12(2) CRPD). It embraces equality by demanding legal capacity on an equal basis for all (Article 12 (2) CRPD). In these ways, the right to legal capacity parallels liberal feminism in its adoption and adaptation of liberal political theory. It is, therefore, similarly vulnerable to the critiques of liberal feminism and liberal political theory more broadly.

Legal capacity, at its core, envisions an atomistic privileged male operating to develop and extinguish legal relationships in such a way that maximises benefit to himself and allows him to live his version of the 'good life'—as described by theorists such as Dworkin, Galston, and Rawls (Lund 1996; Nussbaum 2001; Wilsdon 2010; Arstein-Kerslake 2017). The concept of legal capacity was—in essence—not created with women or other minorities groups in mind. In fact, it can be argued that it was created—and has evolved—in a liberal political landscape that embraces and relies upon capitalism and, in fact, is predicated on an underclass of working people—largely minorities—whose legal capacity is not recognised on an equal basis with the upper class privileged males. These connections to liberal theory cannot be denied—and the weakness of liberal theory is therefore carried forward in the concept of legal capacity. However, those critiques do not render legal capacity any less significant for the individual living in our neo-liberal world in which individual rights reign and power and privilege is, to some degree, predicated on the liberty and autonomy of the individual.

The right to legal capacity, as articulated in Chap. 1, may hold more depth than simply existing as a vessel of liberal political theory. It embraces the liberal political values of autonomy and liberty but it also asserts a right to recognition of legal personhood for all people. Liberal political theory espouses the importance of individual autonomy, liberty, rights, and equality—but it often falls short of guaranteeing those things for all people (Kittay 2005; Naffine 2011). The right to legal capacity, however, goes farther and deeper and may provide a new landscape from which to seek equality for these groups—one that has not yet been envisioned in liberal political theory. The right to legal capacity guarantees autonomy and liberty on an equal basis for all—not a privileged few. It may be the tool that allows for the realisation of these liberal political ideals for minority groups such as women, disabled people, and gender minorities—even though they were not originally envisioned in early emanations of liberal political theory as persons for the purpose of theories of justice and the manner in which we organise our socio-legal world.

Liberal political theory may provide us with a justification for the removal of barriers to the legal capacity of women, disabled women, and gender minorities—however, it does not provide an explanation or justification for the state obligation to provide access to support for the exercise of legal capacity. Liberal political theory and liberal feminism gives us reason to seek an equal right to legal capacity for all in order to achieve—or take steps towards achieving liberty, autonomy, and equality for all. It does not take into consideration the complex web of relationships and interdependencies that we all live within and that for some people—and, maybe, all people—are essential in order for them to exercise their legal capacity and engage with the socio-legal world. It can be argued that we are all part of this web of interdependency. It can also be argued that minority groups such as women, disabled women, and gender minorities experience this web of interdependence uniquely, and possibly to a greater degree than those whom are experiencing high levels of social privilege, like white, able-bodied, cisgender men. A view of personhood from relational feminist theories may give us some insight into this web of interdependency and how the right to legal capacity and the accompanying state obligation to provide support for the exercise of legal capacity may allow us to envision a new socio-legal order that values the individual and individual rights to autonomy and liberty but also takes into account that individuals are inherently interconnected and even when autonomy is being exercised it is not done in a vacuum.

2.3.1.2 Relational Feminism and Personhood

Relational feminism—sometimes also known and cultural feminism—is a reaction to liberal political theory and it may provide some solutions for the gaps left by liberal political theory. Unlike liberal feminism, it does not embrace liberal political theory. Instead, it reimagines the structure of society and the role of the law. Liberal political theory operates under the premise that the law serves to protect individual rights—it protects the individual from incursions on their rights by other individuals or entities. It prioritises liberty and creating independence for the individual over interdependence—some would argue that it even seeks to protect the individual from interdependence. Relational feminism, in contrast, is premised on a system of interdependence and mutual responsibility.

Relational feminism is rooted in Carol Gilligan's work examining differences in the moral development of girls and boys (Gilligan 1993; McConnell 1996). Her work was, in part, a reaction to work by psychology professor Lawrence Kohlberg. Kohlberg conducted a study on the development of morality. In his study he only examined boys—not girls. He concluded that the correct course of moral development for human beings is the recognition that the pursuit of individual rights is the paramount model of justice (Kohlberg and Hersh 1977; McConnell 1996, p. 302). Gilligan's work challenged Kohlberg's findings—particularly his emphasis on one correct moral process and his examination of only moral development in boys and not girls. Gilligan used boys and girls and developed a counter theory—that there are two distinct moral analytic processes. One model that favours a justice model that focuses on the individual and individual rights—and a second model that favours relational care (Gilligan 1993). Her work was at the forefront of the emergence of relational feminism, which sought to argue for a new system of values that prioritise a society and legal system that is based on love, connection, interdependence and care (McConnell 1996, p. 303).

The pioneering legal theory that was essential in the development of relational feminism was created by Robin West. West argues that women are uniquely inseparable from other human beings—by virtue of biologically determined phenomena such as pregnancy, menstruation, penetrative sex, and breast feeding. She argues that a theory of justice—of the overarching social and legal order—cannot adequately apply for women if it is premised on the divisibility of human beings—on their separateness (West 1988). In fact, West argues that it likely cannot adequately apply to anyone of any gender because we are all interconnected (West 1988, pp. 70–71). In West's work, and relational feminism theory more broadly, a person cannot be an isolated atomistic individual as has been envisioned by liberal political theorists. A person must be recognised as inherently interconnected with other people. West argues that all forms of life should be recognised, respected, and honoured (West 1988, p. 72).

Robin West describes relational feminism this way:

> We might summarize . . . [relational] feminism in this way: women's potential for a material connection to life entails (either directly, as I have argued, or indirectly, through the reproduction of mothering) an experiential and psychological sense of connection with other human life, which in turn entails both women's concept of value, and women's concept of harm. Women's concept of value revolves not around the axis of autonomy, individuality, justice and rights, as does men's, but instead around the axis of intimacy, nurturance, community, responsibility and care. For women, the creation of value, and the living of a good life, therefore depend upon relational, contextual, nurturant and affective responses to the needs of those who are dependent and weak, while for men the creation of value, and the living of the good life, depend upon the ability to respect the rights of independent co-equals, and the deductive, cognitive ability to infer from those rights rules for safe living. Women's concept of harm revolves not around a fear of annihilation by the other but around a fear of separation and isolation from the human community on which she depends, and which is dependent upon her. (West 1988, p. 28)

Relational feminism sees the person as inherently interconnected. All actions that are taken and all relationships that are created and extinguished are not done so in a vacuum—instead, every action and every relationship created or extinguished is part of an intricate web of dependency and support that we all receive from those around us. In the beginning of our lives—we receive life, nourishment, and care from our mothers, and sometimes we receive much the same from our fathers or other caregivers—in different ways. Later in life, we rely on our caregivers for safety, guidance, shelter, and other forms of assistance. Throughout our lives we rely on friends, teachers, counsellors, caregivers, the government, educational institutions, and others for our formation and our security as members and participants in a thriving and complex social order. As West discusses in the quote above, women experience these relationships differently than privileged white, cisgender men—similarly, disabled women and gender minorities often experience these relationships uniquely.

Similarly, women, disabled women, and gender minorities experience legal capacity uniquely. They do not necessarily see themselves as, or act as, separate legal entities—isolated and seeking to exercise liberty and autonomy to seek the good life for themselves. Instead, women, disabled women, and gender minorities are often exercising their liberty and autonomy—their personhood and agency—in collaboration with others and, sometimes, in order to serve others, not themselves. They may actively relinquish their legal agency to another to make a decision on their behalf—often not out of weakness or confusion, but because their lives are built on relationships of trust and interdependence and decisions are made accordingly—knowing that those in their webs of interdependence and trust can act on their behalves. They often exercise legal agency not to serve their own interests or to seek the good life for themselves, but instead to attempt to prepare the way for those around them, in their interdependent webs, to be able to seek the good life for themselves.

It has been argued that the division between liberal feminism and relational feminism is false. That the relational elements can be read into liberal feminism and that relational feminism fails—on a practical level—if there is no protection for individual rights, such as the right to reproductive autonomy (McClain 1991; Karlan and Ortiz 1992; McConnell 1996, p. 303; Christman 2004; Anderson 2009). My view is that relational feminism presents a wonderful view of the world—one in which interdependence is celebrated and individuals are rewarded for care work. It presents the possibility for a complete revolution in how personhood is envisioned—no longer relying on recognition of the individual and their rights, but instead reimagining a person as a piece of something larger—an interdependent social order. However, I find this difficult to envision on a practical level. This may be because I am so accustomed to and entrenched in the neo-liberal world that prioritises the individual. It may also be because I find it hard to envision how some men, in particular, would fit in to—or react to—a world in which they were forced to live with the possibility that interconnectedness could be prioritised over the individual. I imagine that many of the men that would be most resistant to such a restructured system would be men with a considerable degree of power—men that I would like to be protected from. This instinct forces me to circle back around to the desire to have individual rights recognised in order to have a tool to protect myself from such powerful men—albeit an imperfect tool, due to challenges in adjudication of individual rights and appropriate construction of the content of individual rights. In essence, I find the liberal political emphasis on individual rights imperfect, but convincing, and I would be uncomfortable giving it up. Unfortunately, I don't believe that we can seek equality or even safely exist without individual rights. I feel we need tools for protecting ourselves against each other and against the socio-legal systems that we have created. However, I also feel that the individual rights systems currently in place in many jurisdictions do not adequately account for the reality of the relational elements of all of our lives, and particularly those of minorities such as women, disabled women, and gender minorities.

Although, we are still operating within an individual rights framework that does not comport with West's and other relational feminist's views of the socio-legal order, I believe we can draw on relational feminism to create individual rights that better protect and provide more power to women, disabled women, and gender minorities. One way to do this, is to ensure that the rights framework accounts for the interdependence of all human beings and incorporates it into its demands of states and individuals.

The right to legal capacity is a powerful example of how relational feminism can be incorporated into an individual rights system. The right to legal capacity, as interpreted by the CRPD Committee, acknowledges that individuals are interconnected. It does not view a person as an individual, atomistic, island—seeking to take actions to benefit themselves and provide maximum efficiency and profit to themselves. Instead, it accepts that many people exist in a web of dependency—with their family, friends, caregivers, co-workers, community, and others. It recognises that an individual's personhood is sometimes intricately tied to and reliant on this web of dependency. For example, their wellbeing may be so closely tied to another individual's wellbeing that one cannot exist without the other. They may make decisions based on what is best for those around them, as well as themselves. This interconnection of individuals is recognised in the right to legal capacity in its requirement that states provide access to support for the exercise of legal capacity, which is described in detail in Chap. 1 (Flynn and Arstein-Kerslake 2014a; Watson 2016).

It is important to acknowledge that not all women, disabled women, and gender minorities experience the socio-legal world in exactly the manner that I am describing. I also acknowledge that there are many other individuals and groups that may experience the socio-legal world in a similar manner to how I am describing it for women, disabled women, and gender minorities. For example, racial minorities, sexual minorities, or even those from more privileged groups, such as white men. The experience of interdependence, in particular, is quite universal in its application—it can even be argued that there is no one that is truly free from social dependencies. However, in this book, I am attempting to draw conclusions based on societal norms and expectations that are largely externally thrust upon us by long histories of oppression. This oppression has targeted—or impacted—particular groups uniquely, such as women, disabled women, and gender minorities. In this book, I am seeking to describe this general experience—the impact of systemic oppression on women, disabled women, and gender minorities, in the form of denial of the right to legal capacity.

2.3.1.3 Other Feminist Theories and Personhood

Legal scholar, Saru Matambanadzo has also tackled the topic of personhood from a feminist perspective (Matambanadzo 2012). Matambanadzo takes the body and embodiment as her starting point and draws on insights from vulnerability studies and embodiment theory to reimagine legal personhood (Matambanadzo 2012, p. 71). Vulnerability studies examines vulnerability under the assumption that vulnerability is a universal constant for human beings. It argues for a legal system that is premised on the dependency created by this inherent vulnerability of human beings. It also rejects the liberal political notion of isolated individualism—instead it recognises the vulnerability and dependency that we all exist within and that connects us to those around us and to an interconnected web of reciprocity with other human beings. Philosopher Judith Butler has written about how we are defined, in part, by such embodied vulnerabilities (Matambanadzo 2012, p. 75). Matambanadzo identifies several concepts from vulnerability studies that she draws on:

> Persons are characterized both as individuals and by their connection to others.
>
> Persons possess a human body. They are characterized by embodiment, have been born and have been gestated in the body of another member of their species. Persons are potentially mothers and always the children of mothers.
>
> Persons are sentient creatures that spend some time in their lives with self-awareness.
>
> Persons possess present potential for individual existence and present potential for collective associations.
>
> Persons' bodies are characterized not only by needs and appetites, but also by the limits of sickness, illness and death.
>
> Persons are demonstrably capable of pain and suffering and also pleasure and happiness. (Matambanadzo 2012, pp. 75–76)

Matambanadzo uses these concepts, combined with embodiment theory to develop her own nine non-hierarchical factors to determine when legal personhood should be recognised (Matambanadzo 2012, p. 76).

Embodiment theory is a feminist theory of the body that queries how the self is constructed in relation to the body (Matambanadzo 2005; Lennon 2019). Matambanadzo posits that the body itself influences the boundaries of who is and who is not considered a legal person (Matambanadzo 2012, p. 74). Therefore, taking the body itself as her starting point and premising her work on an assumption of vulnerability of human beings, she developed the following nine non-hierarchical elements of legal personhood:

> Embodied
>
> 'Natural' in so far as it is born of another member of its species
>
> Vulnerable to death, illness, injury and need arising from embodiment
>
> Capable of pain and suffering
>
> Capable of pleasure and joy
>
> Capable of volition
>
> Possessing the potential for individual and collective existence
>
> Possessing the potential for relational capacity under law (willingly enter into contractual relationships and mutual obligations) and potential to understand the ramifications of such relations
>
> Possessing self-awareness (Matambanadzo 2012, pp. 76–77)

Matambanadzo begins her analysis with a presumption of personhood—she says that all individuals, entities, or collectives whose existence mirrors that of a human being in terms of body and embodiment should enjoy a presumption of personhood. For this class of individuals, entities, or collectives, when they are seeking to be newly recognised as legal persons or they are already recognised as legal persons but they are seeking an expansion of rights and responsibilities within legal personhood, they should be entitled to a presumption of legal recognition for the rights and responsibilities of legal personhood at least to the level of quasi-personhood. She says that those that do not mirror the embodied capacities and vulnerabilities of human beings should have the burden of proving that they resemble human bodies and are similarly situated to embodied human beings. She proposes that the nine elements listed above can determine which individuals, entities, or collectives are entitled to this presumption of personhood. If some, but not all, of the elements exist, then the individual, entity or collective could be deemed a quasi-person entitled to a particular range of rights and/or responsibilities. If none of the elements are met—meaning that the individual, entity, or collective does not display the sorts of vulnerability or the types of potential that arise from the body—then, the individual, entity, or collective is not granted legal personhood and may only enjoy the rights and responsibilities of legal personhood as a matter of privilege and not as a matter of right (Matambanadzo 2012, pp. 76–77). Matambanadzo says that her framework restructures legal personhood in a manner that is centred on human embodiment and vulnerability but it can also be used to identify and ascribe legal personhood to non-human entities and collectives that demonstrate sufficiently similar attributes to human bodies and their vulnerability (Matambanadzo 2012, p. 77).

I have included Matambanadzo's work here to demonstrate the vastness of literature and theories on legal personhood and the potential to create and adapt such theories to comport with what may be a new understanding of legal personhood introduced in CEDAW with the right to legal capacity in Article 15 and developed further in the CRPD in Article 12. While Matambanadzo's theory does not substantively engage with human rights law—her attempt appears to be to reconstruct the boundaries of legal personhood to better incorporate minority groups, such as women, disabled women, and gender minorities by utilising embodiment theory and vulnerability studies. Embodiment theory allows her to include minority groups as full legal persons by virtue of their humanness. Vulnerability studies allows her to adapt the elements of legal personhood—her nine non-hierarchical elements—to reflect a definition of legal personhood that incorporates elements that are lacking from previous definitions—such as those created largely by white, able-bodied, cisgender men, like liberal political theory. For example, she has included the elements, "Possessing the potential for individual and collective existence" and "Possessing the potential for relational capacity under law," which both emphasise a relational view of personhood—focusing on the role of the legal person in social spaces and not merely the individual capabilities of the legal person (Matambanadzo 2012, pp. 76–77).

Matambanadzo's view of the legal person relates to the right to legal capacity in that it includes the relational elements described above. Her theory of legal personhood does not stray too substantively from traditional liberal political theory views of legal personhood—she stills largely maintains elements of cognition, rationality, and volition—as can be seen (and are problematic for the reasons described in Chap. 1, such as the conflation between a right to legal capacity and an assessment of mental capacity) in the last four elements that she lists. In addition, she maintains the prioritisation of individualism in some respects—she discusses legal personhood in the context of an individual right (although, she leaves the potential for it to be ascribed to collectives and other entities). This is similar to the right to legal capacity in international human rights law—it maintains the liberal political theory emphasis on the rights of the individual—it is, after all, an individual right to legal capacity. In addition, the relational elements that she brings in—discussed above—do, at least, give a nod to the possibility that legal personhood could be held and exercised across multiple actors. These relational elements align with the state obligation to provide access to support for the exercise of legal capacity in Article 12(3) of the CRPD.

I, myself, am not completely convinced by Matambanadzo's nine elements—I'm not sure that they adequately incorporate the needs of all minority groups—including women, disabled women, and gender minorities. For example, some disabled women—and some disabled people, more broadly—may be perceived to be excluded by the elements of 'understanding' and 'self-awareness.' Conversely, I would be happy to argue that all people—including all disabled people with cognitive impairments—can be assumed to possess self-awareness and the potential to understand—even where the communication of such skills is not always clear (Flynn and Arstein-Kerslake 2014b; Arstein-Kerslake 2017). However, I am not confident that all parties would argue in such a manner when implementing Matabanadzo's elements and they may then exclude some disabled people from legal personhood on the basis that they are perceived to not understand or have sufficient self-awareness. I would also query the necessity of such elements for legal personhood. I would instead argue, in line with what I see the text of Article 12 of the CRPD requiring, that we can assume legal personhood and then—in recognition of the relational existence of everyone—seek to provide support for the exercise of personhood and tailor that support to the needs of each individual. As I have mentioned previously, this maintains the liberal political notion of the individual as possessor of rights—such as the right to legal capacity—yet does so while challenging the liberal political notion that individuals operate in isolation.

2.3.1.4 Application of Liberal Political Theory of Rights to Women

Critical feminist theory also queries whether 'rights' can meaningfully apply to women, when the conception of legal personhood is so profoundly rooted in the notion of the male (Ahmed 2016; Naffine 2019). This raises the question of whether the right to legal capacity can meaningfully apply to women. In many ways, no, rights cannot meaningfully apply to women or any other minority group—at least not in the same way that they do to men—because the concept of rights has, as its foundation, principles that are overwhelmingly attached to a patriarchal history that prioritised the personhood of men and the needs and desires of men (McConnell 1996). As discussed previously, the concept of individual rights largely stems from a liberal political history that was, in many ways, created by and for men—embracing a long line of male dominated legal and political theory.

However, individual rights have evolved to become a rousing cry for equality for all. This originally strongly patriarchal notion of rights has been ascribed to minority groups—including women—and is utilised to demand equality for these groups on an equal basis with others—'others' are usually the dominant white male, cisgender, heterosexual individuals that exist in a realm of privilege that is largely untouchable for other groups. It is easy to see the irony of using the rights framework to attempt to create equality—when the framework itself came from a place of extreme privilege. This theory of individual rights created by the privileged is now being applied (often by the privileged) to seek to provide equality for the underprivileged minorities. How could such a framework encompass the needs of underprivileged minorities? Men created the rights framework in line with their values of individual strength, isolated autonomy, and liberty. Many minorities—women, in particular—don't share the same values. Women and other minorities often value community and family driven ideals more than individual ideals, partly because women and other minorities have had to band together in response to oppression. For example, women, at all levels of social classes, are often charged with rearing children and caring for the health and welfare of the entire family unit. As such, they may value law and policy reform that provides assistance with childcare, healthcare, and caregiving responsibilities—this provides benefit to people other than themselves—it may not directly fulfil an individual right—however, it may be the means that women need and/or desire to improve their lives and improve the lives of those that they love. The rights framework, in contrast, is structured to primarily provide a means to improve the individual's life—in classic white, able-bodied, heterosexual, cisgender male fashion.

It may be worth mentioning at this point that even this discussion is taking place within what is, of course, the remnants (or, perhaps, more than remnants—perhaps the ongoing dominant form) of patriarchal legal and social theory. It is almost inescapable in its dominance because there is very little in the way of alternative dialogues or alternative systems. When you do venture down these alternative roads, you run very quickly into a feeling of futility—so much of our social and legal systems are built on the dominant hegemony of patriarchy—or systems that were established in this hegemony—that venturing outside of it renders your work impactless aside from those fringe few that may also be interested in an alternative system. While this is unfortunate in some respects—in other respects, it makes sense and lends itself to societal efficiency and consistency. We all likely relate to each other better and work more effectively together when we are working within a common system—or at least within common ideologies. Because men, and the patriarchal system have held positions of power and privilege for so long—it is their system of patriarchy that has become—or been imposed—as our common system.

Recognising that patriarchy remains the dominant system—or at least heavily influences our common social, legal, and political theories and systems—in order to have an impact, it is often most effective to work within these systems of patriarchy. For this reason, we might answer 'yes, to some degree' to the question of whether 'rights' can meaningfully apply to women, when the conception of legal personhood is so profoundly rooted in the notion of the male as a 'person'. While it is rooted in the notion of a male as a person—it is also deeply committed to equality. Of course, this was originally a conception of equality that only applied to a privileged male class of people—however, the principles of equality may be able to apply beyond that group.

2.3.1.5 Right to Legal Capacity and Critical Feminist Theories of Personhood

Feminist theories do not all support the current reality of the neo-liberal emphasis on the primacy of the individual, as mentioned above. They do all provide a more holistic picture of what personhood means from a feminist perspective and an explanation for why women have often been excluded from theories of personhood—women do not nicely slot into the patriarchal creation that is modern legal or moral personhood, as we know it. We would very likely benefit from a conception of legal and moral personhood that more widely embraces these feminist theories. Such a change to the conception of legal and moral personhood would likely also necessitate—or precipitate—a change to the conception of legal capacity.

Some ideas from feminist theories of personhood are already embraced and encompassed in the right to legal capacity. Such as the possibility to exercise autonomy relationally—in concert or in cooperation with others—which is inherent in the state obligation to provide access to support for the exercise of legal capacity, discussed above and in Chap. 1. Recognising and enforcing these concepts may begin to push the world toward a recognition of personhood that is more closely aligned with feminist theories of personhood. This may provide a world in which personhood can be more easily attributed to a wider diversity of individuals and, hopefully, can then precipitate a more equitable society because more individuals will have access to the power that is inherent in recognition as a legal person.

Understanding that the current notion of personhood is largely reflective of patriarchal norms of individualism and economic competition, it is important to also recognise that legal capacity similarly encompasses some of these norms—which makes legal capacity a particularly powerful concept, because it is a tool of the dominant strata of our society. Individuals who have their legal capacity recognised, are recognised as persons and actors in our socio-legal lifeworld—they have the power of the dominant strata. It is, therefore, essential that all peoples have this dominant form of personhood recognised on an equal basis with others in order for any semblance of equality to be achieved.

I do not want to give the impression that I am endorsing a neo-liberal, patriarchal conception of personhood. I would love to live in a world in which feminist theories of personhood dominate in our legal system and the granting or denying of personhood falls along those feminist lines. For example, in line with relational feminist theory, acknowledging the personhood of a family unit and providing some form of legal recognition for the family unit as a legal person. If such a broader conception of personhood was enacted, the boundaries of legal capacity would similarly need to be re-examined and re-defined. Alas, this is not the system that we currently live within, and, as such, in Chap. 3, I will discuss denials of personhood and legal capacity within the current system that exists today—which is one that continues to largely maintain neo-liberal patriarchal notions of personhood.

2.3.2 *Critical Disability Theory and Personhood*

Critical disability theory does not have the same clarity as critical feminist theory in the development of various schools of thought regarding different theories of personhood. Instead, it appears that critical disability theory on personhood is a piecemeal body of literature in which many individual scholars have discussed the topic, but until the discussion of legal capacity spurred by Article 12 in the CRPD, there had not been large bodies of scholarly literature developed on theories of disabled personhood. Since Article 12, there has been a flurry of writing on legal personhood and disability—this scholarship has developed with a common thread, which is the universal recognition of personhood, by virtue of being born human (Dhanda 2012; Quinn and Arstein-Kerslake 2012; Flynn and Arstein-Kerslake 2014b; Quinn and Rekas-Rosalbo 2016). Much of that scholarship was discussed in Chap. 1. In this section, I discuss scholarship related to disability and personhood that is primarily pre-CRPD or emanating from sources other than the CRPD.

2.3.2.1 Exclusion from Moral Personhood of Disabled People

Moral philosophers have thoroughly debated the personhood of disabled people. Unfortunately, many of those debates have taken as their starting point an assumption that there is an argument for *not* including disabled persons as full moral persons. In fact, it appears that more philosophers have discussed excluding disabled people than they have discussed including them. This exclusion has spurred responses from critical disability theorists and fellow philosophers (Kittay 2005; Kittay and Carlson 2010; Wong 2010; Flynn and Arstein-Kerslake 2014b).

Liberal theorist and moral philosopher, John Rawls, provides one of the most inclusive liberal attempts to rationalise how political and social institutions should define personhood (Kukathas and Pettit 1990; Nussbaum 2006). However, he assumes that personhood only includes those who are considered "normal and fully cooperating members of society over a full life" with the "requisite capacities for assuming that role" (Rawls 2005, p. 21). There has long been a difficulty in determining what this definition of personhood means for disabled people—

particularly those that some conceptualise as non-participating members of society. Rawls himself called this one of "the problems on which justice as fairness may fail" (Rawls 2005, p. 21). However, he also suggested that "perhaps we simply lack the ingenuity to see how the extension [of justice to disabled people] may proceed" (Rawls 2005, p. 21).

Some scholars, including Martha Nussbaum, Eva Kittay and Cythia Stark have argued that Rawls' conception of personhood particularly excludes people with intellectual disability or may require differential treatment for people with intellectual disability. They argue that other theories, such as Amartya Sen's work that is based on enhancing human capabilities, provides for better inclusion of disabled people (Kittay 1999; Nussbaum 2006; Stark 2007). However, others argue that Rawls' theory can be interpreted in a way which includes disabled people in definitions of personhood and does not require differentiating between disabled people and those without disabilities (Wong 2010; Flynn and Arstein-Kerslake 2014b).

In Rawls' theory of justice as fairness, one of the primary characteristics of those he conceptualises as persons is that they have the potential to develop what he calls the two 'moral powers': (1) the capacity for a sense of justice (the ability to regard others as equals and engage with them on fair terms) and (2) the capacity for a conception of the good (the ability to determine ones goals and work towards achieving them) (Rawls 1999, p. xii). Nussbaum argues that these two moral powers required for personhood may exclude some disabled people (Nussbaum 2006). Conversely, Sylvia Wong argues that we should read Rawls' work as including the possibility that all human beings have the potential to develop these moral powers—she calls this the potentiality view (Wong 2010). Wong argues that the potentiality view means that all persons should be supported to develop these two moral powers and that this can be done through securing 'enabling conditions' which allow individuals to express their will and preferences.

Rawls himself acknowledged that, according to what he calls 'the principle of need,' citizens' basic needs—such as food, shelter, and access to social and cultural opportunities—must be met before liberty and equality can be meaningfully sought (Rawls 1993, p. 7). Wong argues that 'enabling conditions' fit within the principle of need and therefore must be secured before equality or liberty can be sought for disabled people. Wong states that 'enabling conditions' include opportunities such as: belonging to social groups, interacting with adults who are already exercising the two moral powers, developing relationships with family members, classmates, friends and co-workers, and taking ample time to develop skills (Wong 2010, p. 133).

Building upon Wong's theory, scholar Eilionóir Flynn and I argue that the enabling conditions specified by Wong can include what we conceptualise as a continuum of support for the exercise of legal capacity—or support for legal decision-making as outlined in Article 12(3) of the CRPD (Flynn and Arstein-Kerslake 2014b). We argue that this support for the exercise of legal capacity is an 'enabling condition' because it is "necessary for citizens to understand and to be able fruitfully to exercise . . . rights and liberties" (Rawls 1993, p. 7).

In addition, Flynn and I argue that support for the exercise of legal capacity can allow individuals to express their will and preferences in such a manner that allows them to develop Rawls' two moral powers that he theorises as prerequisites for personhood. In other words, people can be supported to exercise legal capacity to develop an understanding of others as equals, to engage with them on fair terms, and to determine their own goals and work towards them. This allows for the utilisation of Rawls' liberal theory of justice while also including disabled people as moral subjects within the theory and recognising their moral and legal personhood (Flynn and Arstein-Kerslake 2014b).

2.3.2.2 Interpersonal Exclusions from Personhood of Disabled People

Heikki Ikäheimo, discusses 'interpersonal personhood.' He says that recognising your own personhood is essential for fulfilment in life. He also identifies that recognition of your own personhood is often dependent upon others receiving and accepting you as a person (Ikäheimo 2008, p. 87). He explores the experience of disability and identifies the importance of the simple experience of others not treating you and acting towards you in the way that they would for those they consider full persons. He says that this, itself, is a manifestation of a granting or denial of personhood (Ikäheimo 2008, p. 83). For example, he discusses the experience of some disabled people:

> It is as if you were not included, in the implicit countings or accountings of others in concrete context of interactions, among the persons present. It is the way they look at you, the fact that they talk *about* you, rather than *to* you (though they may talk to your assistant). When you try to speak to them, you seldom see the light of understanding in their faces, but more often a humiliating mixture of pity and confusion. Indeed, how would they count, if someone asked them to count the number of persons in a room where you are? (Ikäheimo 2008, p. 84)

He identifies this as the epitome of social exclusion. If an individual is formally recognised as a legal person—and theoretically recognised as a moral person—but is excluded in interpersonal interactions, they may experience profound social exclusion as a result of the denial of this 'interpersonal personhood.' The denial of personhood in this way may have an even greater negative effect on the individual than the more systemic denials of personhood at the legal or moral levels. Ikäheimo asserts that merely recognition of the right to legal personhood may not assist in denials of this type of 'interpersonal personhood.' His solution to such denials is to create an open dialogue about such denials in order to raise awareness in those that may be perpetrating such interpersonal denials of personhood (Ikäheimo 2008, p. 86). He asserts that the recognition of an individuals' personhood is worth fighting for—and it is better to respond when an interpersonal denial of personhood occurs rather than resign oneself to such denials (Ikäheimo 2008, p. 87).

Other scholars have also identified similar denials of personhood on an interpersonal level for disabled people (Luborsky 1994; Murphy 2001, 2016). Anthropologist Robert Murphy writes drawing on literature as well as personal experience of acquired disability and identifies both the self and the social environment as possible limiting factors on a disabled individual's personhood. He says,

> The disabled have become changed in the minds of the rest of society into a kind of quasi-human. In only a few months, I had moved subtly from the centre of my society to its perimeter. I had acquired a new identity that was contingent on my defects and that either compromised or radically altered my prior claims to personhood. In my middle age, I had become a changeling, the lot of all disabled people. They are afflicted with a malady of the body that is translated into a cancer within the self and a disease of social relationships. They have experienced a transformation of the essential condition of their being in the world. They have become aliens, even exiles, in their own lands. (Murphy 2016, p. 260)

Murphy focuses strongly on external forces in the social environment that devalue and dehumanise the disabled individual and the disabled body (Murphy 1995).

Anthropologist Mark Luborsky undertook a qualitative study of middle aged and elderly polio survivors and found that personhood can be eroded on a social, interpersonal level for disabled people. He asserts that personhood cannot be individually ascribed, but instead is dependent upon recognition and affirmation by others. He identifies that there are certain roles that an individual must be able to perform in order to be recognised and accepted as a full person—including being a responsible and productive worker, spouse, family and community member (Luborsky 1994, p. 240). Lubrorsky identifies that this social exclusion from consideration as a full person is a key aspect in disabling the individual (Luborsky 1994, p. 251). This fits in with the social model of disability, which presents its own framework for viewing personhood in the context of disability.

2.3.2.3 Social Model of Disability and Personhood

Critical disability theorists utilise the social model of disability to theorise the relationship between disabled people and our socio-legal world. The traditional medical model of disability places the burden of disability on the individual. It pathologizes human difference and labels individuals as disabled. It seeks to fix or cure those individuals by altering the individual in such a way that they better fit with a preconceived notion of normal. In contrast, the social model of disability places the burden of disability on society rather than on the individual. The social model views disability as simply a result of an unaccommodating society. It theorises that disability occurs where an individual's impairments—physical or mental—are not sufficiently accommodated in society. The theory surmises that it is only these social barriers that create disability. If the social barriers were broken down, disability would not exist (Hughes and Paterson 1997; Oliver 2013; Shakespeare 2016).

The conception of personhood has not been thoroughly explored among social model theorists. However, the social model has the potential to be an important platform for the conceptualisation of personhood from the perspective of critical disability theory. It inherently requires the full recognition of legal personhood in disabled people because it assumes that disabled people are due equal rights and responsibilities to others. This is clear because there would be no obligation to alter social environments to achieve equality for non-persons—or, at least, the impetus would be much less to do so. Therefore, for the effective implementation of the social model of disability, disabled people must be recognised as full legal persons—they must be entitled to equal rights.

The demand for full moral personhood can also be identified in social model theory because it views disabled people as individuals who merely have impairments. In this way, they are full persons, who are merely experiencing impairment of some kind—physical or mental. As stated above, it is social barriers that turn those impairments into disabling conditions. It can be argued that Wong's potentiality view, discussed above, fits in well with the social model. In order for the social model to be consistent, all people must be thought of as people—or that they at least have the potential to have all the characteristics that one would require for the ascription of personhood. This starting point of recognising moral personhood is required in order to then go on to apply the social model and examine what impairment the individual has and how it interacts with the social environment to disable that individual. In other words, it would be largely irrelevant if non-persons experience social barriers—because we are generally not seeking equality for non-persons (this ties in with liberal political theory's emphasis on equality). Therefore, if there were people who could be disregarded has not having sufficient potential for human traits in order to be considered moral persons, the analysis of their impairment and the impairment's interaction with social barriers would be meaningless—which would make the social model meaningless. In this way, the recognition of moral personhood of disabled people is a foundational element of the social model—the model assumes moral personhood and would not apply if disabled people were not recognised as moral persons.

The very delineation of personhood is a delineation that we use in order to understand who we consider our equals and who we are willing to accept as members of our society—as part of our social contract—and who we have a moral obligation to ensure enjoys equal participation with others and who we, in turn, are obligated to ensure protection of their liberty, privacy, property, etc. Therefore, the social model demand for barriers to be broken down—is dependent upon an assumption that disabled people are equal contracting members in the social world and are, therefore, entitled to equal participation and recognition.

2.3.2.4 Diagnosis and Its Impact on Personhood

There is also a line of scholarship that identifies the ascription of diagnoses and labelling of disability as precipitating denials of personhood (Hacking 1986; Hughes 2012). They highlight the sometimes arbitrary nature of medical diagnoses and the importance of taking the individual as a whole person—a blank slate—whom a diagnosis has been foisted upon. Philosopher Ian Hacking identifies several diagnoses and labels that have been created by the medical profession and other sciences—

for example, multiple personality disorder and autism. He discusses how they are developed, how they evolve, and how they are applied to individuals. He states,

> numerous kinds of human beings and human acts come into being hand in hand with our invention of the categories labelling them (Hacking 1986, p. 236)

He explores what these labels mean for the individual and how that impacts their relative personhood and their position in the world (Hacking 1998a, b). He examines these, not necessarily out of a desire to achieve social justice or equality, but, out of a philosophical curiosity about how we 'make up people' (Hacking 1986). This suggests that personhood is, at least in part, constructed externally by social forces—as many of the other theories discussed in this chapter also suggest. It also highlights the transience of such labels and the sometimes highly subjective and socially biased creation of such diagnoses and labels.

The ascription of identities—via diagnoses and labels of disability—have a profound impact on how personhood is or is not recognised in both interpersonal dimensions (described above) as well as socio-legal dimensions (such as legal personhood being denied via guardianship that is imposed on the basis of a particular diagnosis, such as dementia or mental health diagnoses). The underlying reason for this impact on personhood, in such ascription of identities, is the profound discrimination that exists against people with actual or perceived cognitive disability and mental health disability. It may be illusory labels that are ascribed to individuals at the whim of the medical profession—or that are constructed by the medical profession—but it is this discrimination and prejudice that precipitates the removal of personhood as a result. (These phenomena are not discrete—it is likely that the creation of disabling labels was influenced by strong discriminatory desires against those perceived as different. Once the labels are created, it then becomes easier to discriminatorily deny personhood based on those labels because the power of science and medicine then lies behind the force of the denial of personhood.)

Well-known disability scholar, Tom Shakespeare, identifies both the illusory nature of disability and the reality of the disability experience. He does not venture into formulating a new theory of personhood—however, he does discuss the impact that diagnosis has on personhood, while also heavily emphasizing that it is not only diagnosis that constructs disability. Although he is not specifically creating a theory of personhood—his theory can be applied to personhood in that his arguments imply that socially imposed diagnosis or other disability labelling, paired with physical, bodily experiences of disability make up the 'disability personality'—or personhood in the context of disability. In other words, the social construction and the physical embodiment make up disabled personhood (Shakespeare 2013, pp. 59–67).

2.3.2.5 Right to Legal Capacity and Critical Disability Theories of Personhood

Arguably, even more so than for women, the story of disability and personhood is largely a story of exclusion. Much of the scholarship is defensively attempting to amend existing theories of personhood to ensure that disabled people are included. In contrast, significant lines of inquiry in feminist theory are seeking to revolutionise personhood and completely re-imagine personhood from a feminist perspective—for example, relational feminism, discussed above. Such re-imagining has the potential to bring the benefit of feminist thought and apply it to a conception of personhood that applies to everyone—it has the potential to not only benefit women but also to transform our socio-legal world by providing new meaning to how we define and support personhood. Critical disability theory has yet to achieve such a substantial body of work in which conceptions of disability may lead the way in redefining personhood. However, the scholarship and lines of inquiry that I have outlined above present the potential for such a transformation of personhood.

This scholarship combined with right to legal capacity as developed by the CRPD Committee, may provide the fuel for a new line of inquiry into re-imaging personhood based on critical disability theory. As Flynn and I have argued, the right to legal capacity and support to exercise that capacity can be 'enabling conditions' for the potential of all individuals to be included as moral persons (Flynn and Arstein-Kerslake 2014b). In addition, theories of interpersonal personhood highlight the history of oppression that disabled people face in daily interactions and the necessity to overcome that discrimination in order to realise the right to legal personhood—as part of the right to legal capacity. The social model of disability similarly highlights the social barriers—external to the individual—that also must be overcome to realise the rights to legal personhood and legal capacity. A part of overcoming this discrimination and breaking down these social barriers is ensuring that the conception of the individual is divorced from any diagnosis or label of disability—that the personhood is attached to the individual and is not dependent upon the existence or absence or certain diagnoses or labels. These insights apply to the context of disability, but they can apply much more broadly than that as well.

Critical feminist theory reflects a re-imagining of personhood with the inclusion of relational elements. This is reflected in the right to legal capacity in the obligation for the state to provide support for the exercise of legal capacity. Critical disability theory discusses these relational elements much less, but instead focuses on the profound discrimination and exclusion that disabled people face in regard to recognition as full persons. Combining these, as well as the following contribution of critical queer theory to conceptions of personhood may begin to provide a picture of what the right to legal personhood—and legal capacity—means for women, disabled women, and gender minorities, as well as how insights developed from critical social theory related to these groups may give us a new understanding of personhood.

2.3.3 *Critical Queer Theory and Personhood*

There is relatively limited scholarship available about how gender minorities fit in to existing theories of personhood—or, indeed, how personhood may be conceptualised from the perspective of gender minorities. However, critical queer theory does provide some insights. It examines the social world from the perspective of the queer community—usually conceived of as including sexual minorities (including gay, lesbian, and bisexual people) and gender minorities (including transgender, intersex, and non-binary people). It is focused on the philosophy of difference and marginality and its roots include the works of Michel Foucault and Judith Butler (Foucault 1990; Butler 1999; Jackson and Hogg 2010).

2.3.3.1 Michel Foucault and Personhood

Foucault's *History of Sexuality* makes an argument that has parallels with critical disability studies scholars who argue that the pathologizing of difference have a profound impact on self-imposed and socially constructed perceptions of an individual's personhood, discussed above (Hacking 1986; Foucault 1990; Hughes 2012; Shakespeare 2013). He distinguishes sexuality from sex—he identifies sex as a physical act and sexuality as an internal characteristic of the individual. He argues that psychiatry played a pivotal role in constructing sexuality as a means of categorizing persons and pathologizing non-heterosexual sex. With the rise of the medical establishment and psychiatry in the mid nineteenth century, came the classification of sexual desires. People's desires were pathologized if they did not fit in with the heteronormative dominant culture. They began to be labelled according to their sexual desires and those labels had the potential to create a differential standing of person—a lesser form of personhood.

In particular, Foucault identifies homosexuality as merely an invention of heterosexuality—as simply a label for those who deviate from what is considered to be the norm of heterosexuality. Foucault's work explores the impact on personhood of labelling and categorizing people based on sexuality. It highlights the ever-present issue that those labelled with some form of deviation from the dominant norm often experience problems with personhood—either others treating them as not being full persons, either formally or on interpersonal levels, or self-imposed denigration of personhood based on such socially constructed and subsequently internalised labels (Foucault 1990; Jackson and Hogg 2010).

2.3.3.2 Judith Butler and Personhood

Judith Butler's *Gender Trouble* tackles personhood from a different angle. From her work, we can draw additional conclusions regarding the role of identity in constructing personhood. In *Gender Trouble*, she addresses identity in feminism—she asserts that an identity category, such as 'women' has boundaries that may lend coherence to the movement but may serve to exclude some of the most marginalised individuals. She identifies that white, heterosexual women with families were the category of person that was most clearly included in the feminist movement. This preferred identity of the movement excluded transwomen, women of colour, lesbians, and others. In this way, Butler argues that identity is permanently troubled and can be utilised as a weapon of exclusion.

I believe that Butler's work can be extrapolated to personhood. The feminist movement was only willing to ascribe its version of personhood to the identity of women that it chose—white, heterosexual women with families. It effectively relegated all others to a category of non-person—or at least to a category of person that was not worthy of inclusion in a feminism rights movement. To solve this, Butler proposes to leave identity categories permanently open and undefined. She argues for defining who to include in social movements based on common aims and struggles, as opposed to common identities (Butler 1999; Jackson and Hogg 2010). She seems to be asking for personhood to be conceptualised universally. If we assume inclusion in personhood of all those born human, there is no possibility for exclusion from social movements based on identity or group membership. In a liberal political landscape—such as the one that dominates much of the world-—those recognised as having personhood are entitled to equal rights (Gutmann 1980). If all humans are designated as persons, then they are all entitled to equal rights and it must be their struggles that define their social movements because to define it otherwise would run counter to an assertion that all persons are entitled to equal recognition and equal rights.

In this way, in *Gender* Trouble, Butler establishes that it is not only the medical profession that can ascribe labels that impact our personhood—as discussed in critical disability theory and by Foucault. It may be a social movement that creates a category of person that it will include and others that it will exclude. The individuals whose identities are excluded may have their personhood doubly impacted—the dominant cultural has rejected them and so has the minority group that they potentially could have sought refuge with.

In Butlers 2004 book, *Undoing Gender*, she tackles personhood in a more explicit manner. She identifies that the oppressed subject enjoys recognition—in order to be oppressed by a dominant culture or group, one must be recognised as a person or subject. However, the denial of recognition presents an even more profound instance of social exclusion. She says,

> To find that you are fundamentally unintelligible (indeed, that the law of culture and of language find you to be an impossibility) is to find that you have not yet achieved access to the human, to find yourself speaking only and always *as if you were* human, but with the sense that you are not, to find that your language is hollow, that no recognition is forthcoming because the norms by which recognition takes places are not in your favour. (Butler 2004, p. 30)

Butler identifies that the struggle for sexual minorities and gender minorities is not merely for rights—but for recognition in the first instance (Butler 2004, p. 32). She also queries the usefulness of the conception of personhood as it exists with the dominant heteronormative patriarchal culture and the likely impossibility that sexual and gender minorities could fit into such notions of the person. Instead, she says that the struggle for sexual and gender minorities is not merely to be recognised as persons, but to first create a social transformation of what it means to be a person—in order for the definition of personhood to be able to meaningfully include sexual and gender minorities. She argues that international human rights law is a means for intervening into the social and political process that creates and articulates personhood. It has the power to redefine and renegotiate what it means to be a human (Butler 2004, pp. 32–33). The right to equal recognition before the law and the right to legal capacity may be one of the most direct and the most effective ways to reconceptualise the human—or the definition of legal personhood.

2.3.3.3 Queer People, Liberal Political Theory, and Personhood

It has also been argued that queer people can and do fit into the liberal political notion of a 'person' and that the rights framework that accompanies liberal political personhood can and should be applied to queer people (Phelan 2000). Shane Phelan argues that queer people necessarily must be accepted into liberal political theory and use it to their benefit. Liberal political theory promotes individual rights and sanctity for the private severe and for individual liberty. Phelan argues that it is essential for minorities—including queer people—to engage with liberal political theory because it continues to dominate much of our legal and political systems. He also argues that these concepts of individual rights and sanctity for the private sphere are areas of liberal political theory that are particularly important and beneficial for queer people. He argues that there is no need for queer people—or any minority group—to adhere to or endorse a particular view of liberal political theory. Instead, he argues that liberal political theory can be adapted to include the needs of queer people and other groups who may place higher importance on relationships and recognition than traditional (white, male, cisgender) liberal political theorists have done.

It is important to recognise that Phelan discusses primarily sexual minorities and not gender minorities. Sexual minorities are individual who have sexual preferences other than the majority group experience of heterosexuality. Gender minorities—as discussed previously—are those that do not ascribe to the gender binary, for various reasons. In this book, I am focusing my analysis on gender minorities and not sexual minorities because my main concern in this book is the impact of gender on the realisation of the right to legal capacity. However, there are likely similarities between the oppression experienced by sexual minorities and gender minorities and—as such—theories of inclusion in personhood for sexual minorities may have some parallels for gender minorities.

In relation to Phelan's work, his assertions can likely apply to gender minorities, as well as other minority groups. As I have discussed elsewhere in this book, I am leaving aside the opportunity to substantially critique liberal political theory—however tempting it may be. Instead, in this book, I am accepting that liberal political theory plays a prominent role in many of our modern legal systems and therefore engaging with it may provide the best way to create reform towards the realisation of the right to equal recognition before the law of women, disabled women, and gender minorities (of course, this is debatable as well, and I look forward to future opportunities to engage with such debates).

Assuming that we are accepting that liberal political theory plays a significant role in modern legal systems and that minority groups, such as gender minorities, may benefit from engaging with liberal political theory, I believe that—as Phelan suggests—gender minorities can and should fit in to modern conceptions of personhood in liberal political theory. In addition, similar to Phelan's arguments related primarily to sexual minorities—for gender minorities, I believe that the protection of individual rights and preserving the sanctity of the private sphere are also elements of liberal political theory that are important. This is largely because gender minorities often experience gross intrusions into their private spheres. For example, intersex people are subjected to forced genital modification and sterilisation (Karkazis 2008); and intersex and transgender people are often in situations where the law requires intrusions into the private sphere, such as divorce and forced sterilisation before recognition of gender (Karkazis 2008; Lee 2015; Honkasalo 2018; Rowlands and Amy 2018).

2.3.3.4 Right to Legal Capacity and Critical Queer Theories of Personhood

Critical queer theory adds important insights for a reconstruction of personhood in light of gender. Foucault's arguments that personhood can be denigrated by socially imposed norms and labels related to gender and sexuality parallels critical disability studies arguments that medical diagnoses and disability labelling can lead to denials of personhood. Butler's work emphasises the importance of initial recognition—the concept that the first struggle for gender and sexual minorities is often simply recognition as people in the first instance—recognition that they exist. Her work also highlights the necessity that any definition of personhood is sufficiently inclusive of all people, including those that do not conform to the gender binary. In addition, some concepts from liberal political theory may be beneficial to gender minorities in considering a reconstruction of personhood—for example, the importance of the protection of individual privacy and the protection of individual rights. A reconstruction of personhood in light of these insights, would include consideration that labels can denigrate personhood, the need for holistic recognition of all people—regardless of gender identity, and the maintenance of individual rights that attach to the person—including the right to privacy.

This relates to the right to legal capacity in many ways. First, it is an individual right, as discussed previously, and therefore fits in with liberal political theory and may be the tool necessary for the protection of personhood for gender minorities—as suggested by Butler and Phelan (Phelan 2000; Butler 2004, pp. 32–33). Second, the universal nature of the right to legal capacity, as discussed above, and by Dhanda, can encompass the need to overcome labels as well as the need to provide initial recognition to gender minorities. If a right is truly universal, it must apply to all individuals (Dhanda 2012).

2.3.4 *Conclusion on Personhood and Critical Feminist, Disability, and Queer Theory*

Drawing on critical feminist, disability, and queer scholarship, personhood may be able to be reimagined to better encompass the reality of the lives of women, disabled women, and gender minorities. Relational elements can be included from critical feminist theory. Drawing on critical disability theory and queer theory, the impact of labelling based on medical diagnosis or social norms can be limited and discrimination can be taken into consideration from both an interpersonal and systemic perspective. Critical queer theory has also highlighted the need for initial recognition—to ensure that there are not groups, such as some gender minorities, that are completely overlooked when defining, granting, and asserting personhood. This has the potential to create a new conception of personhood that better includes women, disabled women, and gender minorities—and may better reflect the reality of all individuals lives because the experiences of individuals in these three minority groups may be reflective of some part of the lives of most individuals. For example, the reality of exercising autonomy in relation to others (from feminist theory); the need to combat discrimination (from disability theory and queer theory); and the need to be flexible in the definition of personhood in order to maximise and ensure inclusion (from queer theory).

2.4 Power and Privilege: Importance of Legal Personhood

Power and privilege are both complex concepts that have been defined in various ways across scholarly literature and social spaces (Bierstedt 1950). As the movement for social equality grows—and, in particular the movement for racial equality—the concepts of power and privilege are becoming increasingly prevalent. The broad idea is that discussions of power and privilege are discussions of an individual's social capital and their position in society. Minority groups generally have less power and privilege and dominant groups have the highest amounts of power and privilege—most often white, able-bodied, heterosexual cisgender men (Johnson 2005; Kimmel and Holler 2011; Rosenkranz 2012; Kimmel 2017). However, power varies by individuals, depending on the unique mix of privilege and social marginalisation that each individual experiences based on their mix of group membership and their social environment.

Power is often a mix of many factors—for example: the potential to influence others; the possession or control of valuable resources; and the relative control over other individuals and the things that they value (Bierstedt 1950; Fiske and Berdahl 2007). Privilege is the idea that some people benefit from unearned, often unrecognised, advantages (Rothman 2014; McFeeters 2019). These advantages do not necessarily come from discrimination against other groups—they are sometimes merely the product of a hierarchical class system in which some groups hold more power than others. In other words, those who are privileged hold power and those with power are privileged.

Personhood is a predictor of power and privilege because it is what allows the individual to be recognised as more than an object to be controlled by others. When an individual—or entity—is recognised as possessing legal personhood, they suddenly become a potential holder of rights and responsibilities. When they are recognised as a moral person, they are included in theories of justice and they are respected as being able to determine right from wrong and be held responsible for their actions. As a legal person who holds rights and responsibilities the individual has the necessary standing to engage the power of the legal system and to create, modify and extinguish legal relationships. (However, to act on these things, the full realisation of legal capacity is needed because the recognition of legal agency is also needed.) As a moral person, the individual is recognised by others and can take actions that are recognised by others. These freedoms and abilities are often necessary to gain power via the control of resources or other individuals.

In our world that remains dominated by liberal political theory, the social contract is a reality of our daily lives. Social contract theory says that we all exist within society under a largely unspoken agreement between ourselves and society. The agreement—or social contract—says that the individual can exist with all the benefits of living within a society, such as social protection, shared resources, collaboration, as well as the liberty to create and extinguish legal relationships to better one's own position and seek the 'good life' for oneself. In exchange, the individual must obey the laws of society (Riley 2013). This remains a strong thread of liberal political theory (Boucher and Kelly 2003)—we are separate, isolated individuals that are tied together via a social contract that gives us each the freedom to exercise our liberty and take actions towards the realisation of the 'good life' for ourselves with the main constraint being the code of law that we democratically agreed to be ruled by. In different jurisdictions and within different cultures there are varying levels of adherence to such liberal political theory—however, most of the western democratic world is dominated by some form of such social order. It is important to engage with critiques of such theory and the systems that embrace them—however, here, I would simply like to acknowledge the dominance of social contract theory in our current systems and the ongoing importance of individual personhood for securing a place in such a system. It is only those who are recognised as having legal personhood who will be able to engage in the social contract and to seek a good life for themselves.

It is important to discuss at this point one of the critical errors with this line of reasoning. As highlighted by relational feminist theory (West 1988; McConnell 1996)—it can be argued that no matter how much effort is put into securing personhood for minority groups such as women, disabled women, and gender minorities, they will never be on equal footing in the hegemony of white, able bodied, heterosexual cisgender men (McConnell 1996; Kimmel and Holler 2011; Rosenkranz 2012). This may very well be true. However, the reality of our current system is such that I believe that the course of action that will feasibly result in improved levels of equality for women, disabled women, and gender minorities, is accepting that we live in a world dominated by liberal political theory created by and created to suit white, able-bodied, heterosexual cisgender men—and seeking power within this system may be the most effect way to change such a system or gain some power within the system—even if power and privilege at the level of white, able-bodied, heterosexual cisgender men is eternally out of reach. I suppose my goal is to use the system to slowly build power for minorities such as women, disabled women, and gender minorities and then seek to overthrow—or maybe, more accurately, gently topple—the hegemony of white, able-bodied, heterosexual cisgender men and the existing form of liberal political theory that dominates our socio-world.

2.5 Conclusion

In this chapter, I have attempted to explore various theories of personhood in order to provide insight into how personhood can be constructed in such a way that better reflects the lives of women, disabled women, and gender minorities—and, thereby, better includes them in definitions of personhood. I have done this in order to ensure that the remaining discussion of the right to legal capacity for individuals in these groups is couched in these overarching theories. Although I am accepting the reality of the power and prevalence of liberal political theory, I also see the need to ensure that we are constantly questioning its foundations. That we are constantly breaking down the elements created to suit a dominant class that frequently does not include women, disabled women, and gender minorities. To achieve this, I think the concept of personhood is critical. As previously discussed, liberal political theory has been constructed in such a way that often excludes women, disabled women, and gender minorities from personhood—or upholds definitions of personhood that do not match with the lived experiences of individuals in these groups. For this reason, it is critical to reevaluate and reconstruct existing definitions of who is considered a person and who is considered a member of our society worthy of equality, liberty, and justice. It is particularly critical when we are exploring the right to legal capacity—which includes the right to personhood and agency. For these reasons, these theories of personhood will influence the subsequent chapters, in which I will explore the right to legal capacity and how it has been denied to women, disabled women, and gender minorities.

References

Agger, Ben. 2006. *Critical Social Theories*. 2nd ed. Paradigm Publishers.

Ahmed, Sara. 2016. *Deconstruction and Law's Other: Towards a Feminist Theory of Embodied Legal Rights: Social & Legal Studies*. Thousand Oaks, CA: Sage CA. https://doi.org/10.1177/096466399500400103.

Anderson, Elizabeth. 2009. Toward a Non-Ideal, Relational Methodology for Political Philosophy: Comments on Schwartzman's "Challenging Liberalism". *Hypatia* 24: 130–145. JSTOR.

Arstein-Kerslake, Anna. 2017. *Restoring Voice to People with Cognitive Disabilities*. Cambridge University Press.

Arstein-Kerslake, Anna, and Eilionóir Flynn. 2017. The Right to Legal Agency: Domination, Disability and the Protections of Article 12 of the Convention on the Rights of Persons with Disabilities. *International Journal of Law in Context* 13: 22–38. https://doi.org/10.1017/S1744552316000458.

Assassi, Libby. 2009. Property and Gender: Irrational Women and Rational Men. In *The Gendering of Global Finance*, ed. Libby Assassi, 49–68. London: Palgrave Macmillan UK. https://doi.org/10.1057/9780230246690_3.

Bierstedt, Robert. 1950. An Analysis of Social Power. *American Sociological Review* 15: 730–738. JSTOR. https://doi.org/10.2307/2086605.

Blair, Margaret M. 2013. Corporate Personhood and the Corporate Persona Symposium: In the Boardroom. *University of Illinois Law Review*: 785–820.

Bohman, James. 2019. Critical Theory. In *The Stanford Encyclopedia of Philosophy*, ed. Edward N. Zalta. Metaphysics Research Lab, Stanford University, Winter 2019.

Boucher, David, and Paul Kelly. 2003. *The Social Contract from Hobbes to Rawls*. Routledge.

Butler, Judith. 1999. *Gender Trouble: Feminism and the Subversion of Identity*. Routledge.

———. 2004. *Undoing Gender*. Routledge. https://doi.org/10.4324/9780203499627.

Calhoun, Craig. 1995. *Critical Social Theory: Culture, History, and the Challenge of Difference*. Cambridge, MA, USA: Wiley-Blackwell.

Campbell, Josephine. 2020. Critical Theory. In *Salem Press Encyclopedia*. Salem Press.

Cannoot, Pieter. 2019. '#WontBeErased': The Effects of (De)pathologisation and (De)-medicalisation on the Legal Capacity of Trans* Persons. *International Journal of Law and Psychiatry* 66: 101478. https://doi.org/10.1016/j.ijlp.2019.101478.

Christman, John. 2004. Relational Autonomy, Liberal Individualism, and the Social Constitution of Selves. *Philosophical Studies: An International Journal for Philosophy in the Analytic Tradition* 117: 143–164. JSTOR.

Collins, Patricia Hill. 2019. *Intersectionality as Critical Social Theory*. Duke University Press.

Dhanda, Amita. 2012. Universal Legal Capacity as a Universal Human Right. In *Mental Health and Human Rights: Vision, Praxis, and Courage*, ed. Michael Dudley, Derrick Silove, and Fran Gale. Oxford University Press.

Dunn, John. 1982. *The Political Thought of John Locke: An Historical Account of the Argument of the "Two Treatises of Government"*. Cambridge University Press.

Epstein, Richard A. 2002. *Animals as Objects, or Subjects, of Rights*. SSRN Scholarly Paper ID 359240. Rochester, NY: Social Science Research Network.

Fiske, Susan T., and Jennifer Berdahl. 2007. Social Power. In *Social Psychology: Handbook of Basic Principles*, 2nd ed., 678–692. New York, NY, US: The Guilford Press.

Fisse, Brent. 1995. Corporations, Crime and Accountability. *Current Issues in Criminal Justice* 6: 378–386. https://doi.org/10.1080/10345329.1995.12036668.

Flynn, Eilionoir, and Anna Arstein-Kerslake. 2014a. The Support Model of Legal Capacity: Fact, Fiction, or Fantasy. *Berkeley Journal of International Law*: 124–143.

———. 2014b. Legislating Personhood: Realising the Right to Support in Exercising Legal Capacity. *International Journal of Law in Context* 10: 81–104. https://doi.org/10.1017/S1744552313000384.

Foucault, Michel. 1990. *The History of Sexuality. Penguin History*. Penguin.

Frenkel, David A., and Yotam Lurie. 2001. Culpability of Corporations - Legal and Ethical Perspectives Articles and Addresses. *Criminal Law Quarterly* 45: 465–487.

Gilligan, Carol. 1993. *In a Different Voice: Psychological Theory and Women's Development*. Harvard University Press.

Green, Frederick. 1945. Corporations as Persons, Citizens, and Possessors of Liberty. *University of Pennsylvania Law Review* 94: 202–237.

Gutmann, Amy. 1980. *Liberal Equality*. CUP Archive.

Hacking, Ian. 1986. Making Up People. In *Reconstructing Individualism: Autonomy, Individuality, and the Self in Western Thought*, ed. Thomas C. Heller, Morton Sosna, and David E. Wellbery, 222–236. Stanford University Press.

———. 1998a. *Rewriting the Soul. F Second Printing Used Edition*. Princeton, NJ: Princeton University Press.

———. 1998b. *Mad Travelers: Reflections on the Reality of Transient Mental Illnesses*. Charlottesville, Va: University of Virginia Press.

Honkasalo, Julian. 2018. Unfit for Parenthood? Compulsory Sterilization and Transgender Reproductive Justice in Finland. *Journal of International Women's Studies* 20: 40–52.

Horkheimer, Max. 1972. *Critical Theory: Selected Essays*. A&C Black.

Hudson, Barbara. 2006. Beyond White Man's Justice: Race, Gender and Justice in Late Modernity. *Theoretical Criminology* 10: 29–47. https://doi.org/10.1177/1362480606059981.

Hughes, Bill. 2012. Civilising Modernity and the Ontological Invalidation of Disabeld People. In *Disability and Social Theory*, ed. Bill Hughes, Dan Goodley, and Lennard J. Davis, 17–32. Springer.

Hughes, Bill, and Kevin Paterson. 1997. The Social Model of Disability and the Disappearing Body: Towards a Sociology of Impairment. *Disability & Society* 12: 325–340. https://doi.org/10.1080/09687599727209.

Ikäheimo, Heikki. 2008. Personhood and the Social Inclusion of People with Disabilities: A Recognition-Theoretical Approach. In *Arguing about Disability: Philosophical Perspectives*, ed. Kristjana Kristiansen, Simo Vehmas, and Tom Shakespeare, 77–92. Routledge.

Jackson, Ronald, II, and Michael Hogg. 2010. Queer Theory. In *Encyclopedia of Identity*, 612–616. Thousand Oaks: SAGE Publications, Inc. https://doi.org/10.4135/9781412979306.

Jaworska, Agnieszka, and Julie Tannenbaum. 2018. The Grounds of Moral Status. In *The Stanford Encyclopedia of Philosophy*, ed. Edward N. Zalta. Metaphysics Research Lab, Stanford University, Spring 2018.

Johnson, Allan G. 2005. *The Gender Knot: Unraveling Our Patriarchal Legacy*. Temple University Press.

Karkazis, Katrina Alicia. 2008. *Fixing Sex: Intersex, Medical Authority, and Lived Experience. E-Duke Books Scholarly Collection*. Duke University Press.

Karlan, Pamela S., and Daniel R. Ortiz. 1992. In a Diffident Voice: Relational Feminism, Abortion Rights, and the Feminist Legal Agenda. *Northwestern University Law Review* 87: 858–896.

Kimmel, Michael. 2017. *Angry White Men: American Masculinity at the End of an Era*. PublicAffairs.

Kimmel, Michael, and Jacqueline Zuzann Holler. 2011. *The Gendered Society*. Oxford University Press.

Kittay, Eva Feder. 1999. *Love's Labor: Essays on Women, Equality, and Dependency*. Routledge.

———. 2005. At the Margins of Moral Personhood. *Ethics* 116: 100–131. JSTOR. https://doi.org/10.1086/454366.

Kittay, Eva Feder, and Licia Carlson, eds. 2010. *Cognitive Disability and Its Challenge to Moral Philosophy*. 1st ed. Chichester, West Sussex; Malden, MA: Wiley-Blackwell.

Kohlberg, Lawrence, and Richard H. Hersh. 1977. Moral Development: A Review of the Theory. *Theory Into Practice* 16: 53.

Kramer, Matthew H. 2008. *Where Law and Morality Meet*. Oxford University Press.

Kukathas, Chandran, and Philip Pettit. 1990. *Rawls: A Theory of Justice and Its Critics*. Stanford University Press.

Lee, Rebecca (I). 2015. Forced Sterilization and Mandatory Divorce: How a Majority of Council of Europe Member States' Laws Regarding Gender Identity Violate the Internationally and Regionally Established Human Rights of Trans People. *Berkeley Journal of International Law* 33: 114–152.

Lennon, Kathleen. 2019. Feminist Perspectives on the Body. In *The Stanford Encyclopedia of Philosophy*, ed. Edward N. Zalta. Metaphysics Research Lab, Stanford University, Fall 2019.

Locke, John. 1794. *The Works of John Locke*. T. Longman, B. Law.

Luborsky, Mark R. 1994. The Cultural Adversity of Physical Disability: Erosion of Full Adult Personhood. *Journal of Aging Studies* 8: 239–253. https://doi.org/10.1016/0890-4065(94)90002-7.

Lund, William R. 1996. Politics, Citizens, and the Good Life: Assessing Two Versions of Ethical Liberalism. *Political Research Quarterly* 49: 479–504. JSTOR. https://doi.org/10.2307/449094.

Mackenzie, Catriona, and Natalie Stoljar. 2000. *Relational Autonomy: Feminist Perspectives on Autonomy, Agency, and the Social Self*. Oxford University Press.

Macklin, Ruth. 1983. Personhood in the Bioethics Literature. *The Milbank Memorial Fund Quarterly. Health and Society* 61: 35–57. JSTOR. https://doi.org/10.2307/3349815.

Maitland, Frederic Wiliam. 1905. Moral Personality and Legal Personality. *Journal of the Society of Comparative Legislation* 6: 192–200. JSTOR.

Matambanadzo, Saru. 2005. Engendering Sex: Birth Certificates, Biology and the Body in Anglo American Law. *Cardozo Journal of Law & Gender* 12: 213–246.

Matambanadzo, Saru M. 2012. Embodying Vulnerability: A Feminist Theory of the Person. *Duke Journal of Gender Law & Policy* 20: 39.

McClain, Linda C. 1991. Atomistic Man Revisited: Liberalism, Connection, and Feminist Jurisprudence. *Southern California Law Review* 65: 1171–1264.

McConnell, Joyce E. 1996. Relational and Liberal Feminism: The Ethic of Care, Fetal Personhood and Autonomy Symposium: Farley v. Sartin and Fetal Personhood. *West Virginia Law Review* 99: 291–310.

McFeeters, Belinda Bennett. 2019. White Privilege: The Invisible Advantages and Apparent Disadvantages. In *Salem Press Encyclopedia*. Great Neck Publishing.

Minow, Martha. 1987. Justice Engendered. *Harvard Law Review* 101: 10.

Minow, Martha, and Mary Lyndon Shanley. 1996. Relational Rights and Responsibilities: Revisioning the Family in Liberal Political Theory and Law. *Hypatia* 11: 4–29. JSTOR.

Murphy, Robert. 1995. Encounters: The Body Silent in America. In *Disability and Culture*, ed. Benedicte Ingstad and Susan Reynolds Whyte, 140–158. University of California Press.

———. 2016. The Damaged Self. In *Understanding and Applying Medical Anthropology*, ed. Peter J. Brown and Svea Closser, 249–260. Routledge.

Murphy, Robert F. 2001. *The Body Silent: The Different World of the Disabled*. New York: W. W. Norton & Company.

Naffine, Ngaire. 2009. *Law's Meaning of Life: Philosophy, Religion, Darwin and the Legal Person*. Bloomsbury Publishing.

———. 2011. Women and the Cast of Legal Persons. In *Gender, Sexualities and Law*, ed. Jackie Jones, Anna Grear, Rachel Anne Fenton, and Kim Stevenson, 15–25. Routledge.

———. 2019. *Criminal Law and the Man Problem*. Bloomsbury Publishing.

Nussbaum, Martha. 2001. The Enduring Significance of John Rawls. *The Chronicle of Higher Education* 7.

Nussbaum, Martha Craven. 2006. *Frontiers of Justice: Disability, Nationality, Species Membership*. Harvard University Press.

O'Donnell, Erin, and Julia Talbot-Jones. 2018. Creating Legal Rights for Rivers: Lessons from Australia, New Zealand, and India. *Ecology and Society* 23. https://doi.org/10.5751/ES-09854-230107.

Oliver, Mike. 2013. The Social Model of Disability: Thirty Years on. *Disability & Society* 28: 1024–1026. https://doi.org/10.1080/09687599.2013.818773.

Phelan, Shane. 2000. Queer Liberalism? Edited by Mark Blasius, Morris Kaplan, Valerie Lehr, Steven Seidman, Andrew Sullivan, and Jeffrey Weeks. *The American Political Science Review* 94: 431–442. JSTOR. https://doi.org/10.2307/2586023.

Quinn, Gerard, and Anna Arstein-Kerslake. 2012. Restoring the 'Human' in "Human Rights": Personhood and Doctrinal Innovation in the UN Disability Convention. In *The Cambridge Companion to Human Rights Law*, ed. Connor Gearty and Costas Douzinas, 36–55. Cambridge University Press.

Quinn, Gerard, and Abigail Rekas-Rosalbo. 2016. Civil Death: Rethinking the Foundations of Legal Personhood for Persons with a Disability. *Irish Jurist* 56: 286–325.

Rawls, John. 1993. *Political Liberalism*. Columbia University Press.

———. 1999. *A Theory of Justice*. Oxford University Press.

———. 2005. *Political Liberalism*. Columbia University Press.

Riley, Patrick. 2013. *Will and Political Legitimacy: A Critical Exposition of Social Contract Theory in Hobbes, Locke, Rousseau, Kant, and Hegel*. Harvard University Press.

Rosenkranz, Mark Steven. 2012. *White Male Privilege: Fourth Edition*. Law Dog Books.

Ross, Loretta, and Rickie Solinger. 2017. *Reproductive Justice: An Introduction*. Univ of California Press.

Rothman, Joshua. 2014. The Origins of "Privilege". *The New Yorker*, May 12.

Rowlands, Sam, and Jean-Jacques Amy. 2018. Preserving the reproductive potential of transgender and intersex people. *The European Journal of Contraception & Reproductive Health Care* 23: 58–63. https://doi.org/10.1080/13625187.2017.1422240.

Scott, G.E. 1990. *Moral Personhood: An Essay in the Philosophy of Moral Psychology*. SUNY Press.

Shakespeare, Tom. 2013. *Disability Rights and Wrongs Revisited*. Routledge.

———. 2016. The Social Model of Disability. In *The Disability Studies Reader*, ed. Lennard J. Davis, 195–203. Taylor & Francis.

Shaver, Sheila. 1996. *Liberalism, Gender and Social Policy*. Social Policy Research Centre Discussion Paper No. 68. Social Policy Research Centre, University of New South Wales.

Smith, Adam. 1987. *The Essential Adam Smith*. W. W. Norton & Company.

Smith, Bryant. 1928. Legal Personality. *The Yale Law Journal* 37: 283–299. JSTOR. https://doi.org/10.2307/789740.

Stark, Cynthia A. 2007. How to Include the Severely Disabled in a Contractarian Theory of Justice. *Journal of Political Philosophy* 15: 127–145. https://doi.org/10.1111/j.1467-9760.2005.00257.x.

Wahlert, Lance, and Autumn Fiester. 2012. Queer Bioethics: Why Its Time Has Come. *Bioethics* 26: ii–iv. https://doi.org/10.1111/j.1467-8519.2011.01957.x.

Warren, Mary Anne. 2000. *Moral Status: Obligations to Persons and Other Living Things. Issues in Biomedical Ethics*. Oxford University Press.

Watson, Joanne. 2016. Assumptions of Decision-Making Capacity: The Role Supporter Attitudes Play in the Realisation of Article 12 for People with Severe or Profound Intellectual Disability. *Laws* 5: 6. https://doi.org/10.3390/laws5010006.

West, Robin. 1988. Jurisprudence and Gender. *The University of Chicago Law Review* 55: 1–72. JSTOR. https://doi.org/10.2307/1599769.

Whitney, Shiloh Y. 2011. Dependency Relations: Corporeal Vulnerability and Norms of Personhood in Hobbes and Kittay. *Hypatia* 26: 554–574. https://doi.org/10.1111/j.1527-2001.2011.01188.x.

Wilsdon, Emily A. 2010. *Feminism and Personhood*. SSRN Scholarly Paper ID 1632926. Rochester, NY: Social Science Research Network.

Wong, Sophia Isako. 2010. Duties of Justice to Citizens with Cognitive Disabilities. In *Cognitive Disability and Its Challenge to Moral Philosophy*, ed. Eva Feder Kittay and Licia Carlson, 127–146. John Wiley & Sons, Ltd. https://doi.org/10.1002/9781444322781.ch7.

Chapter 3
Gender, Disability and Decision-Making: Historical Discrimination

3.1 Introduction

Chapter 1 laid out the history and definition of the human right to legal capacity—including the specification that it encompasses both legal personhood and agency. This definition laid the foundation for the application of the right throughout this book. Chapter 2 focused on the theoretical underpinnings of personhood; how it has traditionally excluded women, disabled women, and gender minorities; and how insights from critical feminist, disability, and queer theory provide the potential for a new understanding of personhood that may facilitate the realisation of the right to legal personhood—as part of the right to legal capacity—for women, disabled women, and gender minorities.

From a more practical perspective, the recognition of an individual's legal capacity bestows the holder with decision-making power. When legal capacity is fully recognised—personhood is recognised and agency is permitted to be exercised. The individual (or entity) is then free to make decisions and to have those decisions legally recognised. In this chapter, Chapter 3, I will begin to explore this more practical implication of denials of legal capacity and exclusions from personhood and agency. Specifically, I will explore the historical prejudices that have led to the denial of decision-making power to women, disabled women, and gender minorities. In the following chapter, Chap. 4, I will explore the denials of decision-making power themselves and discuss how they are denials of the right to legal capacity.

This chapter will introduce the historical discrimination that women, disabled women, and gender minorities have experienced regarding their decision-making skills. It will discuss the myth of female hysteria and irrationality that permeated our culture in the past and continues to be seen in law, policy, and practice that de-values the decision-making and cognitive skills of women (Devereux 2014). It will then discuss the myth of incapacity in relation to disabled people (Arstein-Kerslake 2017). It will cover the illusory bright line between capacity and incapacity, and the disproportionate amount of disabled people that are determined to lack capacity.

A. Arstein-Kerslake, *Legal Capacity & Gender*,
https://doi.org/10.1007/978-3-030-63493-3_3

This will build on my past work in which I have critiqued functional capacity laws and proposed a 'continuum of support' for the exercise of legal capacity for people with various levels of decision-making abilities (Flynn and Arstein-Kerslake 2014a, b). The chapter will also examine the myth of illness that gender minorities are forced to combat. It will examine the pathologisation of the lives of gender minorities. It will conclude with a discussion of how these prejudicial notions have contributed to the creation of law, policy, and practice that excludes women, disabled women, and gender minorities from decision-making and denies their legal capacity.

3.2 Women and Decision-Making: Myth of Hysteria

There is a long history of women being perceived as having inferior cognitive skills to that of men (Micale 1995). At many points in history, women have been viewed as prone to 'hysteria' or other mental health issues that would lead to decision-making impairments (Lerner 1974; Gilman 1993; Micale 1995; Devereux 2014, p. 20). 'Hysteria' was used as supposed evidence of the instability of the female mind and the purported limitations of women, which were often perceived to be due to their reproductive organs (Devereux 2014, p. 20). It can be debated whether this perception of women as irrational led to restrictions of legal capacity—or whether restrictions on legal capacity led to an inability to demonstrate decision-making skills on an equal basis with men, which led to perceptions of irrationality. It may be that one contributed to another in a vicious cycle of deeply imbedded prejudice and accompanying rights denial.

The term 'hysteria' has multiple meanings. One is its use in common parlance to delineate overemotional people—predominately women or people displaying what is perceived as 'female behaviour.' Another is the disease of hysteria, described by French physician and psychologist, Pierre Brique, in 1859 (Chodoff 1974, p. 1074). Sometimes, hysteria is perceived to be caused by the functioning and distress of female reproductive organs and sometimes simply attributed as an inherent element of being female (Micale 1995).

The father of psycho-analysis, Sigmund Freud, is often credited with the modern ascription of hysteria to woman (Gilman 1993; Micale 1995, p. 3). He coined the term 'anxiety hysteria' (Chodoff and Lyons 1958, p. 734). Much of his work pathologized the experiences and expressions of women and largely discarded them as 'hysterical' or irrational (Schafer 1974; Makari 1991; Slipp 1993). He is credited with the creation of the concept of 'hysterical conversion,' which emphasised the repression of unpleasant and traumatic experiences that are 'converted' into physical symptoms (Chodoff 1974, p. 1073; Freud and Breuer 2004; North 2015, p. 499). He argued that hysteria was caused by repressed traumatic memories that were likely sexual in nature. One of the most famous cases that Freud wrote about was 'Anna O.' She displayed 'hysterical' symptoms and after discussing the traumatic events that led to her hysterical symptoms, the symptoms disappeared—this was the beginning of 'the talking cure' and was a part of the creation of Freud's psychoanalysis that remains heavily influential on modern psychology. (Micale 1995, p. 27).

Freud, however, was by no means the first to attribute hysteria or irrationality to women. From almost the earliest written records, there has been an association between femininity and hysteria (Chodoff 1982, p. 545). For example, the word 'hysteria' is derived from the Greek word for uterus, 'hystera,' and has been associated with female psychological dysfunction ever since (Chodoff 1982, p. 545; Micale 1995, p. 19; Cramer 2019, p. 705). The Greek use of the word was derived from the Sanskrit word for stomach or belly. There is evidence that Egyptian medicine from around 1900 bc documented what was perceived as abnormal behaviour in adult women and interpreted it as abnormalities caused by the movement of the uterus, in an autonomous manner, upward, which put pressure on the diaphragm. Treatment for such 'hysteria' included placement of scented substances on the vulva to lead the uterus back down and the smelling and consumption of foul tasting and rotting substances to move the uterus away from the diaphragm (Micale 1995, p. 19). These Egyptian views on hysteria formed the foundations for the classical Greek medical and philosophical theories of hysteria (Micale 1995, p. 19). In referring to the 'nature' of women—which, one could argue, relates to a view of the personhood of women—Plato wrote:

> The womb is an animal which longs to generate children. When it remains barren too long after puberty it is distressed and sorely disturbed and straying about in the body and cutting off the passages of the breath, it impedes respiration and brings the sufferer into the extremest anguish, and provokes all manner of diseases besides. [The disturbance continues until the womb is appeased by passion and love.] Such is the nature of women and all that is female. (Plato and Jowett 360AD; Chodoff 1982, p. 546)

Women were viewed as burdened with their reproductive organs, which were perceived to control their lives—both physically and mentally. They were perceived as incapable of rational thought on par with men—in part, because it was believed that their biology would not allow it (Chodoff 1982, p. 546; Cramer 2019, p. 705). Therapy for such perceived illness was often immediate marriage (Micale 1995, p. 19).

Ancient Romans also wrote about hysteria. They moved on from the Greek notion of a wandering uterus—however, it remained an illness tied exclusively to the female reproductive tract, which is termed gynaecological determinism of hysteria. Cases were identified primarily in unmarried women, in particular—virgins, those never married, and widows—and the treatment prescribed was often marital fornication. The Egyptian, Greek, and Roman conceptions of hysteria provide the basis for the concept of hysteria in western civilisation. Until the early twentieth century, the notion of gynaecological determinism of hysteria remained (Micale 1995, p. 20).

From the fifth to the thirteenth centuries, with the increasing strength of Christian civilization in Europe, there was a shift towards viewing hysteria as a manifestation of evil and a consequence of original sin. The female hysteric was seen either as a victim of bewitchment to be pitied or a soul mate of the devil to the feared. In the late medieval and Renaissance periods, there was a shift from treating hysteria as a medical condition to subjecting women deemed hysterical to the courtroom. Women were tortured and executed on the basis of being a witch or hysteric. In response to this, in the following period—during the scientific revolution—hysteria was returned to the field of medicine and become re-pathologised and was, once again, treated as a medical disorder and mental illness. In the mid-1800s, medical scholars began to treat hysteria as a behavioural disorder, as opposed to a physical illness. Traits that were ascribed to hysteria during this time included: eccentricity, impulsiveness, emotionality, coquettishness, deceitfulness, and hypersexuality. It wasn't until the late 1800s that hysteria began to be discussed as a psychological phenomenon. (Micale 1995, pp. 21–26).

Just prior to Freud's work on hysteria, which took place in the 1880s and 1890s, Briquet was one of the first to discuss 'hysteria' as a disease. He identified it as a disease of women that has an onset before the age of 35. He claimed that it is characterised by multiple physical complaints and hospitalisation (Chodoff 1974, p. 1074). He defined hysteria as "neurosis of the brain in which the observed phenomena consist chiefly of a perturbation of vital activities, which serve as the manifestation of affective feeling and passions" (Briquet 1859, p. 3; Mai and Merskey 1980, p. 1401). Briquet based much of his work on a study he conducted with 430 cases of 'hysteria' over a ten-year period at the Hôpital de la Charité in Paris. In this study he identified several predisposing factors of hysteria: sex; age; heredity; physical constitution and 'moral disposition'; social class; mode of education; influence of emotions and 'moral affections'; occupation; sexual continence; and general health (Mai and Merskey 1980, pp. 1401–1402). He claimed that women are at least 20 times more at risk of becoming hysterics than men (Briquet 1859, p. 36). He notes,

> Amongst women, there exists a more lively sensitiveness than amongst men. Feelings are more easily aroused, are experienced more intensely, and have more repercussions in the whole economy than amongst men. Everything is an occasion for feeling, and all feelings exercise their influences on the splanchnic viscera. (Briquet 1859, p. 47; Mai and Merskey 1980, p. 1401)

Briquet found that there were certain phenomena that provided alleviation of hysteria:

> The return of regular menses, an improvement in social position, the development of an intercurrent disease (e.g., tuberculosis), "violent moral emotions," and the imagination and the will had a favorable effect on the course of hysteria, whereas marriage and pregnancy had an unfavorable effect. In general, those influences that calmed the nervous system improved hysteria, and those that excited the nervous system aggravated the illness." (Briquet 1859, pp. 498–514; Mai and Merskey 1980, p. 1403)

In his work, there is a clear connection between assumptions about women, rationality, and illness.

Prominent psychiatrist and scholar, Paul Chodoff, engaged in significant scholarly work exploring the history, meaning, and application of hysteria (Chodoff and Lyons 1958; Chodoff 1974, 1982). In the early 1980s, he queried whether hysteria was inherently female or whether it was, in fact, predominantly seen in women due to social and cultural forces such as male domination (Chodoff 1982). His work, at the time, appears to be quite progressive for the psychiatric profession—he concludes that hysteria is not a natural attribute of women. Instead, he finds that hysteria is developed in women under the stress of male dominance. I find this significant for two reasons. The first is that he doesn't appear to significantly engage with the question of whether 'hysteria' exists at all—or whether it is merely a creation of the male dominated medical and psychiatric professions. He doesn't question whether it is simply a gendered label to further stigmatise and oppress the already marginalised female population. Of course, Chodoff is from the male dominated and historically patriarchal medical and psychiatric professions and is not a critical theorist or feminist—at least I have not found evidence that he is either of these.

Feminists at the time, had, of course, already began to query the foundations of 'hysteria' and its use as a tool of oppression (Devereux 2014). Interestingly (and cleverly), in the 1970s and 1980s, in the midst of the second wave of feminism, feminist scholars began to reclaim hysteria. The involuntary, physical symptoms of hysteria that had been ascribed as a medical condition, were being re-understood as a cultural phenomenon—an embodied manifestation of paternalistic oppression. They were beginning to be understood as an individual assertion of feminism—a kind of individual rebellion against the patriarchy (Gilman 1993, p. 21; Devereux 2014). It is paradoxical that this coincided with the removal of the diagnosis of 'hysteria' from the Diagnostic and Statistical Manual of Mental Disorders (DSM). Both the conservative medical profession and radical feminists were asserting that hysteria is something other than a physical malady (Devereux 2014, p. 21).

The evolution of the concept of hysteria in the DSM is evidence of the ongoing modern prevalence of the remnants of the notion of females being inherently cognitively flawed. The DSM is the classification of what are believed to be 'mental disorders' using a common language and standard criteria. It is published by the American Psychiatric Association (APA) and it is widely used by clinicians, researchers, psychiatric drug regulation agencies, health insurance companies, pharmaceutical companies, the legal system, and policy makers (American Psychiatric Association 2013). The DSM included some form of hysterical (histrionic) personality disorder until 1980 (American Psychiatric Association 1987; Devereux 2014, p. 19; North 2015, p. 503; Cramer 2019, p. 705; Cherry 2020). The current version, *DSM-5*, does not include a specific reference to hysteria. However, it has retained 'conversion disorder,' which is drawn from Freud's psychoanalytic theory and, as described above, was developed from notions of female hysteria (North 2015, p. 503). This ongoing maintenance in the DSM of concepts derived from the notion of female hysteria evidentiates the continued prevalence of the prejudicial notion of women as irrational. It also indicates that the modern medical profession continues to view women as, at least, potentially lacking in decision-making skills.

Hysteria is far from an antiquated, under-used concept. In 1995, scholar Mark Micale wrote of the 'new hysteria studies'—documenting a new surge in academic interest in hysteria (Micale 1995). In addition, hysteria is ever-present in popular culture—including recent feature films and television series centred on the concept

(Devereux 2014, p. 41). Hysteria is still very much a part of modern vernacular and the oppression inherent in hysteria's insistence that women are irrational and cognitively unstable continues to permeate the social consciousness.

This is only a snapshot of the long and winding history of the discreditation of female cognition. On the basis of their gender, women's intellects, rationality, and decision-making skills have been questioned pervasively and continuously (Devereux 2014). They have also been denied the opportunity to exercise decision-making skills through the denial of legal capacity in various ways, which will be discussed in Chap. 4. This denial of decision-making power coupled with the disregard and disrepute for their decision-making skills have had a profound effect on women's power and privilege—it has decidedly held them back, as was discussed at the end of Chap. 2.

3.3 Disability and Decision-Making: Myth of Incapacity

Disabled people have experienced similar prejudice to that of women—potentially to a greater degree. Here, I think it is more relevant to describe how and why disabled people are ascribed with poor decision-making skills, rather than to undertake a review of the history of such assumptions—as I did in the last section related to women and the ascription of labels of 'hysteria' and assumptions related to irrationality. I have chosen to focus on the how and why in the context of disability because of the ongoing prevalence of assumptions regarding poor decision-making skills as well as the pervasive existence of laws that enshrine such assumptions. For women, there are ongoing assumptions of irrationality, as I discussed in the previous section—however, they are now quite rarely seen explicitly in law. Instead, women more frequently face insidious assumptions regarding their irrationality in interpersonal relationships as well as indirectly in laws that more subtly restrict their decision-making rather that explicitly disregarding it. Disabled people, however, are faced with laws such as guardianship, mental health law, and mental capacity law that explicitly allow disabled people's decision-making to be denied.

People with physical disability as well as cognitive disability are often perceived of as lacking decision-making skills. Many assume that disability inherently includes a lack of decision-making skills. This is often termed a lack of 'capacity'—which usually refers to a lack of mental capacity. However, the use of the term 'capacity' in this context is often conflated with the concept of legal capacity. In this way, disabled people are often described as 'lacking capacity' when referring to decision-making skills—they are often then assumed to also not be entitled to legal capacity. As I have written elsewhere (Flynn and Arstein-Kerslake 2014b; Arstein-Kerslake 2017) this conflation is leading to the disproportionate denial of legal capacity to disabled people. It is also leading to the maintenance and perpetuation of systems that deny legal capacity to disabled people because it allows people to ask the question 'do they have capacity?'—and then attempt to test disabled people's decision-making skills in order to determine that they lack mental capacity and therefore are not entitled to legal capacity. (For example, the *Mental Capacity Act 2005* in England and Wales) (Series 2013; Donnelly 2016). There are two critical errors with this. The first is the fallacy that any functional test of decision-making skills is accurate. The second is that legal capacity can be denied on the basis of mental capacity.

A functional test of decision-making skills presents significant problems for various reasons. It assumes that a test can be created to accurately determine whether an individual is appropriately making decisions according to a process that is deemed acceptable. It also assumes that there is a set manner in which decisions are made. The abundance of scholarship on the difficulty of assessing an individual's decision-making skills indicates that the area is fraught and existing tests may be lacking accuracy and effectiveness (Spar and Garb 1992; Glass 1997; Martin and Hickerson 2013; Series 2013; Owen et al. 2017; Spencer et al. 2017; Owen et al. 2018). It is likely that it will always be very difficult to determine whether an individual is capable of making decisions—this is because of the wide variety in the functioning of the human mind as well as the difficulty in communicating what is inside the mind. For these reasons, any test of the functioning of the human mind should be viewed with some degree of scepticism, or at least should be closely scrutinised.

Such functional tests usually assume that decisions should be made using a rational, logically sound decision-making process. They then attempt to create a test that can determine if a particular individual is able to undertake a rational and logically sound decision-making process. This is erroneous for two reasons. The first is that there is evidence that a significant portion of all of our decision-making is not based on rational or logical processes. The second is that there are substantial liberty and equality problems that arise when we force only a certain group of people to undergo tests of their decision-making in order to be respected as full legal persons and legal agents.

Research has repeatedly shown that people very frequently do not make decisions based on a rational, logically sound process. Instead, people often make decisions according to emotions or instinct and do not at all in engage in a weighing of options or even seek to choose the most optimal path according to efficiency or expediency (Gladwell 2007; Yang and Lester 2008; Ariely 2009; Lehrer 2010). It is possible that this is a cause for celebration—some of the most profound and impactful decisions we make in life are often not made due to rationality or logic—for example, falling in love, taking risks, and acting out of instinct when coming to someone's aid. However, the level of rationality that goes into individual decision-making is not the core issue that I would like to tackle here. What I would like to address is the reality that we all, at least sometimes, act according to emotion, instinct, or factors other than rationality and logic—and we enjoy the freedom to do so. It is likely important for the development of our personalities and our interpersonal relationships. As such, it feels deeply unequitable to require disabled people to pass a test to prove that they are engaging in a rational and logical decision-making process before their decisions will be respected and recognised in law. In addition, in a liberal political environment, it is essential for equality and liberty that we all have equal enjoyment of all types of decision-making.

In line with a liberal political view—discussed in Chaps. 1 and 2—as much of the world does, we place value on liberty and the freedom of the individual to engage with the socio-legal world as they choose. Although there are quite significant and well-reasoned critiques of liberal political theory—again, discussed in Chap. 2—our systems are, nonetheless, significantly influenced by liberal political theory, which make it worth engaging with. In addition—the value of liberty is often one aspect of liberal political theory that is often celebrated by even some of its staunchest critics. Part of the right to liberty is the freedom to make decisions as one wishes—to not be tied to a particular process for decision-making. Those experiencing privilege—often white, able-bodied, heterosexual cisgender males—rarely have their decision-making processes questioned. They are more or less free to make decisions according to a rational process of logically determined weighing of options and information or—conversely—to make decisions based on emotion, instinct, or anything else. However, disabled people, in particular, are often assumed to lack decision-making skills and are subject to functional tests of capacity that profess to determine whether they are using rational decision-making processes when others are not required to do so. In order to respect the liberty and equality of disabled people—they must not be asked to past functional test of their decision-making skills that others are not required to pass.

Eilionóir Flynn and I successfully advocated for this to be included in the United Nations Convention on the Rights of Persons with Disabilities (CRPD) Committee General Comment on the Right to Equal Recognition Before the Law. As discussed in Chap. 1, the General Comment states that mental capacity must not be conflated with legal capacity. Mental capacity is an individual's decision-making skills and legal capacity is the recognition of an individual's legal personhood and agency. The General Comment states that legal capacity must not be denied on the basis of mental capacity (Committee on the Rights of Persons with Disabilities 2014, p. 3). This obviates the need for tests of functional cognitive capabilities because legal capacity must be respected regardless. Instead, there is a need for robust and sensitive assessments of what supports individuals may need for the exercise of their legal capacity (Flynn and Arstein-Kerslake 2014a, b).

Disabled women are particularly affected by these historical and modern prejudices because they are subjected to both discrimination related to the mental capacity of disabled people as well as the long history of women being labelled as hysteric and lacking rationality. As such, specific attention must be paid to the situation of disabled women and their status as legal persons and legal agents. They are experiencing uniquely profound marginalisation in this area and they are, therefore, in need of uniquely stringent rectification and tailored support for the recognition and exercise of their legal capacity.

3.4 Gender Minorities and Decision-Making: Myth of Illness

Gender minorities experience a different—but equally detrimental—form of prejudice that leads to others questioning their decision-making skills. Gender minorities—transgender people, in particular, but intersex and other gender minorities have experienced it as well—have been erroneously labelled as having mental health illnesses as a result of their gender identity and the way that they experience gender. This has happened on both a formal level with the psychiatric profession, as well as an informal, interpersonal level with widespread misunderstanding and prejudice expressed in popular culture and in interpersonal interactions (Reicherzer 2008, p. 328; Pfäfflin 2015; Spade 2015; Cannoot 2019b).

The existence of gender minorities is not a new phenomenon. Throughout human history there is evidence of non-binary and non-traditional gender identity and expression. Many cultures did not have negative associations with non-binary gender expression. Some cultures have even revered such experiences and expressions as having important religious or spiritual value. However, European centric cultures have relatively consistently pathologized non-binary gender experiences and expressions (Reicherzer 2008, p. 327). In these cultures, non-conforming gender identity has been considered a medical condition to be treated instead of simply an individual characteristic (Cannoot 2019a, p. 3). The late 1800s and early 1900s saw an increase in the medicalisation of non-binary and non-traditional gender expression, which came about with the advent of Forensic Psychiatry and Sexology in Europe—particularly in Austria and Germany. During this time, patients with non-binary or non-traditional gender identities or gender expression were often classified as having delusions. In addition, because transsexual individuals, in particular were often having sexual relationships with people of their same biologically expressed gender, their sexual relationships were criminalised and there were many individuals that were imprisoned (Pfäfflin 2015).

In order to understand the pathologisation and medical classification of non-binary and non-traditional gender expressions and experiences, it helps to understand the history of the treatment of sexuality and gender more broadly. While gender minorities vary significantly in their sexualities and sexual expression—including heterosexual, homosexual, and bisexual individuals—the history of treatment of sexuality provides a window into the oppressive atmosphere that exists in relation to non-traditional sexual and gender identities and expressions. It was in the late 1940s and 1950s that Alfred Kinsey and Evelyn Hooker produced some of the first substantial research work on sexuality. Both were highly controversial and professionally censured by many in the academic and psychological communities of the time. This history demonstrates the lack of knowledge and the resistance to seeking knowledge regarding gender and sexuality identity and expression (Reicherzer 2008, p. 327).

Just over a decade later, in 1968, the gay rights movement was well underway—demonstrated by the Stonewall Rebellion in which a demonstration for the human rights of gay, lesbian, and transgender people erupted into riots prompted by violence by police against protestors in the iconic gay bar, the Stonewall Inn in New York City (Manalansan 1995; Bullough 2014; Faderman 2016). While this struggle for recognition and equality was gathering momentum, sexuality and gender was also being increasing medicalised. In 1968, the DSM produced a new volume that included the diagnosis of "Sexual orientation disturbance [Homosexuality]" (the DSM continued to include some form of diagnosis of homosexuality until 1987) (Reicherzer 2008, p. 327). It was amidst this climate of prejudice and ignorance that the ongoing medicalisation of gender minorities was taking place.

Medicalisation of non-binary gender experiences and expressions began occurring via formal identification and classification of what was considered gender nonconformity in the early 1900s (Reicherzer 2008, p. 330). Some of the first sex reassignment surgeries also occurred in Europe in the early 1900s. Two were performed in London, England on two individuals that were born with male genitalia and identified as female. The decision to perform the surgery was made due to the doctor's concern that the individuals would self-mutilate otherwise (Reicherzer 2008, p. 330). Several other reassignment surgeries were performed around the same time in Berlin, Germany at Magnus Hirshfield's Institute for Sexual Science (Reicherzer 2008, p. 330; Pfäfflin 2015; Cannoot 2019b, p. 3). Hirshfield has been described as a "Jew, transvestite, and effeminate homosexual" and his institute sought to both provide scientific rigor to studies of gender and sexuality as well as to provide assistance to gender minorities and to begin to seek equality and equal rights for gender and sexual minorities (Hirschfeld 1914; Dose 2014; Hirschfeld 2017). It appears that sex reassignment surgeries were occurring both at the behest of individuals themselves that sought to have their physical bodies altered to better reflect their gender identities as well as at the behest of medical professionals who sought to correct non-conforming gender binary behaviour that they perceived to be an illness.

World War II impacted this medicalisation of non-binary gender expression and experiences. In 1933, Hirshfield's Institute and his work was largely dismantled by the Nazi's in Germany (Reicherzer 2008, p. 331). This was effectively the loss of the first significant hub of progressive work towards the realisation of gender minority rights. It was also the loss of one of the first significant efforts toward scientific discovery in the area of sexuality and gender. Scientific medical research continued in the area, but most of it did not include the same effort towards social justice for gender and sexual minorities. For example, Dr. David Cauldwell a sexologist who worked on gender non-conforming individuals from 1947 to 1956, began to classify gender non-conforming expression and experiences as "psychopathia transexualis" (Reicherzer 2008, p. 331)—he made the following assertions:

> When an individual fails to mature according to his (or her) proper biological and sexological status, such an individual is psychologically (mentally) deficient. The psychological condition is in reality the disease. . . . When an individual who is unfavorably affected psychologically determines to live and appear as a member of the sex to which he or she does not belong, such an individual is what may be called a psychopathic transexual. This means,

> simply, that one is mentally unhealthy and because of this the person desires to live as a member of the opposite sex. (Cauldwell 2006, p. 41)

Cauldwell concluded that individuals who he labelled as 'psychopathic transexuals' acquired this disease as a result, largely, of unfavourable childhood environments and overindulgent caregivers. He believed that a cure for psychopathic transexualis was inevitable and imminent (Cauldwell 2006, p. 41; Reicherzer 2008, p. 331). Cauldwell's pathologisation of non-binary gender expression and experiences assumes that individuals having such experiences and generally not conforming to the gender binary are unwell and 'mentally unhealthy.' It is easy to see how such pathologisations and assumptions can lead to gender minorities being considered to be unable to make decisions for themselves or that they generally lack decision-making skills because they are mentally unwell.

There were also two widely known cases of sex reassignment surgery that brought significant medical attention to the transgender world, in particular. The first was Christine Jorgensen, a transwoman from the United States who travelled to Denmark to receive sex reassignment surgery in 1952—and a transman, Laurence Michael Dillon, from the United Kingdom who underwent sex reassignment surgery in the 1940s and published a book on his experience (Dillon 2013; Pfäfflin 2015; Cannoot 2019b, p. 3). Paradoxically, gender reassignment surgery became increasingly available for those that sought to exercise agency and choose to change their physical gender characteristic—while, at the same time, the increased medicalisation of non-binary gender experiences and expressions also served to increasingly discredit and disregard the experiences of gender minorities as delusions or struggles of the mentally ill. This likely has contributed to the de-valuing of the cognition and decision-making skills of gender minorities.

Until the mid-1960s, psychotherapy to 'cure' non-conforming gender expression was the dominant form of treatment for what was considered a disease and mental illness. In 1966 endocrinologist and sexologist Harry Benjamin published his book, *The Transsexual Phenomenon*, which became the foundation of the modern medical approach to non-conforming gender expression. He argued that the physical body should be changed to match the gender that the individual identifies with psychologically. However, he believed that this should only be done for those that he designated as 'true transsexuals'—and he only believed that the individual's experience could be designated as 'true' via diagnosis by a psychiatrist. This continues to be a prevalent requirement for those undergoing sex reassignment surgery and those seeking to legally change their gender. The requirement of a diagnosis for sex reassignment or legal gender recognition inherently pathologizes non-conforming gender expression and experiences. It makes having a non-conforming gender identity a medical problem to be cured instead of simply an aspect of identity (Benjamin 1966; Cannoot 2019b, p. 3). It also devalues the personhood and agency of the individual who has a non-conforming gender identity. The decisions of the individual themselves regarding sex reassignment surgery and legal gender recognition are not sufficient—they are given full legal recognition. Instead, the decisions of a psychiatrist are used to make decisions on behalf of the individual. This devaluing of the decision-making of those who have non-conforming gender experiences or expression is particularly striking when compared with other individuals who seek cosmetic plastic surgery. Generally, there is no requirement for a psychiatrist or other doctor to provide a diagnosis before an individual can undergo significant plastic surgery that has significant health implications and may alter their appearance significantly. As long as an individual is seeking surgery that conforms with the gender binary, generally no diagnosis is needed. In this way, because gender minorities do not fit in to traditional gender expression and roles, they are pathologized and their decision-making is often discredited.

Judith Butler discusses the myth of illness in relation to gender minorities. She acknowledges that from a practical perspective there are many advantages to being diagnosed with what the medical profession calls gender identity disorder (GID). For example, the medicalisation of gender non-conforming expressions and experiences into GID can provide a means for some to access medical and technological means for transitioning. Medical diagnosis is often required for health insurance companies to cover costs of sex reassignment surgery or other medical treatment related to gender identity needs. For these reasons, and others, it can be critical that medical treatment and sex reassignment surgery is not conceived of as 'elective.' However, she cautions that a diagnosis is an instrument of pathologization (Butler 2004, p. 75). She asserts that,

> To be diagnosed with GID is to be found, in some way, to be ill, sick, wrong, out of order, abnormal, and to suffer a certain stigmatization as a consequence of the diagnosis being given at all. (Butler 2004, p. 76)

She notes that those that argue for the continued inclusion of the GID in the DSM and as a medical illness, often do so because they are seeking the means to conform appropriately to external societal and legal obligations before they can exercise their autonomy in choosing to undergo treatment or surgery that will allow them to express their gender as they choose. She also notes that those that seek to stop the pathologisation of non-bianray gender experiences and expressions also often do so in order to have their autonomy recognised. They seek for their gender expression to be recognised as an exercise of their autonomy and to be understood as simply an aspect of human diversity—not a sickness to be cured (Butler 2004, pp. 76–77).

Butler also notes that the two positions—one arguing for a medical diagnosis of gender dysphoria, and one arguing against any diagnosis—have fundamentally different views of autonomy. Those arguing against a medical diagnosis are often coming from a individualistic perspective—similar to liberal political theory. They seek for non-binary gender identity and experiences to be recognised as a natural part of the human experience in order for each individual to be free to exercise autonomy and make their own choices regarding their gender identity and experiences. Those arguing for the inclusion of gender dysphoria as a medical diagnosis are acknowledging that there are material conditions for the exercise of liberty. They would like GID to remain a medical diagnosis in order for them to be able to have the medical community and insurance companies, in particular, recognise and provide resources towards the potential necessity of medical treatments in order for people to have the gender expressions and experiences of their choosing. In this way, the resources gained from insurance companies are a material condition for the expression of autonomy (Butler 2004, p. 85). The medicalisation of non-binary gender expression and experiences, therefore, inhibits autonomy assuming illness instead of choice—and also fosters autonomy, when it is the means by which an individual can access the medical treatment necessary in order for them to exercise autonomy in gender expression (Butler 2004, p. 92).

Butler's work provides a succinct analysis of the impact of medicalising non-binary gender expression and experiences. It both hampers freedom and facilitates it. However, it only facilitates it within a world in which the gender binary and heteronormativity dominate. In a changed world—where gender expression was not stigmatised, the gender binary was broken down, and same sex relationships were accepted in the same manner as heterosexual relationships—there would be do need for the medicalisation of non-binary gender expression and experiences to facilitate autonomy or, in other words, to facilitate the exercise of legal capacity to choose gender expression. This would be vastly preferable because while the medicalisation of non-binary gender expression and experiences can facilitate autonomy in the way described, it even more frequently and insidiously undermines autonomy. Similar to stigmatisation from disability labelling described above (Hacking 1986; Winick 1995), pathologizing and medicalising non-binary gender expression experiences can be profoundly damaging. When something is medicalised or pathologized, it is a label of wrongness—of something that needs to be corrected; of a person who is not whole. It is socially and psychologically dehumanising. As Butler puts it, "the diagnosis intensifies the very suffering that requires alleviation" (Butler 2004, p. 100). It sends a message to the world that the individual is not complete, and when the label is one of a mental health diagnosis—as GID is—it sends a message to the world that the individual cannot make decisions for themselves and should not be allowed to make decisions for themselves. It is easy, in such a context, for an individual to be denied legal capacity to make decisions—either minute decisions or significant decisions, such as medical or financial decisions. In this way, the myth of non-binary gender expression and experiences as an illness significantly contributes to the widespread erection of barriers to and denial of legal capacity for gender minorities.

3.5 Conclusion

In this chapter, I have attempted to discuss three myths that have led to the de-valuing of the decision-making of women, disabled women, and gender minorities. Women have suffered from the myth of hysteria. Women's cognition and their decision-making skills have, for centuries, been disregarded as hysterical—sometimes due to the belief that women's reproductive organs cause cognitive instability and other times due to the systematic pathologisation of what are deemed to be female characteristics. Disabled people have been subjected to the myth of incapacity. They are frequently considered to lack 'capacity'—or sufficient decision-making skills—often on the basis that they have a disability. Disability is perceived as being inherently associated with an inability to make decisions. They have their decision-making skills called into question via legal mechanisms for the removal of their right to make decisions. Gender minorities face oppression from the myth of illness. Due to historical prejudice and misconceptions, gender minorities continue to be perceived of as having a mental illness that is the root of their non-binary gender expressions or experiences. This myth of illness is associated with deficiency in mental capabilities, including decision-making skills. In these ways, women, disabled women, and gender minorities suffer under historical and on-going prejudicial notions of their cognitive skills and decision-making capabilities. These have likely led to barriers to legal capacity and, in some cases, the systematic denial of legal capacity. Those barriers and denials will be discussed in the next chapter.

References

American Psychiatric Association. 1987. *Diagnostic and Statistical Manual of Mental Disorders (DSM-3®)*. 3rd ed. rev. Washington, DC: American Psychiatric Publishing.

———. 2013. *Diagnostic and Statistical Manual of Mental Disorders (DSM-5®)*. 5th ed. rev. Washington, DC: American Psychiatric Publishing.

Ariely, Dan. 2009. *Predictably Irrational: The Hidden Forces that Shape Our Decisions*. HarperCollins UK.

Arstein-Kerslake, Anna. 2017. *Restoring Voice to People with Cognitive Disabilities*. Cambridge University Press.

Benjamin, Harry. 1966. *The Transsexual Phenomenon*. Julian Press, Incorporated Publishers.

Briquet, Pierre. 1859. *Traite de l'Hysterie*. Paris: JB Bailliere et Fils.

Bullough, Vern L. 2014. *Before Stonewall: Activists for Gay and Lesbian Rights in Historical Context*. Routledge.

Butler, Judith. 2004. *Undoing Gender*. Routledge. https://doi.org/10.4324/9780203499627.

Cannoot, Pieter. 2019a. The Pathologisation of Trans* Persons in the ECtHR's Case Law on Legal Gender Recognition. *Netherlands Quarterly of Human Rights* 37: 14–35. https://doi.org/10.1177/0924051918820984.

———. 2019b. '#WontBeErased': The Effects of (De)pathologisation and (De)medicalisation on the Legal Capacity of Trans* Persons. *International Journal of Law and Psychiatry* 66: 101478. https://doi.org/10.1016/j.ijlp.2019.101478.

Cauldwell, David O. 2006. Psychopathia Transexualis. In *The Transgender Studies Reader*, ed. Susan Stryker and Stephen Whittle, 40–44. Routledge.

Cherry, Kendra. 2020. Understanding Hysteria in the Past and Present. *Verywell Mind*, March 16.

Chodoff, Paul. 1974. The Diagnosis of Hysteria: An Overview. *American Journal of Psychiatry* 131: 1073–1078. https://doi.org/10.1176/ajp.131.10.1073.

———. 1982. Hysteria and women. *American Journal of Psychiatry* 139: 545–551. https://doi.org/10.1176/ajp.139.5.545.

Chodoff, Paul, and Henry Lyons. 1958. Hysteria, the Hysterical Personality and "Hysterical" Conversion. *American Journal of Psychiatry* 114: 734–740. https://doi.org/10.1176/ajp.114.8.734.

Committee on the Rights of Persons with Disabilities. 2014. General Comment No. 1 – Article 12: Equal Recognition Before the Law. UN Doc. No. CRPD/C/GC/1.

Cramer, Phebe. 2019. What Has Happened to Hysteria? *The Journal of Nervous and Mental Disease* 207: 705–706. https://doi.org/10.1097/NMD.0000000000000850.

Devereux, Cecily. 2014. Hysteria, Feminism, and Gender Revisited: The Case of the Second Wave. *English Studies in Canada* 40: 19–45. https://doi.org/10.1353/esc.2014.0004.

Dillon, Michael. 2013. *Self: A Study in Ethics and Endocrinology*. Elsevier.

Donnelly, Mary. 2016. Best Interests in the Mental Capacity Act: Time to say Goodbye? *Medical Law Review* 24: 318–332. https://doi.org/10.1093/medlaw/fww030.

Dose, Ralf. 2014. *Magnus Hirschfeld: The Origins of the Gay Liberation Movement*. 1st ed. New York: Monthly Review Press.

Faderman, Lillian. 2016. *The Gay Revolution: The Story of the Struggle*. Reprint edition. New York London Toronto Sydney New Delhi: Simon & Schuster.

Flynn, Eilionoir, and Anna Arstein-Kerslake. 2014a. The Support Model of Legal Capacity: Fact, Fiction, or Fantasy. *Berkeley Journal of International Law*: 124–143.

———. 2014b. Legislating Personhood: Realising the Right to Support in Exercising Legal Capacity. *International Journal of Law in Context* 10: 81–104. https://doi.org/10.1017/S1744552313000384.

Freud, Sigmund, and Joseph Breuer. 2004. *Studies in Hysteria*. Penguin Classics.

Gilman, Sander L. 1993. *Hysteria Beyond Freud*. University of California Press.

Gladwell, Malcolm. 2007. *Blink: The Power of Thinking Without Thinking*. 1st ed. New York: Back Bay Books.

Glass, Kathleen Cranley. 1997. Refining Definitions and Devising Instruments: Two Decades of Assessing Mental Competence. *International Journal of Law and Psychiatry* 20: 5–33. https://doi.org/10.1016/S0160-2527(96)00020-9.

Hacking, Ian. 1986. Making Up People. In *Reconstructing Individualism: Autonomy, Individuality, and the Self in Western Thought*, ed. Thomas C. Heller, Morton Sosna, and David E. Wellbery, 222–236. Stanford University Press.

Hirschfeld, Magnus. 1914. *Die Homosexualität des Mannes und des Weibes*. L. Marcus.

———. 2017. *Berlin's Third Sex*. Rixdorf Editions.

Lehrer, Jonah. 2010. *How We Decide*. Houghton Mifflin Harcourt.

Lerner, H.E. 1974. The Hysterical Personality: A "Woman's Disease". *Comprehensive Psychiatry* 15: 157–164. https://doi.org/10.1016/0010-440x(74)90032-7.

Mai, Francois M., and Harold Merskey. 1980. Briquet's Treatise on Hysteria: A Synopsis and Commentary. *Archives of General Psychiatry* 37: 1401–1405. https://doi.org/10.1001/archpsyc.1980.01780250087010.

Makari, George J. 1991. German Philosophy, Freud, and the Riddle of the Woman. *Journal of the American Psychoanalytic Association* 39: 183–213. https://doi.org/10.1177/000306519103900109.

Manalansan, Martin F. 1995. In the Shadows of Stonewall: Examining Gay Transnational Politics and the Diasporic Dilemma. *GLQ: A Journal of Lesbian and Gay Studies* 2: 425–438. https://doi.org/10.1215/10642684-2-4-425.

Martin, Wayne, and Ryan Hickerson. 2013. Mental Capacity and the Applied Phenomenology of Judgement. *Phenomenology and the Cognitive Sciences* 12: 195–214. https://doi.org/10.1007/s11097-011-9242-y.

Micale, Mark S. 1995. *Approaching Hysteria: Disease and Its Interpretations*. Princeton University Press.

North, Carol S. 2015. The Classification of Hysteria and Related Disorders: Historical and Phenomenological Considerations. *Behavioral Sciences* 5: 496–517. https://doi.org/10.3390/bs5040496.

Owen, Gareth S., Fabian Freyenhagen, Wayne Martin, and Anthony S. David. 2017. Clinical Assessment of Decision-Making Capacity in Acquired Brain Injury with Personality Change. *Neuropsychological Rehabilitation* 27: 133–148. https://doi.org/10.1080/09602011.2015.1053948.

Owen, Gareth S., Fabian Freyenhagen, and Wayne Martin. 2018. Assessing Decision-Making Capacity After Brain Injury: A Phenomenological Approach. *Philosophy, Psychiatry, and Psychology* 25: 1–19. https://doi.org/10.1353/ppp.2018.0002.

Pfäfflin, Friedemann. 2015. Transgenderism and Transsexuality: Medical and Psychological Viewpoints. In *The Legal Status of Transsexual and Transgender Persons*, ed. Jens M. Scherpe, 11–24. Intersentia. https://doi.org/10.1017/9781780685588.003.

Plato, and Benjamin Jowett. 360AD. *Timaeus*. Champaign, Ill: Project Gutenberg.

Reicherzer, Stacee. 2008. Evolving Language and Understanding in the Historical Development of the Gender Identity Disorder Diagnosis. *Journal of LGBT Issues in Counseling* 2: 326–347. https://doi.org/10.1080/15538600802502035.

Schafer, Roy. 1974. Problems in Freud's Psychology of Women. *Journal of the American Psychoanalytic Association* 22: 459–485. https://doi.org/10.1177/000306517402200301.

Series, Lucy. 2013. *The Mental Capacity Act 2005 and the Institutional Domination of People with Learning Disabilities*. University of Exeter.

Slipp, Samuel. 1993. *The Freudian Mystique*. NYU Press.

Spade, Dean. 2015. *Normal Life: Administrative Violence, Critical Trans Politics, and the Limits of Law*. Duke University Press.

Spar, James E., and Andrew S. Garb. 1992. Assessing Competency to Make a Will. *The American Journal of Psychiatry* 149: 169–174. https://doi.org/10.1176/ajp.149.2.169.

Spencer, Benjamin W.J., Gareth Wilson, Ewa Okon-Rocha, Gareth S. Owen, and Charlotte Wilson Jones. 2017. Capacity in Vacuo: An Audit of Decision-Making Capacity Assessments in a Liaison Psychiatry Service. *BJPsych Bulletin* 41: 7–11. https://doi.org/10.1192/pb.bp.115.052613.

Winick, Bruce J. 1995. The Side Effects of Incompetency Labeling and the Implications for Mental Health Law. *Psychology, Public Policy, and Law* 1: 6–42. https://doi.org/10.1037/1076-8971.1.1.6.

Yang, Bijou, and David Lester. 2008. Reflections on rational choice—The existence of systematic irrationality. *The Journal of Socio-Economics* 37. Behavioral Dimensions of the Firm Special Issue: 1218–1233. https://doi.org/10.1016/j.socec.2007.08.006.

Chapter 4
Gendered Denials: Law, Policy and Practice

4.1 Introduction

The aim of this chapter is to explore the role of gender in historical and modern legal capacity denials. It discusses law, policy and practice that lead to these denials. It adopts the United Nations Convention on the Rights of Persons with Disabilities (CRPD) Committee definition of the right to legal capacity as described in their General Comment and as outlined in Chap. 1 of this book (Committee on the Rights of Persons with Disabilities 2014; Arstein-Kerslake and Flynn 2016b). It uses this definition to examine the history of gendered denials of legal capacity and explore where existing systems continue to deny legal capacity in unique ways to women, disabled women, and gender minorities. Chapter 5 then explores how this may be creating vulnerability in various contexts. The recommendations for reform in Chap. 6 are then based on the denials identified in this chapter.

There is a long history of gender being used as a basis for the denial of legal capacity. One commonly used justification for this is the inherent lack of rationality inaccurately associated with women, disabled people, and gender minorities, as was discussed in Chap. 3 (Assassi 2009; Prokhovnik 2012; Spade 2015). These notions of deficient cognitive skills in women, disabled people, and gender minorities are both erroneous and prejudicial. Their use as a justification for the denial of legal capacity to these groups has likely contributed substantially to the ongoing oppression and inequality that these groups face, as discussed at the end of Chap. 2.

The perception that women, disabled women, and gender minorities lack the requisite level of cognition to be included as full legal persons—and to be granted full legal capacity—is consistent with dominant theories in moral philosophy and liberal political theory that prioritise and glorify the rational autonomous actor who deftly negotiates his way through the world and through social relationships in pursuit of his own version of the good life, as discussed in Chap. 2 (Nussbaum

Portions of this chapter are drawn from (Arstein-Kerslake 2019).

A. Arstein-Kerslake, *Legal Capacity & Gender*,
https://doi.org/10.1007/978-3-030-63493-3_4

2004; Silvers and Francis 2005; Rawls 2009; Wong 2010). This myth of the autonomous rational actor, which was perpetuated by largely male theorists, excluded women and continues to exclude women because of its inaccuracy—there is arguably no autonomous rational actor. Instead, autonomy is almost always relational (for example, it is often work that is traditionally conceived of as women's work that supports an individual—traditionally, a man—to be able to have the freedom to be a decision-maker and leader). In addition, we often make decisions using emotion rather than rationality—which makes rationality an imprecise requirement for the recognition of an individual as a decision-maker via the recognition of their legal capacity. For these reasons, it is often problematic that our legal, political, and economic systems are premised on the idea of the autonomous rational actor. In order to gain a better understanding of the impact of such male-dominated theory, it is pertinent to undertake a gendered analysis of legal capacity law—and the right to equal recognition more broadly. This is essential in order to understand the premise under which such laws are operating and why they are sometimes both ineffective and exclusionary. It also important in order to provide a better picture of the unique barriers that are faced by women, disabled women, and gender minorities in exercising legal capacity and in having their right to legal capacity recognised and realised.

It must also be noted that, in line with the CRPD Committee's General Comment, an individual's decision-making skills cannot be a justification for the denial of legal capacity (Committee on the Rights of Persons with Disabilities 2014, p. 3). Therefore, even if there was truth to the perception that women, disabled women, and gender minorities possess inferior decision-making skills or lack sufficient rationality, according to the CRPD Committee's interpretation of the right to legal capacity, they would still be entitled to the right to legal capacity on an equal basis with others.

4.2 Historical Denials

This section explores historical barriers to and denials of legal capacity to women, disabled women, and gender minorities. Many of these historical barriers and denials are ongoing or have led to other ongoing barriers or violations, as will be discussed in the next section.

4.2.1 Women: Voting, Contracting and Marriage

Historically, gender has been a predicate to full legal personhood and autonomy (Matambanadzo 2012). Women have been systematically denied legal capacity on the basis of their gender. This can be seen in various areas of law, including voting rights as well as laws that remove a woman's legal capacity upon marriage, which affects their ability to contract, inherit, and other legal actions that require the recognition of legal capacity. These areas are only a few examples of how women's right to legal capacity has been denied throughout history, but they provide a good picture of the severity of the deprivation of the right and the recency with which these deprivations have begun to be rectified.

4.2.1.1 Voting

Voting requires that an individual be recognised as a legal person and legal agent—the full recognition of their legal capacity. In order to be added to the electoral roll, you must first be recognised as a legal person. The act of voting is then an exercise of legal agency. It is only in quite recent history that women have been recognised as full legal persons and legal agents for the purpose of voting.

In 1893, New Zealand became the first self-governing country in the world to allow women to vote in parliamentary elections (Grimshaw 1972). Women were not given the right to vote in the United Kingdom until 25 years later with enactment of the *Representation of the People Act 1918*—and even then, it was only women over 30 who met a property qualification. Interestingly, the same Act, expanded voting rights to almost all men over the age of 21 (Hubback 1928; Blackburn 2011). It wasn't until the *Equal Franchise Act of 1928* that almost all women over 21 were given the right to vote and women finally had equal voting rights to that of men in the United Kingdom (Hubback 1928; Takayanagi 2018). In this way, it has been less than 100 years that women have been considered full legal persons for the purpose of political participation and the exercise of their legal agency via voting in the United Kingdom. Similarly, in the United States, after several decades of struggle from activists, the 19th Amendment became part of the United States Constitution on 18 August 1920. It states, "The right of citizens of the United States to vote shall not be denied or abridged by the United States or by any State on account of sex" (Kennedy 2020). At the time of writing this book, it is nearly exactly 100 years that women have formally enjoyed an equal right to vote in the United States. Across the globe, many countries recognised the right of women to vote in the mid-1900s (Morgan 1996; Rupp 1997; D'Itri 1999). However, there were some countries that took much longer to grant women the right to vote—for example, women in Saudi Arabia were only granted the right to vote in 2015 (Briscoe 2016; Karolak and Guta 2020). The recognition of the right to vote was a significant advancement in the realisation of the right to legal capacity on an equal basis for women—although it is pertinent to highlight how recent in our history the right to vote has actually been realised for women. In addition, women's right to vote has rarely (if ever) been framed as a part of the right to legal capacity.

It is also critical to note that many indigenous women and other racial minority group women were denied the legal capacity to vote for much longer than white women. For example, in Canada, indigenous women and women of Asian descent were specifically excluded from voting rights that were granted to other women in 1918. They did not gain the right to vote until much later in the 1940s and 1960s (Janovicek and Thomas 2019). In the United States in 1870, several decades before the 19th Amendment was passed that prohibited the denial of the right to vote on the basis of sex, the 15th Amendment to the Constitution was passed. It prevents states from denying the right to vote on grounds of "race, colour, or previous condition of servitude" (Gillette 2019). As such, with the enactment of the 19th Amendment in 1920, women of all races had their right to vote formally recognised in the Constitution.

However, in practice, in the United States, women from racial minority groups struggled for many decades to have their right to vote realised. Women from racial minority groups had their legal personhood recognised for the purpose of voting—via the 19th Amendment. However, their ability to exercise their legal capacity to vote, or their legal agency, was hampered by various barriers at the state and federal level—including a series of precedent setting court cases that gave power to opponents of Black voting rights. Black women spent several decades struggling to be able to register to vote; to vote without fear for their bodily safety; and to overcome various discriminatory obstacles to voting (Gidlow 2018). In addition, Native Americans were not formally granted the right to vote until the Indian Citizenship Act in 1924—and some states prevented Native Americans from voting up until the 1965 Voting Rights Act (VRA) (Wolfley 1991; McCool et al. 2007). Therefore, Native American women did not enjoy the recognition of their legal capacity to vote until 45 years after most other women in the United States received such recognition with the passage of the 19th Amendment in 1920. Indigenous women and women from racial minorities were denied the right to legal capacity to vote for much longer than others—in particular, much longer than white women.

4.2.1.2 Contracting and Marriage

In addition, until relatively recently in history, women were often considered to be property of their fathers or husbands (Gardner 1986; Kittell 1998; Zaher 2002; Matambanadzo 2012). They often did not enjoy separate legal personhood from these men, instead the law viewed women as objects and these men held the power to make legal decisions on their behalf (Matambanadzo 2012). This was a denial of women's legal capacity because their personhood was generally not independently recognised and their legal agency was largely divested to their father or husband.

For example, the practice of coverture dictated that a woman's legal rights and obligations were subsumed by her husband upon marriage—husband and wife became one legal person. The wife was no longer a separate legal person. She had no legal rights or obligations separate from her husband. She could not own property, inherit, enter contracts, or keep a wage (Holcombe 1983; Zaher 2002; Erickson 2005; Matambanadzo 2012). The first major reform of coverture in England came in 1870 with the Married Women's Property Act. The Act came about after significant lobbying and activism by feminist groups (Shanley 1993; Shammas 1994). The Act allowed women to keep their own wages and to inherit a certain amount of wealth (Combs 2005). Shortly thereafter, the Married Women's Property Act of 1882 further secured the right of married women to own, buy, and sell property. It also established married women as separate legal entities from their husbands—it granted legal personhood to wives (United Kingdom 1882; Shanley 1993). It is notable that coverture was not significantly reformed in England until the late nineteenth Century—meaning that women in England have only been guaranteed legal capacity separate from their husbands for less than 150 years (Shanley 1993).

The coverture laws of England heavily influenced common law countries. Similarly, the Married Women's Property Act in England coincided with a cascade of reforms to coverture laws across common law jurisdictions (Shammas 1994). However, in the United States the last significant laws related to coverture were not reformed until the 1950s and 60s (Basch 1986; Flexner and Fitzpatrick 1996; Matambanadzo 2012). In California, for example, the 1954 case of *Follansbee v. Benzenberg* (122 CalApp.2d 476, 265 P.2d 183) was the landmark decision which secured separate legal capacity for women from their husbands. It states, "The legal status of a wife has changed. Her legal personality is no longer merged in that of her husband. Generally a husband and wife have, in the marriage relation, equal rights which should receive equal protection of the law" (Wilson 1961). As such, women in some parts of the United States have only enjoyed a formal recognition of their legal capacity independent of their husbands for less than 75 years (Vogel 1990). In addition, as will be discussed below in Sect. 4.3.1, the legacy of coverture laws can be seen in modern immigration law, which disproportionately impacts the right to legal capacity of women from racial minorities and those with diverse national origins.

Coverture laws were often propagated by the notion that women are objects incapable of reason or self-governance. Women were viewed to need a male counterpart to provide the cognitive capabilities necessary for the exercise of legal capacity (Assassi 2009; Cheu 2012; Ward 2014). While many such laws have been abolished or significantly stripped back, the notion that women are less able to make legal decisions appears to continue to permeate modern legal capacity law, which is further discussed below in Sect. 4.3.1.

4.2.2 Disabled Women: Institutionalisation, Eugenics, and Reproductive Choice[1]

There is a long history of denying legal personhood and legal agency to disabled women. This has manifested itself as the denial of decision-making and autonomy in various contexts. In addition, self-determination has often been replaced with the profound overregulation of the lives of disabled women (Arstein-Kerslake 2015; Arstein-Kerslake and Flynn 2016a; Arstein-Kerslake 2019).

As discussed above, the dark cloud of 'hysteria' has been hovering over women for centuries. Of course, one of the ironies of a label of hysteria is that a woman

[1]Portions of this section are drawn from (Arstein-Kerslake 2015).

becomes a disabled woman when she receives a label of hysteria. She is foisted into a realm where her identity is dictated by a diagnosis and society creates disabling barriers to her participation and equality with others. In this way, the line between women and disabled women may not be as clear as it may sometimes seem. In the context where women are on the precipice of being labelled as hysterical and disregarded as irrational and mentally ill, much of the barriers that they face, are identical to those of disabled people and disabled women. Of course, this is not to say that able-bodied women do not have a unique and privileged position that is often distinct from that of disabled women. As women gain more as a minority group—which they have done over the last several decades, in particular—their social position to that of disabled people and disabled women becomes more and more disparate. It becomes disparate because the social position of disable people, arguably, is not keeping pace with that of women. Of course, this is not true for all women or all disabled people. There are, of course disabled individuals who experience more privilege than some women—however, it is largely true that women, as a whole, likely experience more privilege than disable people, as a whole.

Disabled women have experienced not only the oppression and prejudice that women experience, as well as the oppression and prejudice that disabled people experience, but also a version of oppression and prejudice that is unique to disabled women. They face the history of eugenics, the ongoing assumptions of the inferiority of disabled people's decision-making skills, combined with the legacy of hysteria ascribed to women, and the long history of laws restricting women's legal personhood and legal agency.

4.2.2.1 Institutionalisation

The industrial revolution brought about a unique situation for disabled people—with the emphasis on capitalism and economic productivity, those who experienced disadvantage because of social barriers that interacted with their impairments to disabled them became less valuable. They were seen as economically unproductive and various methods were developed to manage such unproductive members of society (Oliver 1990; Borsay 1998).

The methods for managing these 'unproductive' members of society ranged from complete disregard—which resulted in extreme poverty and death—to institutionalisation (Borsay 2004; Wagner 2005; Wise 2013). An examination of the population of people that were institutionalised and the rationales for their institutionalisation combined with the emerging eugenics movement, points strongly towards the use of institutionalisation for managing those deemed to be 'undesirables' and 'defectives' (Woodhouse 1982; Jackson 2003). The institutionalisation of women, disabled people—and disabled women, in particular, was widespread (Walsh 1999; Finnegan 2004; K. Johnson and Traustadottir 2005; Appignanesi 2011).

Women and disabled women were not the only ones institutionalised. As described above, disable people, in general, were institutionalised in a systemic manner that had largely not been seen before in history (Oliver 1990; Walmsley 2005). In addition, individuals experiencing poverty were also systemically institutionalised—both in 'poor houses' as well as in workhouses (Longmate 2003; Driver 2004; Wagner 2005; Crowther 2016). Many individuals that were institutionalised had overlapping identities—they were experiencing poverty and were disable people—or were disabled women—or experiencing other variations of multiple layers of disadvantage and discrimination (Jackson 2003). Women were institutionalised in more than one setting as well. The wealthy were institutionalised under the premise of 'hysteria,' as discussed in Chap. 3 (Appignanesi 2011). Women experiencing poverty were institutionalised in a very different way—primarily on the basis of their poverty, as opposed to assumptions regarding their cognitive skills or level of rationality (Driver 2004; Fowler 2014). In some places, both wealthy women and those experiencing poverty were institutionalised for pregnancy outside of wedlock and other socially unacceptable experiences (Finnegan 2004; Appignanesi 2011).

Institutionalisation of disabled people during the industrial revolution appears to have developed in parallel for those with physical and intellectual disability and for those with actual or perceived mental health disabilities. The industrial revolution inspired the rise of asylums where people with actual or perceived mental health disabilities were institutionalised (Wise 2013). Separate from asylums, there were institutional settings that were reserved for people with physical and intellectual disability (Gleeson 1999; Borsay 2004).

The history of institutionalisation of women and disabled people is relevant to an exploration of the history of legal capacity denials for these groups because the complete denial of legal personhood and legal agency generally accompanied institutionalisation – and often continues to do so today (Lewis 2011, 706). In addition, the development of modern guardianship law and mental health law coincides with the mass institutionalisation of women and disabled people (Fry 1864; Bartlett 1999; Glen 2012, p. 104; Lush 2019, p. 138; Moran 2019). In this way, the development of institutionalisation led to the development of legal mechanisms that are still used today to deny legal capacity—as discussed more in Sect. 4.3.2.

4.2.2.2 Eugenics and Reproductive Choice

The regulation of sexual intimacy of women with intellectual disability has been particularly invasive and harmful and was historically legitimised by the eugenics movement (Waxman 1994; Heslop and Macaulay 2009, pp. 39–40; Hough 2012, p. 136). I have chosen to use this as an example of the denial of legal personhood and legal agency to disabled women because of the severity of the denial of these rights—and because sexual relationships are at the core of how humans develop partnerships and meet basic human sexual needs (Plummer 2002).

People with intellectual disabilities have been subject to a long history of denial of the right to sex (Brown 1994, pp. 123–128). The eugenics movement in the late nineteenth and early twentieth centuries was one of the most profoundly discriminatory eras. The movement considered reproduction by people with intellectual disabilities a danger to society. The misguided concern was that people with intellectual disabilities that reproduced would be threatening the 'heritage of intelligence' (Murphy and O'callaghan 2004; Goodman 2005). The movement caused discrimination and abuse of people with intellectual disabilities (Pfeiffer 1994). It also deepened and facilitated the growth of stigma related to intellectual disabilities to such a great extent that its effects can still be felt over a hundred years later (Shakespeare 1998).

The eugenics movement contributed to an increase in the segregation of disabled people into institutions, as discussed above (Tredgold 1909; Fennell 1992, p. 213; Murphy and O'callaghan 2004, p. 1347). It also brought on mass compulsory sterilization of women with intellectual disabilities. In the United States alone, it is estimated that at least 50,000 women were sterilized in the first half of the twentieth century (Kempton and Kahn 1991). In the United Kingdom, guardianship law itself was a product of a desire to have a legal mechanism to sterilize people with intellectual disabilities (Fennell 1992, pp. 213–218). There was a sense that the world needed to be protected from the sexual activity of people of intellectual disabilities.

Conversely, there is also a long history of people with intellectual disabilities being thought of as asexual. Along with this, came a sense that people with intellectual disabilities actually need to be protected from sex. There was a perception that people with intellectual disabilities are perpetual children and should not be exposed to adult sexual activity (McCarthy 1999). While these perceptions have largely fallen out of favour, there is legislation that contains remnants from this era (Irish Criminal Law (Sexual Offences) Act, 1993, Section 5). In addition, there continue to be cases of parents subjecting their children to treatments to keep them small and child-like (Liao et al. 2007, pp. 16–20). The continuing use of the concept of 'capacity to consent to sex' seems to be a remaining plague of this era where society wanted to de-sexualize people with intellectual disabilities—either under the auspices of the protection of the individuals with intellectual disabilities themselves or under the auspices of protecting the world from the sexual activity of people with intellectual disabilities that can lead to reproduction (Perlin and Lynch 2014, p. 298).

Disabled women have been uniquely affected by the eugenics movement. As disabled people, they are devalued and dehumanised by the eugenics movement—eugenics, in many ways, seeks to eliminate the existence of disabled people. As women, they carry children and are reproductive beings—eugenics seeks to utilise reproduction to eliminate characteristics that are deemed undesirable. Therefore, disabled women are burdened with the eugenics movements desire to eradicate them as well as the movement's desire to control and manipulate their reproduction.

4.2.2.3 Conclusion

This history is related to the right to legal capacity in multiple ways. It demonstrates deprivations of legal capacity for disabled women throughout history. It also begins to provide the story of how the position of disabled women exists as it does today—why disabled women are often so profoundly undervalued, so frequently assumed to lack decision-making, and so often denied legal capacity.

When disabled women are institutionalised, their legal capacity is removed. This is true of all people. Institutionalisation itself is a denial of legal capacity because it is done against the will of the individual. Their decision-making is denied, their liberty is removed, and they are forced to enter the institutional setting. Within the institutional setting, individuals largely experience total denial of legal capacity. Frequently, the staff of the institution is formally vested with the legal capacity of the individuals residing in the institution. Virtually all decisions—ranging from daily meals and clothing choices to medication and financial decisions—are managed by the staff of the institution. While all people in institutional settings experience this—it is uniquely and, arguably, more profoundly experienced by disabled women because they were and are disproportionately institutionalised (Kothari 2005).

Disabled women also often experience greater denial of legal capacity related to reproductive choice than disabled men. This is likely, at least in part, because of the eugenics movement's devaluing of the lives of disabled people and the strong desire during that time to inhibit the reproduction of disabled women. It is also because the nature of being a woman means that you have a greater number of choices—including choices that have legal implications—in relation to your body and to reproduction.

4.2.3 Gender Minorities: Forced Treatment and Criminalisation

Gender minorities have their own, unique history of prejudice and legal capacity denial. Much of it centres around forced treatment for what was perceived to be mental illness, as discussed in Chap. 3, and the criminalisation of non-gender conforming behaviours (Lennox and Waites 2013; Map of Countries that Criminalise LGBT People | Human Dignity Trust 2020). In addition, as will be discussed below in Sect. 4.3.3, law, policy, and practice that continues to prevent gender minorities from having their gender identity legally recognised creates barriers to the recognition and exercise of their legal capacity in many ways—including the inability to obtain legal identification and documentation, which is often a prerequisite for the recognition of legal personhood and the exercise of legal agency (Cannoot 2019b).

4.2.3.1 Forced Treatment

Forced treatment, as discussed in Chap. 3, has been an unfortunate presence in the lives of gender minorities. In the late 1800s and early 1900s, sex reassignment surgery began to be available and the medical profession began to pay attention to non-binary gender experiences and expressions (Cannoot 2019b). This attention from the medical profession—including surgeons and psychiatrists—facilitated the exercise of autonomy for some transgender people because they were able to get medical assistance to achieve, physically, their gender identity (Pfäfflin 2015). However, for other transgender people and other gender minorities, it accompanied a medicalisation of non-binary gender experiences and expressions that led both to informal pressures to undergo medical treatment as well as formal legal requirements of medical treatment and surgery (Butler 2004, pp. 75–77). For example, intersex infants and children began to be surgically altered to adhere to the dominant gender binary expectations (Suresh 2015). In addition, some jurisdictions began to require surgery, medical treatment (such as hormone treatment), and psychiatric treatment before an individual could legally change their gender (Spade 2009). Many of these requirements remain today (Ezie 2011).

Some surgery and treatment that gender minorities have been forced to undergo due to informal pressures or formal legal requirements has the potential for significant downsides—including sterilisation, permanence, health risks, and others (Rossi Neto et al. 2012; Morrison et al. 2015; Wang and Poppas 2017). For example, a transgender person may not want to engage in certain surgeries or medical treatment because it poses a risk to fertility or for other reasons—however that individual may identify as a gender other than their birth gender and may have a need to legally change their gender. In some jurisdictions, it may not be possible to legally change their gender without undergoing certain surgeries or medical treatment (Allen 2007; Ezie 2011). This is due, in part to this history of the medicalisation of gender minorities and their non-binary gender experiences and expressions. In addition, the surgical alteration of intersex children that was also precipitated by the medicalisation of non-binary gender experiences or expressions has had profoundly negative impacts—both because it denies the child the ability the autonomy to discover for themselves their gender identity, but also because the medical treatments themselves have similar negative effects as those described above – health risks, permanence, and sterilisation (Karkazis 2008; Suresh 2015).

This history of forced treatment of gender minorities is a history of legal capacity denial. Gender minorities, such as transgender people, experienced overt denial of their legal capacity to consent to medical treatment when they have been subjected to forced mental health treatment and other forced medical treatment on the basis that their non-binary gender experiences and expressions are a form of mental illness. This could fall under the prohibition of legal capacity denial on the basis of disability under Article 12 of the CRPD.

They have also been subjected to more insidious forms of forced treatment via laws that require medical and surgical treatment as a pre-requisite for legal gender recognition. This is a form of legal capacity denial because it places gender minorities in a position that requires them to undergo medical treatment in order to have their legal personhood recognised. Gender recognition is a form of legal personhood recognition when it is required before an individual will be recognised as a legal person. For example, in order to be recognised as a legal person, identity documents are often required. Many jurisdictions required the gender binary identification of gender on identity documents (Hanssen 2017, p. 302). If gender minorities are prevented from having their accurate gender (the gender that they identify with) on their identity documents, then they often cannot get appropriate documents and are then prevented from having the documentation that is often required for others to recognise them as legal persons. If medical treatment—including surgery—is required in order for an individual to be able to access appropriate documentation that accurately reflects their gender and allows them to be recognised as a legal person—then they are being forced into medical treatment in order to be recognised as a legal person. In this way, their legal capacity to consent to medical treatment is effectively denied because the alternative is the inability to have their legal personhood recognised (which is an element of legal capacity).

The denial of legal capacity to consent to medical treatment—including irreversible surgery—of intersex children raises some more complex questions. The first is whether children have the same right to legal capacity as adults. There is not space here to thoroughly address this question. However, if children do enjoy the same right to legal capacity as adults, then this is an impermissible denial of the right to legal capacity on the basis of gender identity and group membership as a gender minority. I am inclined to argue that children are entitled to protection of the right to legal capacity—however, there is language in the Convention on the Rights of the Children (CRC) that could be used to argue otherwise—for example, the consistent use of the "best interest" standard throughout the CRC, which indicates that it is not the will and preference of the child that must be protected (as is required by Article 12 of the CRPD for the protection of the right to legal capacity). The profound impact of forced medical treatment in this area, however, leads me to seek arguments for the protection of the right to legal capacity of children to consent to such medical treatment.

4.2.3.2 Criminalisation

Gender minorities have been impacted by multiple forms of criminalisation. The criminalisation of same-sex sexual activity is perhaps the most widespread form of criminalisation that affects gender minorities. There is a striking correlation between colonisation and the criminalisation of same-sex sexual activity. It was criminalised across the British Empire in the nineteenth Century and decriminalisation did not begin until 1967 in England and Wales (Lennox and Waites 2013, p. 1). Many countries in the British Commonwealth, the former British Empire, and elsewhere continue to criminalise same-sex sexual activity—at the time of writing, there remain 72 countries that criminalise private, consensual, same-sex sexual activity and in 11 of those jurisdictions the death penalty is a potential sentence for these crimes (Map of Countries that Criminalise LGBT People | Human Dignity Trust 2020). Gender minorities are also impacted by laws that criminalise the gender identity and expression of transgender people. This criminalisation occurs via laws that criminalise 'cross-dressing,' 'impersonation,' and 'disguises' (Map of Countries that Criminalise LGBT People | Human Dignity Trust 2020). For example, in Brunei, *Syariah Penal Code Order 2013, Section 198* criminalises anyone who "dresses and poses" as the opposite sex in a public place. In Lebanon, *Article 521* of the *Penal Code 1943* makes it an offense for a man to "disguise himself as a woman." In Indonesia, *Article 281* of the *Penal Code 1999* criminalises any person who "offends against decency" and in Sri Lanka, Section 399 of the *Penal Code 1883* criminalises cheating "by pretending to be some other person"—both of which can be used to criminalise non-binary gender experiences or expression (Map of Countries that Criminalise LGBT People | Human Dignity Trust 2020).

Laws that criminalise non-binary gender experiences or expressions are also often rooted in colonial history (Kirby 2013; Lennox and Waites 2013; Gichki 2020, p. 33). For example, in the 1800s in Iran, gender was much more fluid, there was not a strict binary between female and male. In addition, same-sex sexual relationships were common—in fact, homoeroticism was a large part of Persian literature. With increased contact with the West—and with Britain, in particular—Iranian culture began to disavow same-sex practices and began to solidify the gender binary categories of female and male. This was reflected in laws, such as the criminalisation of sodomy (Gichki 2020, p. 34). In addition, in countries that were under colonial rule, such as Pakistan and India, explicit laws were created to criminalise non-binary gender experiences and expressions. Prior to these laws, non-binary gender experiences and expressions were often celebrated and sometimes even deified (Gichki 2020, pp. 33–35).

The criminalisation of same-sex sexual activity has had significant implications for sexual minorities—it has also made the position of many gender minorities very difficult. Not all gender minorities engage in same-sex sexual relationships—although, some do. Many gender minorities also engage in sexual relationships that they may not consider same-sex, due to the gender that they identify with—however, the law may consider them same-sex and may have criminalised them in some circumstances. This could occur because in a particular jurisdiction there was not appropriate legal mechanisms for altering one's gender ascribed at birth. It could also occur because a particular individual did not engage existing gender recognition laws due to the oppressive nature of some laws, as is discussed below in Sect. 4.3.3. Nonetheless, the history of criminalisation of same-sex sexual relations has had an impact on the freedom of gender minorities to exercise sexual agency.

This criminalisation of same-sex sexual activity and non-binary gender experiences and expressions is a denial of the right to legal capacity to consent to sexual activity and to exercise agency in asserting one's gender identity. The right to legal capacity to consent to sex requires that all people have an equal right to consent to sex—therefore, the right to consent to sex cannot be denied on the basis of an individual's group membership (Arstein-Kerslake 2015). In this way, the right to legal capacity to consent to sex requires that gender and sexual minorities have the same right to legal capacity to consent to sex as others. Similarly, it requires that gender minorities have the same right to experience and express their gender identity as others. In this way, the historical (and on-going) criminalisation of same-sex sexual activity and non-binary gender experiences and expression is a denial of the right to legal capacity on an equal basis.

4.3 Modern Denials

The previous section explored historical barriers to or denials of legal capacity for women, disabled women, and gender minorities. Some of those denials are no longer occurring due to law reform and socio-cultural changes. However, some of those denials continue. This section discusses these and other modern denials of legal capacity for women, disabled women, and gender minorities.

4.3.1 Women: Immigration, Inheritance, Contracting, Reproductive Choice, and Consent to Sex

In the modern world, women face ongoing prejudice as a remnant of the history of the myth of hysteria, which continues to taint perceptions of women's decision-making skills. Women continue to be viewed as lesser decision-makers compared to men. This is evidenced by the large disparity in the percentage of women in leadership roles compared to men—both in government and commercial spheres—that are women (Porterfield and Kleiner 2005; Chesser 2019; Catalyst 2020; UN Women).

Some may have the perception that modern women enjoy equal recognition before the law on par with men. However ongoing prejudice, as described above, has resulted in ongoing denials of women's right to equal recognition before the law and legal capacity (Seedat 2013). There are many jurisdictions in which women's recognition as legal persons and legal agents—their legal capacity—is substantially restricted compared to men. In addition, ongoing restrictions on women's legal capacity in various forms are occurring across the globe—including in jurisdictions such as the United States, where many may assume that women enjoy exactly the same legal capacity as men. In this section, I have chosen to focus on the examples of immigration, inheritance, contracting, reproductive choice, and consent to sex. These areas are all particularly poignant and prominent areas of law, policy, and practice where women continue to experience denials of their right to legal capacity.

4.3.1.1 Immigration

Coverture laws, discussed above in Sect. 4.2.1.2, deny the legal capacity of women and invest it in their husbands. The husband 'covered' the wife's legal identity—her legal capacity—completely (Erickson 2005, p. 4). Women's legal personhood became entwined with that of their husband's and their legal agency was granted to their husband—this prevented women from taking independent legal actions and allowed husbands to take legal actions on their behalf (Zaher 2002; Erickson 2005). Coverture laws are largely absent from modern legal systems, however their legacy lives on. For example, the practice of married women taking the last name of their husbands is a remnant from coverture laws in which the married woman completely lost her own legal personhood and changing her name to that of her husband reflected that her personhood was subsumed by that of her husband (Erickson 2005, p. 4).

Early immigration laws in the United States enshrined coverture laws in ways that have been difficult to reform. For example, male citizens and documented male residents were given the right to control the immigration status of their non-citizen wives. A wife's legal immigration status dependent almost completely on her husband. In addition, women could not petition for their husbands to immigrate to the United States—only men could petition for their wives to immigrate (Calvo 1991, p. 600). This demonstrates that, under immigration law, women were viewed as objects under the control of their husbands—as was the case under coverture laws. Reform of these laws has occurred several times—from the 1920s onward there was an attempt to remove the vestiges of coverture laws. However, the basic premise that one spouse is dominant and can control the legal status of the other spouse has never been wholly confronted and rejected (Calvo 1991, pp. 603–606). At the time of writing, one spouse must still petition for the immigration status of the other spouse—giving the petitioning spouse considerable control over the immigration status of the other spouse (Petition for Alien Relative | USCIS 2020).

One effect of these vestiges of coverture in immigration law is significant amounts of abuse experienced by immigrant wives (Calvo 1991, pp. 600, 614, 616–620; Amuedo-Dorantes and Arenas-Arroyo 2019). Because of this, further reform to ameliorate the impact of coverture in immigration law in the United States was attempted under the Violence Against Women Act (VAWA) in 1994. VAWA allows for special consideration for women experiencing domestic violence in the United States, including the option to seek immigration status independent of their spouse (Lakhani 2019; Stupakis 2019). While this is an improvement, it is often unsafe, impracticable, and unfeasible for women to avail of such measures (Amuedo-Dorantes and Arenas-Arroyo 2019; Lakhani 2019).

Immigration status is often a prerequisite for the recognition of an individual's legal personhood and legal agency—their legal capacity. Due to the ongoing patriarchal nature of our society, the effect of laws that give one spouse control of immigration status is that women often receive immigration status via marriage. This effectively creates a modern form of coverture for women immigrating to the

United States via spouse-based immigration laws. The recognition of their legal capacity—legal personhood and agency—is in the control of their husbands.

4.3.1.2 Inheritance and Contracting

The right to legal capacity protects the right to inheritance, contracting, and property via the element of legal agency. Inheritance, contracting, and holding and managing property requires the recognition of legal agency in the individual. All of these activities are essential aspects of participating in our capitalist market economy. Any individual who does not enjoy respect for their right to legal capacity to inherit, contract, and possess and manage property is inhibited from gaining and managing wealth—they are significantly disadvantaged, and social justice and equality is likely fall from reach.

Despite the explicit mention of the right to legal capacity including the exercise of legal agency for inheritance, contracting and possessing and managing property in both CEDAW (Article 15 (2 and 3)) and CRPD (Article 12(5)), women, in particular, continue to face widespread exclusion from protection of these rights. This is evidenced by the fact that women own less than 20% of the world's land (Villa 2017).

Globally, approximately 40% of jurisdictions have at least one legal constraint on women's rights to property, which limits their ability to own, manage, and inherit land (Stone 2018). In addition, approximately half of all women are still denied land and property rights, even though there are legal protections for women's right to exercise legal capacity to inherit, own, and manage property. For example, in the Middle East and Northern Africa region, approximately 25 million women living in urban settings do not enjoy equal constitutional or statutory property rights to that of men (Villa 2017). Around the world, this is due to ongoing discriminatory social norms and practices, as well as poor implementation in some places that provide legal protections (World Bank 2019; UN Women Asia Pacific).

Inheritance for women is equally fraught. According to the World Bank, in at least 36 countries widows are not granted the same inheritance rights as widowers. In addition, in at least 39 countries, daughters are prevented from inheriting the same proportion of assets as sons (*Women, Business, and the Law 2018* 2018).

These issues are rarely framed as a violation of the right to equal recognition before the law or legal capacity. The power of re-framing these issues as violations of these rights is that they become not only issues of rights to property and rights to inheritance, but issues of rights to personhood and equal recognition. I believe this gives weight to these arguments and elevates them from issues of material and economic equality to issues that arrive at the core question of whether women are respected as persons on par with men—or whether they are a sub-class of persons with lesser rights and responsibilities to that of men.

4.3.1.3 Reproductive Choice and Consent to Sex

The ability to decide to have an abortion, to use contraceptives, or other choices related to reproduction are exercises of legal agency—an element of legal capacity—because they are decisions that have legal implications. The overregulation of women's bodies, in particular, has led to reproductive choices having significant legal implications for women (Kelly and Hoerl 2015; Chesney-Lind 2017; Simmonds 2019). However, even if women's bodies were not overregulated, choices regarding reproduction will likely always be exercises of legal agency because they virtually always involve some form of interaction with another individual, which almost always leaves open the potential for legal implications for the regulation of that relationship.

Laws securing the right to exercise legal agency in the context of reproductive choice for women are continually challenged and remain non-existent or ineffectual in many jurisdictions (Petchesky 1990; Smyth 2002; Cheu 2012; Enright et al. 2015). For example, in the United States, significant progress toward the recognition of the right of women to legal agency to choose to have an abortion was made with the landmark Supreme Court Case, *Roe v Wade*, in 1973. However, a series of state and federal court cases since then have slowly stripped back that right, and women in the United States continue to face an uncertain world with respect to protection for their right to legal agency to choose to have an abortion (Forsythe and Morrison 2020; Jacobs 2020; Maveety 2020; Ziegler 2020). 700 million women of reproductive age around the world do not have access to safe and legal abortion—in other words, they do not have their right to exercise legal agency to choose to have an abortion respected or protected (Center for Reproductive Rights 2020).

Conversely, in Ireland, the highest law of the land—the Constitution—prohibited women from exercising legal capacity to choose to have an abortion until May 2018 (Enright et al. 2015; Calkin et al. 2020). At the time of writing, Ireland is now grappling on legal, political, social, and medical levels with how to manage this change (Donnelly and Murray 2020; Taylor et al. 2020). The new law allows women to choose to have an abortion up to 12 weeks of pregnancy and in situations of risk to the life or of serious harm to the health of the pregnant woman and fatal foetal anomaly thereafter (Taylor et al. 2020). This provides significant recognition of a women's right to legal capacity to choose to have an abortion in Ireland. In the United States, the right to legal agency to choose to have an abortion appears to be undergoing increased limitations. Whereas, in Ireland, the opposite is occurring—the right to legal agency to choose to have abortions has recently been recognised to a greater degree than ever before in Irish history. Around the world, overall, the last several decades have seen a marked increase in the number of jurisdictions that provide increasing protection for women's right to legal agency to choose to have an abortion. Nearly 50 countries have liberalised their abortion laws in recent years (Center for Reproductive Rights 2020).

In addition, the exercise of legal capacity to consent to sex is frequently framed as a passive permission that the female may grant to a male who is viewed as the decision-maker and holder of power (Anderson 2010; Arstein-Kerslake 2015; Arstein-Kerslake and Flynn 2016a). This is significant because it impacts the woman's exercise of legal agency—she is respected as an individual with the right to exercise legal agency to take part in sexual activity, but only to the extent that she is passively giving permission to a male to engage in sex with her. This framing of consent grants the male greater legal agency than the women. Instead of requiring that a communication and negotiation take place between two individuals with equal levels of legal agency, it assumes that the male has greater legal agency and only demands that the female has passively acquiesced to the male's sexual advances. This becomes evident when you examine other areas of the law where the concept of consent is used—for example, in patient/doctor relationships and for subjects of research. In almost all uses of the concept of consent, there is a substantial power imbalance between the actors. The individual seeking consent has a great deal of power and the individual providing consent has considerably less power. In order to respect the right to legal capacity to consent to sex on an equal basis for men and women, the concept of consent must be—at a minimum—re-conceptualised in such a way that respects men and women (and people of any and all genders) as possessing equal legal agency and having equal rights to exercise that legal agency.

4.3.2 *Disabled Women: Guardianship, Forced Sterilisation and Consent to Sex*

Disabled women experience, arguably, the most profound and far-reaching denials of their right to legal capacity. They face the history of the myth of hysteria as women and the ongoing assumptions of mental incapacity as disabled people. They face denials of legal capacity—or the potential for denials of legal capacity—in nearly every area of life. In this chapter, I've chosen to focus on guardianship, parental rights, forced sterilisation, and consent to sex because they are all areas in which disabled women face pervasive denials of legal capacity that have a significant impact on many other areas of their lives.

4.3.2.1 Guardianship and Forced Sterilisation[2]

Guardianship, and other forms of interdiction and conservatorship, are one of the most complete forms of legal capacity denial. It occurs when the law provides a mechanism for the removal of legal capacity in relation to one or more decision. The most all-encompassing form is plenary guardianship, where an individual's legal capacity can be completely removed and ascribed to another individual or group of people—for example, a family member, a group home or institution, or a court.

[2]Portions of this section are drawn from (Arstein-Kerslake 2019).

There are also more limited forms which include either limited guardianship or laws, such as the *Mental Capacity Act* in England and Wales, which allows for the removal of legal capacity in regard to either a specific decision or a specified area of life (Series 2013; Flynn and Arstein-Kerslake 2014; Arstein-Kerslake 2017).

There is evidence that women experience guardianship uniquely (Grover 2002; Rosenberg 2009; Victoria Office of the Public Advocate 2017). For example, under guardianship, they may have reproductive choice removed and are often subjected to others choices for them regarding sterilisation, contraception, pregnancy, and abortion (Wingfield et al. 1994a; Grover 2002; Atkinson et al. 2003; Lin et al. 2011). There is also evidence that women may be disproportionately placed under guardianship—potentially, due to the lasting impacts of historical notions of women as less rational and in more need of protection than men (Tavris 1993; Rosenberg 2009; Prokhovnik 2012; Victoria Office of the Public Advocate 2017).

Until recently, it was widely accepted that women with intellectual disability living under guardianship in institutional settings would almost automatically be given either medication to end their menstrual cycle or would undergo surgery for sterilisation or some form of management of the menstrual cycle. This was often done in the 'best interests' of the woman—the individual or entity that maintained guardianship or was ascribed her legal capacity in another form made the decision based on what they believed to be in the woman's best interest (Grover 2002). While, in many places, this policy has changed in institutional settings (Atkinson et al. 2003), young women under guardianship and other substituted decision-making regimes that do not respect the rights, will, and preference of the individual, are still faced with menstrual and sterilisation decisions that are made on their behalf, in their 'best interests' (Wingfield et al. 1994a, b; Grover 2002; Atkinson et al. 2003; Lin et al. 2011).

Legal capacity to exercise reproductive choice is also denied to women in the form of forced sterilisation. This occurs particularly in the context of disabled women and girls. There are laws in some jurisdictions that allow for the forced sterilisation of disabled women and girls (Cepko 1993; Pham and Lerner 2001; Patel 2017). In addition, some disabled women are only offered methods of contraception that may jeopardise their reproductive health (Waxman 1994). There is also evidence that sterilisations are performed at the request of family members or others, without attention paid to the will or preference of the woman or girl (Rosenbaum and Epstein 2019). Both contexts of forced sterilisation result in a denial of the woman's legal capacity to consent to sterilisation, as well as in her legal capacity to make reproductive choices for the remainder of her life.

4.3.2.2 Consent to Sex and Intellectual Disability[3]

Capacity to consent to sex legislation can be a barrier to intimate relationships for people with intellectual disabilities—and women with intellectual disabilities, in particular. In some jurisdictions, such legislation criminalizes most sexual activity of people with intellectual disabilities. In other jurisdictions, it requires people with intellectual disabilities to prove functional capability to consent to sex, which people without intellectual disabilities often do not have to prove and may not be able to prove if they were held to the same high standard. The mere existence of these laws permeates the social consciousness with the message that people with intellectual disabilities are not due the same right to sexual agency as others.

In addition, women with intellectual disabilities are uniquely impacted by consent to sex legislation due to the intersecting marginalisation that they experience as both women and disabled people. As women, they must combat the historical assumptions that their rationality and decision-making skills are lacking (as discussed in Chap. 3). As disabled people, they must combat prejudicial notions that they require a greater degree of protection than others—and the prejudicial notion that, for disabled people, protection is often more important that autonomy or respecting an individual's legal capacity to consent to sex.

The text of Article 12 itself does not mention sex or consent. However, it does state that disabled people have a right to "enjoy legal capacity on an equal basis with others in *all aspects of life*" [emphasis added] (CRPD Article 12(2)). Capacity to consent to sex is a discrete area of the law that regulates legal capacity. Therefore, it must do so on an equal basis for disabled people. According to Article 12, a denial of legal capacity to consent to sex cannot be based on the existence of a disability (CRPD 2014, paras. 25 and 32–34). The challenge is to create law that sufficiently criminalises unwanted sexual encounters that are not understood or agreed to, without making them specific to disabled people.

4.3.2.3 Conflation of Mental and Legal Capacity in Consent to Sex Law

In capacity to consent to sex law, legal capacity and mental capacity has been conflated (CRPD 2014, para. 15), as discussed in Chap. 1. Legal capacity is the state's recognition of the individual as a holder of rights and an actor under the law. Mental capacity is an individual's cognitive abilities and decision-making skills (Committee on the Rights of Persons with Disabilities 2014, p. 3). In capacity to consent law, an individual can be denied legal capacity to consent to sex based on a determination of mental incapacity.

Article 12 provides an opportunity to re-examine whether this is the most effective and rights-protective manner in which to construct the law. The conflation of mental capacity and legal capacity is problematic for several reasons. The first is

[3]Portions of this section are drawn from (Arstein-Kerslake 2015).

that it focuses on the perceived deficiencies of the individual instead of exploring the situation at the given moment in time and the role of other parties. For example, its primary focus is not on what information was available or what efforts were made by the other party to ensure that the individual understood and agreed to the sexual acts. It is also problematic because the determination of mental capacity is often predicated upon the existence of an intellectual disability. This potentially denies people with intellectual disabilities the right to legal capacity to consent to sex based on the diagnosis of disability. A more effective model may be one that is compliant with Article 12 and includes an element of understanding and agreement in all parties to a sexual act, but focuses on the interaction at issue, and does not deny legal capacity to consent to sex on the basis of disability.

4.3.2.4 Non-discrimination in Legal Capacity to Consent to Sex

Respecting legal capacity 'on an equal basis' requires that when legal capacity is denied to individuals, it is done in a way that is non-discriminatory (Committee on the Rights of Persons with Disabilities 2014, pp. 6–8). 'Discrimination on the basis of disability' is defined by Article 2 CRPD as any 'distinction, exclusion or restriction on the basis of disability which has the purpose or effect of impairing or nullifying the recognition, enjoyment or exercise, on an equal basis with others, of all human rights and fundamental freedoms.' Therefore, any restriction on the right to legal capacity to consent to sex must not explicitly be based on the existence of a disability. It must also not have the effect of impairing the recognition of the rights to legal capacity and sexual agency of people with intellectual disabilities.

4.3.2.5 State Obligation to Provide Support for Consent to Sex

Another aspect of the revolution of Article 12 is the articulation of the state obligation to provide access to support for the exercise of legal capacity (CRPD Article 12(3)). The general comment on Article 12 interprets 'support' as including:

> ...various support options which give primacy to a person's will and preferences and respect human rights norms. It should provide protection for all rights, including those related to autonomy (right to legal capacity, right to equal recognition before the law, right to choose where to live, etc.) and rights related to freedom from abuse and ill-treatment (right to life, right to physical integrity, etc.). Furthermore, systems of supported decision-making should not over-regulate the lives of persons with disabilities (Committee on the Rights of Persons with Disabilities 2014, p. 7).

Support for the exercise of legal capacity in sexual decision-making, therefore, should include support that is flexible and has the individual's wishes at its core. It should enable an individual to exercise autonomy in sexual decision-making, while also providing information about how to protect against sexual abuse and resources to avail of when sexual abuse occurs. It should never present an additional barrier to sexual relationships for people with intellectual disabilities. People with intellectual disabilities should not be legally required to accept or use support in order to enjoy the freedom to have sex and develop intimate relationships.

Organizations led and managed by disabled people may provide the best form of support for sexual decision-making for people with intellectual disabilities. For example, the Connect People Network in Ireland holds many events and makes resources available to people with extra support needs, including people with intellectual disabilities. Such support is the type that is mostly likely to be fully compliant with the Article 12 requirement.

4.3.2.6 Legal Landscape of Denials of Capacity to Consent to Sex

Most modern laws that permit the denial of legal capacity to consent to sex are premised on the notion of protecting individuals with intellectual disabilities from sexual abuse. There is a perception that people with intellectual disabilities are not able to protect themselves from others taking advantage of them sexually (Swango-Wilson 2008; Hollomotz 2012). Current law generally denies legal capacity to consent to sex based on a status based or functional approach.

The status approach looks at whether the individual has the status of intellectual disability. If she does, her legal capacity may automatically be denied. It may also look at the IQ of the individual and automatically deny legal capacity to consent to sex based on a certain cut off point (Murphy and O'callaghan 2004, p. 1348).

The functional approach generally looks at whether the individual had the mental capacity to understand the nature and consequences of the sexual act. It denies legal capacity if the individual fails the test of mental capacity—conflating the two concepts, as discussed above. There is often a preliminary requirement of intellectual or other disability before the functional test can be applied. This preliminary requirement means that it is only individuals with these disabilities that can be subjected to the test. In this way, functional tests of legal capacity to consent to sex force people with intellectual disabilities to meet a standard of decision-making that is not applied to the rest of the population.

Understanding the nature and consequences of sexual acts, could be considered quite a high standard. In the context of sexual activity, more so than in other areas of decision-making, most people do not engage in a thought process of decision-making in which they come to understand the nature and consequences of their actions when they decide to engage in sex (Ariely and Loewenstein 2006). Sex is a natural part of human existence, in fact an essential part of human existence, and triggers more instinctual and emotional responses in people than it does rational and well-reasoned processes (Ariely and Loewenstein 2006). If a functional test of mental capacity to consent to sex were applied on an equal basis to all people, many people may be found to lack the requisite capacity to consent. This highlights the inequality in requiring people with intellectual disabilities to meet this standard.

In analysing Article 12 compliance in general legal capacity regulatory regimes, scholars and the CRPD Committee have found that the status and functional approaches are a violation of Article 12 (Dhanda 2006; Committee on the Rights of Persons with Disabilities 2014, p. 4; Flynn and Arstein-Kerslake 2014). Status based approaches do not comply because they directly create a differential basis upon which to deny legal capacity to disabled people. Functional approaches to not comply because they create a differential basis upon which to deny disabled people legal capacity by either (1) creating a functional decision-making standard that only disabled people must meet, or (2) disproportionately applying that standard to disabled people. These approaches operate in the same manner in consent legislation as they do in 'more general legal capacity legislation, such as guardianship. Therefore, the same Article 12 analysis applies, and such approaches are inconsistent with Article 12.

Addressing sexual abuse of people with intellectual disabilities is, of course, a valid and important purpose. However, the denial of legal capacity to consent to sex may serve to further stigmatize and remove agency from individuals with intellectual disabilities. The following section will look at legislative examples from Ireland, England and Wales to explore the status and functional approaches to the denial of legal capacity to consent to sex and whether they are compliant with Article 12.

4.3.2.7 Conclusion

People with intellectual disabilities continue to be seen as a distinct group with different rights and responsibilities than others. It is seen as a group that needs more paternalistic protection from sexual activity than protection for autonomy rights. This is evidenced in laws that deny legal capacity to consent to sex through both functional and status tests. Both approaches disproportionately deny legal capacity to people with intellectual disabilities and apply a different standard of decision-making assessment to them than to people without intellectual disabilities. This is what Article 12 is attempting to correct.

There is a need for the state to provide protection against sexual abuse of all people. There are ways of providing that protection from abuse without further stigmatizing and marginalizing people with intellectual disabilities (Hollomotz 2009). Article 12 provides a framework to achieve this. Support for the exercise of legal capacity to consent to sex, as outlined in Article 12(3), is the first key to preventing abuse. This should include sexual education and empowerment for people with intellectual disabilities (Hollomotz 2012). However, support must be coupled with a respect for the sexual agency of people with intellectual disabilities enshrined in law, as is called for in Article 12(2).

4.3.3 Gender Minorities: Gender Recognition, Marriage, and Reproductive Choice

Gender minorities are also experiencing ongoing modern denials of the right to legal capacity. They are facing the history of assumptions that they are mentally ill (as discussed in Chap. 3), which sometimes has resulted in forced medical treatment (as discussed above in Sect. 4.2.3). They also face historical legal capacity denials in the form of criminalisation of non-binary gender experiences and expressions as well as same-sex sexual activity. Some of these denials of legal capacity continue to today. They are accompanied by other modern forms of legal capacity denial that affect gender minorities. In this section, I've chosen to focus on legal capacity denials related to gender recognition, marriage, and consent. There are likely other ways in which gender minorities face legal capacity denials, however these three areas highlight the challenges that gender minorities face—and legal capacity denials in relation to gender recognition, in particular, goes to the heart of much of the legal capacity denials that gender minorities are subjected to.

4.3.3.1 Gender Recognition

Gender binary requirements for legal documents necessitate identification as either female or male (Romeo 2004; Dvorsky and Hughes 2008). Some gender minorities are nonbinary—they do not identify as female or male (Clarke 2019). In addition, some gender minorities do identify as female or male, however their gender identification does not align with their legal gender as listed on their birth certificate and other documents. In many jurisdictions, there are significant barriers and restrictions to a formal change of gender on such documents (Allen 2007; Spade 2009; Spade 2015). While the intention of gender binary requirements may not explicitly be to remove legal capacity of gender minorities—it can often have this effect.

When there is a requirement of an identification of gender, and a person from a gender minority either is not given the appropriate gender choice, is not legally allowed to make a particular gender choice, or fears the repercussions of identifying as a particular gender, they may be prevented from exercising their legal capacity to make a legal decision regarding their gender. This, in and of itself is a denial of legal capacity. In addition, because they do not have a formal method for the appropriate recognition of their gender, they may be prevented from obtaining legal documentation such as a driver's license or passport, which is required for the exercise of legal capacity in many other circumstances. For example: signing a rental agreement; becoming an employee; entering into most contractual relationships; getting married; voting; and others. Without the required legal documentation and identification, all of these exercises of legal capacity become virtually impossible—creating impediments to the individual's participation in society and their enjoyment of equality (Romeo 2004).

Currently, the law in many jurisdictions is inflexible and does not accommodate gender minorities due to a long history of prejudice and stigma, as discussed above in Sect. 4.2.3 and in Chap. 3 (Stryker and Whittle 2006; Allen 2007; Spade 2009; Spade 2015). Some of this prejudice and stigma is related to the erroneous notion that gender minorities are inherently experiencing mental health disorders that result in gender confusion as well as a decreased ability to reason or make independent decisions regarding their gender identity, as discussed in Chap. 3 (Johnson 2010; Spade 2015; McHugh 2016; Winter et al. 2016). This rejection of the decision-making of gender minorities is similar to the historical assumption, also discussed in Chap. 3, of women's lack of rational decision-making skills—both have resulted in law and policy that does not respect the legal decision-making of individuals in these groups.

It may also be considered a denial of legal capacity when there are laws that require surgery, medical treatment, psychological services, or other prohibitive measures before an individual is legally permitted to change their gender on legal documentation or be legally recognised as a particular gender in another way, such as by a court (Allen 2007; Spade 2009; Ezie 2011, pp. 162–168; Spade 2015; Neuman Wippler 2016). This may be considered a denial of legal capacity because it presents significant barriers to gender recognition—which is often required for the exercise of legal capacity, as described above—and it only applies to gender minorities. Therefore, such requirements for formal gender changes on legal documents is a barrier to legal capacity that only gender minorities experience. It may be considered a denial of legal capacity on the basis of group membership as a gender minority.

Non-binarity in gender requirements on its own may not be sufficient to allow for the full realisation of the right to legal capacity for gender minorities (Cannoot 2019a). There may be a need for a form of gender designation that, instead, actively challenges the gender binary status quo (Neuman Wippler 2016). This could take many different forms; however, the most important quality of any type of gender designations is the freedom for everyone, including gender minorities, to maintain self-determination in their identifications (Hutton 2017). Importantly, breaking down gender binary requirements will likely never occur if gender recognition laws maintain medical and biological definitions of gender or if they simply place all those that do not fit in to gender binary requirements in a category designated as a blank space. This can perpetuate existing stigma and discrimination and further marginalise gender minorities (Neuman Wippler 2016; Katyal 2018; Theilen 2018; Cannoot 2019a). While it may allow for some limited additional exercises of legal capacity for gender minorities, on the whole, it will likely result in more barriers to legal capacity due to the ongoing discrimination that it may engender.

4.3.3.2 Marriage

Gender minorities are denied the right to legal capacity to choose to enter into or maintain a marriage contract via gender recognition laws and laws that prohibit same sex marriage. There are several jurisdictions in which gender recognition laws exist that allow an individual to formally change their gender—however, one of the prerequisites to the formal change of gender is that the individual divorce their partner (Allen 2007; Sharpe 2007; United Nations Free and Equal 2015; Cannoot 2019a). These laws appear to be primarily based on a desire to outlaw same-sex marriages that would result from one partner legally changing their gender to that of the other partner. These laws have the effect of denying individuals the legal capacity to choose to maintain their marriages and their marriage contract.

In addition, restrictions on same sex marriages can deny gender minorities the right to legal capacity to choose to enter into a marriage contract. Some gender minorities are in same sex relationships—if there are legal restrictions on same sex marriage, then they are denied the right to legal capacity to choose to engage in a marriage contract with their same sex partner. In addition, in jurisdictions that allow legal gender changes, but have restrictions on same sex marriages, an individual may be able to legally change their gender to the gender that they identify with, but they may then be restricted from entering into a marriage contract with a partner that is of the same sex as the individual has changed their gender to. This may also amount to a restriction on the right to legal capacity of the individual to choose to engage in a marriage.

4.3.3.3 Reproductive Choice

Gender minorities experience lack of reproductive choice when law or policy require sterilisation before granting gender recognition. In many jurisdictions, there remains no formal options for an individual to change their sex on legal documentation (Allen 2007; Spade 2009, 2015). In some jurisdictions where there is a formal legal entitlement to apply for a change in gender status on legal documentation, there is also a requirement that the individual undergo sterilisation (Spade 2015; Dunne 2017). This denies the individual the opportunity to exercise their legal capacity to make reproductive choices. They are faced with a choice between living an uncertain and often unsafe life with an incorrect gender on legal documents or having their gender accurately reflected on legal documents but losing the ability to exercise legal capacity to make reproductive choices.

4.4 Conclusion

In this chapter, I have endeavoured to utilise the definition of the rights to equal recognition before the law and legal capacity established by the UN Committee on the Rights of Persons with Disability in their General Comment No. 1 and discussed in Chap. 1 of this book. I have applied that definition to an array of areas of law, policy, and practice and identified where I believe the right to legal capacity (and, by extension, the right to equal recognition before the law) is being denied to these groups. As far as I am aware, this has never been done before—as such, it is an imperfect process and there is much more research and analysis that is left to be done regarding the rights to equal recognition before the law and legal capacity of women, disabled women, and gender minorities.

From an analysis perspective, there is more work that remains to be done to examine the exact requirements for fulfilling the demand that all groups enjoy legal capacity on an equal basis. One path would be to merely apply existing discrimination law to legal capacity. This path is fraught because of the variance of discrimination law by jurisdiction—including the unsettled nature of discrimination law even at the international level. It also feels intangibly inadequate. It would imply that the granting of legal personhood must be done in a non-discriminatory manner—however, it would also imply that any denial of personhood would be acceptable if it was carried out in a manner that could be proven to be non-discriminatory. This is somehow unsettling. Instinctively, it feels that all people should be granted legal personhood by virtue of their humanity and there need not be an analysis of the existence or non-existence of discrimination in the granting or denying of such personhood. On the other hand, in this book and elsewhere, I am guilty of identifying various situations in which legal capacity is denied on the basis of group membership and highlighting that these are contrary to a demand for the recognition of legal capacity on an equal basis for all. This is, at least in part, an application of non-discrimination law to the situation of legal capacity recognition. I have done this because, to me, it feels apparent that where legal capacity is denied on the basis of group membership, this is blatantly a non-protection of the right to legal capacity. However, I would like to tackle—or, indeed, have another legal scholar tackle—in more detail, how non-discrimination law and the rights to equal recognition before the law and legal capacity intersect.

In the ways discussed in this chapter, as well as in many other ways, legal capacity has been restricted or denied to women, disabled women, and gender minorities. They are experiencing unique barriers to legal capacity due to histories of marginalisation and ongoing prejudice that perpetuates stereotypes of women, disabled women, and gender minorities as inherently vulnerable and lacking in decision-making skills. While many barriers to legal capacity have been reduced, especially for married women, there are many that still exist. Those barriers that remain may be creating situations of vulnerability for these groups. The next chapter will explore the vulnerability that is created by legal capacity denials for women, disabled women, and gender minorities.

References

Allen, Jason. 2007. A Quest for Acceptance: The Real ID Act and the Need for Comprehensive Gender Recognition Legislation in the United States. *Michigan Journal of Gender & Law* 14: 169–200.

Amuedo-Dorantes, Catalina, and Esther Arenas-Arroyo. 2019. *Police Trust and Domestic Violence: Evidence from Immigration Policies*. SSRN Scholarly Paper ID 3483959. Rochester, NY: Social Science Research Network.

Anderson, Michelle J. 2010. Sex Education and Rape Symposium: Rhetoric & Relevance: An Investigation into the Present and Future of Feminist Legal Theory. *Michigan Journal of Gender & Law* 17: 83–110.

Appignanesi, Lisa. 2011. *Mad, Bad And Sad: A History of Women and the Mind Doctors from 1800 to the Present*. Hachette UK.

Ariely, Dan, and George Loewenstein. 2006. The Heat of the Moment: The Effect of Sexual Arousal on Sexual Decision Making. *Journal of Behavioral Decision Making* 19: 87–98. https://doi.org/10.1002/bdm.501.

Arstein-Kerslake, Anna. 2015. Understanding Sex: The Right to Legal Capacity to Consent to Sex. *Disability & Society* 30: 1459–1473. https://doi.org/10.1080/09687599.2015.1116059.

———. 2017. *Restoring Voice to People with Cognitive Disabilities*. Cambridge University Press.

———. 2019. Gendered Denials: Vulnerability Created by Barriers to Legal Capacity for Women and Disabled Women. *International Journal of Law and Psychiatry* 66: 101501. https://doi.org/10.1016/j.ijlp.2019.101501.

Arstein-Kerslake, Anna, and Eilionóir Flynn. 2016a. Legislating Consent: Creating an Empowering Definition of Consent to Sex That Is Inclusive of People With Cognitive Disabilities. *Social & Legal Studies* 25: 225–248. https://doi.org/10.1177/0964663915599051.

———. 2016b. The General Comment on Article 12 of the Convention on the Rights of Persons with Disabilities: A Roadmap for Equality Before the Law. *The International Journal of Human Rights* 20: 471–490. https://doi.org/10.1080/13642987.2015.1107052.

Assassi, Libby. 2009. Property and Gender: Irrational Women and Rational Men. In *The Gendering of Global Finance, Libby Assassi*, 49–68. London: Palgrave Macmillan UK. https://doi.org/10.1057/9780230246690_3.

Atkinson, Eleanor, Michael J. Bennett, Jan Dudley, Sonia Grover, Kim Matthews, Paddy Moore, Julie Quinlivan, and Tamara Walters. 2003. Consensus Statement: Menstrual and Contraceptive Management in Women with an Intellectual Disability. *Australian and New Zealand Journal of Obstetrics and Gynaecology* 43: 109–110. https://doi.org/10.1046/j.0004-8666.2003.00046.x.

Bartlett, Peter. 1999. *The Poor Law of Lunacy*. A&C Black.

Basch, Norma. 1986. The Emerging Legal History of Women in the United States: Property, Divorce, and the Constitution. *Signs* 12: 97–117.

Blackburn, Robert. 2011. Laying the Foundations of the Modern Voting System: The Representation of the People Act 1918. *Parliamentary History* 30: 33–52. https://doi.org/10.1111/j.1750-0206.2010.00237.x.

Borsay, Anne. 1998. Returning Patients to the Community: Disability, medicine and economic rationality before the Industrial Revolution. *Disability & Society* 13: 645–663. Routledge. https://doi.org/10.1080/09687599826443.

———. 2004. *Disability and Social Policy in Britain since 1750: A History of Exclusion*. Macmillan Education UK.

Briscoe, Imani. 2016. International Women's Suffrage. *Sister Namibia* 28: 29–30.

Brown, Hilary. 1994. 'An Ordinary Sexual Life?': A Review of the Normalisation Principle as It Applies to the Sexual Options of People with Learning Disabilities. In *Disability & Society*, vol. 9, 123–144. Routledge. https://doi.org/10.1080/09687599466780181.

Butler, Judith. 2004. *Undoing Gender*. Routledge. https://doi.org/10.4324/9780203499627.

Calkin, Sydney, Fiona de Londras, and Gina Heathcote. 2020. Abortion in Ireland: Introduction to the Themed Issue. *Feminist Review* 124: 1–14. SAGE Publications. https://doi.org/10.1177/0141778919897684.

Calvo, Janet M. 1991. Spouse-Based Immigration Laws: The Legacies of Coverture. *San Diego Law Review* 28: 593–644.

Cannoot, Pieter. 2019a. The Pathologisation of Trans* Persons in the ECtHR's Case Law on Legal Gender Recognition. *Netherlands Quarterly of Human Rights* 37: 14–35. https://doi.org/10.1177/0924051918820984.

———. 2019b. '#WontBeErased': The Effects of (De)pathologisation and (De)medicalisation on the Legal Capacity of Trans* Persons. *International Journal of Law and Psychiatry* 66: 101478. https://doi.org/10.1016/j.ijlp.2019.101478.

Catalyst. 2020. Female Business Leaders: Global Statistics. *Catalyst*.

Center for Reproductive Rights. 2020. The World's Abortion Laws.

Cepko, Roberta. 1993. Involuntary Sterilization of Mentally Disabled Women. *Berkeley Women's Law Journal* 8: 122–165.

Chesney-Lind, Meda. 2017. Policing Women's Bodies: Law, Crime, Sexuality, and Reproduction. *Women & Criminal Justice* 27: 1–3. Routledge. https://doi.org/10.1080/08974454.2017.1268014.

Chesser, Susan G. 2019. *Women in National Governments Around the Globe: Fact Sheet*. R45483. Congressional Research Service.

Cheu, Maggie. 2012. Now and Then: How Coverture Ideology Informs the Rhetoric of Abortion. *Texas Journal of Women and the Law* 22: 113–130.

Clarke, Jessica A. 2019. They, Them, and Theirs. *Harvard Law Review* 132: 894. Military and Intelligence Database Collection.

Combs, Mary Beth. 2005. "A Measure of Legal Independence": The 1870 Married Women's Property Act and the Portfolio Allocations of British Wives. *The Journal of Economic History* 65: 1028–1057. JSTOR.

Committee on the Rights of Persons with Disabilities. 2014. General Comment No. 1 – Article 12: Equal Recognition Before the Law. UN Doc. No. CRPD/C/GC/1.

Crowther, M.A. 2016. *The Workhouse System 1834-1929: The History of an English Social Institution*. Routledge.

D'Itri, Patricia Ward. 1999. *Cross Currents in the International Women's Movement, 1848-1948*. Popular Press.

Dhanda, Amita. 2006. Legal Capacity in the Disability Rights Convention: Stranglehold of the Past or Lodestar for the Future Symposium: The United Nations Convention on the Rights of Persons with Disabilities. *Syracuse Journal of International Law and Commerce*: 429–462.

Donnelly, Mary, and Claire Murray. 2020. Abortion Care in Ireland: Developing Legal and Ethical Frameworks for Conscientious Provision. *International Journal of Gynecology & Obstetrics* 148: 127–132. https://doi.org/10.1002/ijgo.13025.

Driver, Felix. 2004. *Power and Pauperism: The Workhouse System, 1834-1884*. Cambridge University Press.

Dunne, Peter. 2017. Transgender Sterilisation Requirements in Europe. *Medical Law Review* 25: 554–581. https://doi.org/10.1093/medlaw/fwx028.

Dvorsky, George, and James Hughes. 2008. Postgenderism: Beyond the Gender Binary: 18.

Enright, Máiréad, Vicky Conway, Fiona de Londras, Mary Donnelly, Ruth Fletcher, Natalie McDonnell, Sheelagh McGuinness, Claire Murray, Sinead Ring, and Sorcha Ui Chonnachtaigh. 2015. Abortion Law Reform in Ireland: A Model for Change. *Feminists@Law*: 5.

Erickson, Amy Louise. 2005. Coverture and Capitalism. *History Workshop Journal*: 1–16. JSTOR.

Ezie, Chinyere. 2011. Deconstructing the Body: Transgender and Intersex Identities and Sex Discrimination - The Need for Strict Scrutiny. *Columbia Journal of Gender and Law* 20: 141–200.

Fennell, Phil. 1992. Balancing Care and Control: Guardianship, Community Treatment Orders and Patient Safeguards. *International Journal of Law and Psychiatry* 15. Special Issue: Clinical Criminology: 205–235. https://doi.org/10.1016/0160-2527(92)90015-S.

Finnegan, Frances. 2004. *Do Penance Or Perish: Magdalen Asylums in Ireland*. Oxford University Press.

Flexner, Eleanor, and Ellen Frances Fitzpatrick. 1996. *Century of Struggle: The Woman's Rights Movement in the United States*. Harvard University Press.

Flynn, Eilionoir, and Anna Arstein-Kerslake. 2014. Legislating Personhood: Realising the Right to Support in Exercising Legal Capacity. *International Journal of Law in Context* 10: 81–104. https://doi.org/10.1017/S1744552313000384.

Forsythe, Clarke D., and Rachel N. Morrison. 2020. Stare Decisis, Workability, and Roe v. Wade: An Introduction. *Ave Maria Law Review* 18: 48.

Fowler, Simon. 2014. *The Workhouse: The People, The Places, The Life Behind Doors*. Pen and Sword.

Fry, Danby P. 1864. *The Lunacy Acts: Containing All the Statutes Relating to Private Lunatics, Pauper Lunatics, Criminal Lunatics, Commissions of Lunacy, Public and Private Asylums, and the Commissioners in Lunacy*. Knight.

Gardner, Jane F. 1986. *Women in Roman Law & Society*. Croom Helm.

Gichki, Mahso. 2020. Deconstructing Transgender Identities in Pakistan, India, and Iran in Colonial and Post-colonial Context. *Development* 63: 31–37. https://doi.org/10.1057/s41301-020-00243-3.

Gidlow, Liette. 2018. The Sequel: The Fifteenth Amendment, the Nineteenth Amendment, and Southern Black Women's Struggle to Vote. *The Journal of the Gilded Age and Progressive Era* 17: 433–449. https://doi.org/10.1017/S1537781418000051.

Gillette, William. 2019. *The Right to Vote: Politics and the Passage of the Fifteenth Amendment*. JHU Press.

Gleeson, B.J. 1999. Recovering a 'Subjugated History': Disability and the Institution in the Industrial City. *Australian Geographical Studies* 37: 114–129. https://doi.org/10.1111/1467-8470.00073.

Glen, Kristin Booth. 2012. Changing Paradigms: Mental Capacity, Legal Capacity Guardianship, and Beyond. *Columbia Human Rights Law Review* 44: 93–170.

Goodman, Joyce. 2005. Pedagogy and Sex: Mary Dendy (1855–1933), Feeble-Minded Girls and the Sandlebridge Schools, 1902–33. *History of Education* 34: 171–187. https://doi.org/10.1080/0046760042000338782.

Grimshaw, Patricia. 1972. *Women's Suffrage in New Zealand*. Auckland University Press

Grover, Sonia R. 2002. Menstrual and Contraceptive Management in Women with an Intellectual Disability. *Medical Journal of Australia* 176: 108–110. https://doi.org/10.5694/j.1326-5377.2002.tb04315.x.

Hanssen, Shelby. 2017. Beyond Male or Female: Using Nonbinary Gender Identity to Confront Outdated Notions of Sex and Gender in the Law Notes. *Oregon Law Review* 96: 283–312.

Heslop, Pauline, and Fiona Macaulay. 2009. *Self-Injury and People with Learning Disabilities*. Bristol Crisis Service for Women.

Holcombe, Lee. 1983. *Wives & Property: Reform of the Married Women's Property Law in Nineteenth-Century England*. University of Toronto Press.

Hollomotz, Andrea. 2009. Beyond 'Vulnerability': An Ecological Model Approach to Conceptualizing Risk of Sexual Violence against People with Learning Difficulties. *The British Journal of Social Work* 39: 99–112. Oxford Academic. https://doi.org/10.1093/bjsw/bcm091.

———. 2012. 'A Lad Tried to Get Hold of My Boobs, So I Kicked Him': An Examination of Attempts by Adults with Learning Difficulties to Initiate Their Own Safeguarding. *Disability & Society* 27: 117–129. Routledge. https://doi.org/10.1080/09687599.2012.631801.

Hough, Rebecca Emily. 2012. Adult Protection and 'Intimate Citizenship' for People with Learning Difficulties: Empowering and Protecting in Light of the No Secrets Review. *Disability & Society* 27: 131–144. https://doi.org/10.1080/09687599.2012.631802.

Hubback, Eva M. 1928. The Case for Equal Franchise. Edited by William Leonard Courtney. *Fortnightly review, May 1865-June 1934; London* 123: 526–532.

Hutton, Christopher. 2017. Legal Sex, Self-Classification and Gender Self-Determination. *Law and Humanities* 11: 64–81. https://doi.org/10.1080/17521483.2017.1320037.

Jackson, Mark. 2003. 'A Menace to the Good of Society': Class, Fertility, and the Feeble-Minded in Edwardian England. In *Sex and Seclusion, Class and Custody*, 271–294. https://doi.org/10.1163/9789004333598_011.

Jacobs, Steven Andrew. 2020. *The Future of Roe v. Wade: Have Recent Developments Robbed Roe of its Original Justification?* SSRN Scholarly Paper ID 3550442. Rochester, NY: Social Science Research Network. https://doi.org/10.2139/ssrn.3550442.

Janovicek, Nancy, and Melanee Thomas. 2019. Canada: Uneven Paths to Suffrage and Women's Electoral Participation. In *The Palgrave Handbook of Women's Political Rights*, ed. Susan Franceschet, Mona Lena Krook, and Netina Tan, 169–184. Gender and Politics. London: Palgrave Macmillan UK. https://doi.org/10.1057/978-1-137-59074-9_12.

Johnson, Jaime. 2010. Recognition of the Nonhuman: The Psychological Minefield of Transgender Inequality in the Law Student Article. *Law & Psychology Review* 34: 153–164.

Johnson, Kelley, and Rannveig Traustadottir. 2005. *Deinstitutionalization and People with Intellectual Disabilities: In and Out of Institutions*. Jessica Kingsley Publishers.

Karkazis, Katrina Alicia. 2008. *Fixing Sex: Intersex, Medical Authority, and Lived Experience*. E-Duke Books Scholarly Collection. Duke University Press.

Karolak, Magdalena, and Hala Guta. 2020. Saudi Women as Decision Makers: Analyzing the Media Portrayal of Female Political Participation in Saudi Arabia. *Hawwa* 18: 75–95. https://doi.org/10.1163/15692086-12341371.

Katyal, Sonia K. 2018. The Numerus Clausus of Sex Article Award Winners: The Dukeminier Prize Awarded to. *Dukeminier Awards: Best Sexual Orientation and Gender Identity Law Review* 17: 195–282.

Kelly, Casey Ryan, and Kristen E. Hoerl. 2015. Shaved or Saved? Disciplining Women's Bodies. *Women's Studies in Communication* 38. Routledge: 141–145. https://doi.org/10.1080/07491409.2015.1027088.

Kempton, Winifred, and Emily Kahn. 1991. Sexuality and People with Intellectual Disabilities: A Historical Perspective. *Sexuality and Disability* 9: 93–111. https://doi.org/10.1007/BF01101735.

Kennedy, Nancy B. 2020. *Women Win the Vote!: 19 for the 19th Amendment*. WW Norton.

Kirby, Michael. 2013. The Sodomy Offence: England's Least Lovely Criminal Law Export? In *Human Rights, Sexual Orientation and Gender Identity in The Commonwealth*, 61–82. University of London Press.

Kittell, Ellen E. 1998. Guardianship Over Women in Medieval Flanders: A Reappraisal. *Journal of Social History* 31: 897. https://doi.org/10.1353/jsh/31.4.897.

Kothari, Miloon. 2005. Women and Adequate Housing. United Nations Economic and Social Council. E/CN.4/2005/43.

Lakhani, Sarah M. 2019. Universalizing the U Visa: Challenges of Immigration Case Selection in Legal Nonprofits Notes. *California Law Review* 107: 1661–1712.

Lennox, Corinne, and Matthew Waites, eds. 2013. *Human Rights, Sexual Orientation and Gender Identity in The Commonwealth: Struggles for Decriminalisation and Change*. University of London Institute of Commonwealth Studies. https://doi.org/10.14296/518.9781912250134.

Lewis, Oliver. 2011. Advancing Legal Capacity Jurisprudence. *European Human Rights Law Review*: 700–714.

Liao, S. Matthew, Julian Savulescu, and Mark Sheehan. 2007. The Ashley Treatment: Best Interests, Convenience, and Parental Decision-Making. *The Hastings Center Report* 37. [Hastings Center, Wiley]: 16–20. JSTOR.

Lin, Lan-Ping, Jin-Ding Lin, Cordia M. Chu, and Li-Mei Chen. 2011. Caregiver Attitudes to Gynaecological Health of Women with Intellectual Disability. *Journal of Intellectual & Developmental Disability* 36: 149–155. https://doi.org/10.3109/13668250.2011.599316.

Longmate, Norman. 2003. *The Workhouse: A Social History*. Random House.

Lush, Denzil. 2019. Adult Guardianship and Powers of Attorney in England and Wales. In *Special Needs Financial Planning: A Comparative Perspective*, ed. Lusina Ho and Rebecca Lee, 117–148. Cambridge: Cambridge University Press. https://doi.org/10.1017/9781108646925.005.

Map of Countries that Criminalise LGBT People | Human Dignity Trust. 2020. https://www.humandignitytrust.org/lgbt-the-law/map-of-criminalisation/. Accessed August 10.

Matambanadzo, Saru M. 2012. Embodying Vulnerability: A Feminist Theory of the Person. Duke Journal of Gender Law & Policy 20: 39.

Maveety, Nancy. 2020. Beyond Abortion: Roe v. Wade and the Battle for Privacy. *Journal of American History* 107: 271–272. Oxford Academic. https://doi.org/10.1093/jahist/jaaa160.

McCarthy, Michelle. 1999. *Sexuality and Women with Learning Disabilities*. Jessica Kingsley Publishers.

McCool, Daniel, Susan M. Olson, and Jennifer L. Robinson. 2007. *Native Vote: American Indians, the Voting Rights Act, and the Right to Vote*. Cambridge University Press.

McHugh, Paul. 2016. Transgender Surgery Isn't the Solution. *Wall Street Journal*, May 13, sec. Opinion.

Moran, James E. 2019. *Madness on Trial: A Transatlantic History of English Civil Law and Lunacy. Madness on Trial*. Manchester University Press.

Morgan, Robin. 1996. *Sisterhood is Global: The International Women's Movement Anthology*. Feminist Press at CUNY.

Morrison, Shane D., Thomas Satterwhite, David W. Grant, Johanna Kirby, Donald R. Sr Laub, and Judy VanMaasdam. 2015. Long-Term Outcomes of Rectosigmoid Neocolporrhaphy in Male-to-Female Gender Reassignment Surgery. *Plastic and Reconstructive Surgery* 136: 386–394. https://doi.org/10.1097/PRS.0000000000001459.

Murphy, Glynis H., and Ali O'callaghan. 2004. Capacity of Adults with Intellectual Disabilities to Consent to Sexual Relationships. *Psychological Medicine* 34: 1347–1357. https://doi.org/10.1017/S0033291704001941.

Neuman Wippler, Anna James (aj). 2016. Identity Crisis: The Limitations of Expanding Government Recognition of Gender Identity and the Possibility of Genderless Identity Documents. *Harvard Journal of Law & Gender* 39: 491–554.

Nussbaum, Martha C. 2004. Beyond the Social Contract: Capabilities and Global Justice. An Olaf Palme lecture, delivered in Oxford on 19 June 2003. *Oxford Development Studies* 32: 3–18. https://doi.org/10.1080/1360081042000184093.

Oliver, Michael. 1990. Disability and the Rise of Capitalism. In *The Politics of Disablement, Michael Oliver*, 25–42. London: Macmillan Education UK. https://doi.org/10.1007/978-1-349-20895-1_3.

Patel, Priti. 2017. Forced Sterilization of Women as Discrimination. *Public Health Reviews* 38: 15. https://doi.org/10.1186/s40985-017-0060-9.

Perlin, Michael L., and Alison J. Lynch. 2014. All His Sexless Patients: Persons with Mental Disabilities and the Competence to Have Sex. *Washington Law Review* 89: 257.

Petchesky, Rosalind P. 1990. *Abortion and Woman's Choice: The State, Sexuality, and Reproductive Freedom*. Rev. ed. Northeastern Series in Feminist Theory. Northeastern University Press.

Petition for Alien Relative | USCIS. 2020. August 4.

Pfäfflin, Friedemann. 2015. Transgenderism and Transsexuality: Medical and Psychological Viewpoints. In *The Legal Status of Transsexual and Transgender Persons*, ed. Jens M. Scherpe, 11–24. Intersentia. https://doi.org/10.1017/9781780685588.003.

Pfeiffer, David. 1994. Eugenics and Disability Discrimination. *Disability & Society* 9: 481–499. Routledge. https://doi.org/10.1080/09687599466780471.

Pham, Hoangmai H., and Barron H. Lerner. 2001. In the Patient's Best Interest? Revisiting Sexual Autonomy and Sterilization of the Developmentally Disabled. *Western Journal of Medicine* 175: 280–283.

Plummer, Ken. 2002. *Telling Sexual Stories: Power, Change and Social Worlds*. Routledge.

Porterfield, Jennifer, and Brian H. Kleiner. 2005. A New Era: Women and Leadership. *Equal Opportunities International* 24: 49–56. Emerald Group Publishing Limited. https://doi.org/10.1108/02610150510788150.

Prokhovnik, Raia. 2012. *Rational Woman: A Feminist Critique of Dichotomy*. Routledge. https://doi.org/10.4324/9780203024485.

Rawls, John. 2009. *A Theory of Justice*. Harvard University Press.

Romeo, Franklin H. 2004. Beyond a Medical Model: Advocating for a New Conception of Gender Identity in the Law Note. *Columbia Human Rights Law Review* 36: 713–754.

Rosenbaum, Stephen A., and Julia Epstein. 2019. Revisiting Ashley X: An Essay on Disabled Bodily Integrity, Sexuality, Dignity. *and Family Caregiving. Touro Law Review* 35: 101–138.

Rosenberg, Joseph A. 2009. Poverty, Guardianship, and the Vulnerable Elderly: Human Narrative and Statistical Patterns in a Snapshot of Adult Guardianship Cases in New York City. *Georgetown Journal on Poverty Law & Policy* 16: 315–344.

Rossi Neto, R., F. Hintz, S. Krege, H. Rübben, and F. vom Dorp. 2012. Gender Reassignment Surgery - a 13 Year Review of Surgical Outcomes. *International braz j urol* 38: 97–107. https://doi.org/10.1590/S1677-55382012000100014.

Rupp, Leila J. 1997. *Worlds of Women: The Making of an International Women's Movement*. Princeton University Press.

Seedat, Fatima. 2013. *Sex and the Legal Subject: Women and Legal Capacity in Hanafi Law*. Montreal: McGill University.

Series, Lucy. 2013. *The Mental Capacity Act 2005 and the Institutional Domination of People with Learning Disabilities*. University of Exeter.

Shakespeare, Tom. 1998. Choices and Rights: Eugenics, Genetics and Disability Equality. *Disability & Society* 13: 665–681. Routledge. https://doi.org/10.1080/09687599826452.

Shammas, Carole. 1994. Re-Assessing the Married Women's Property Acts. *Journal of Women's History* 6: 9–30. https://doi.org/10.1353/jowh.2010.0269.

Shanley, Mary Lyndon. 1993. *Feminism, Marriage, and the Law in Victorian England*. Princeton University Press.

Sharpe, Andrew N. 2007. Endless Sex: The Gender Recognition Act 2004 and the Persistence of a Legal Category. *Feminist Legal Studies* 15: 57–84. https://doi.org/10.1007/s10691-006-9042-x.

Silvers, Anita, and Leslie Pickering Francis. 2005. Justice Through Trust: Disability and the "Outlier Problem" in Social Contract Theory. *Ethics: An International Journal of Social, Political, and Legal Philosophy* 116: 40–76.

Simmonds, Alecia. 2019. Sex Smells: Olfaction, Modernity and the Regulation of Women's Bodies 1880–1940 (Or How Women Came to Fear Their Own Smells). *Australian Feminist Studies* 34: 232–247. Routledge. https://doi.org/10.1080/08164649.2019.1576503.

Smyth, Lisa. 2002. Feminism and Abortion Politics: Choice, Rights, and Reproductive Freedom. *Women's Studies International Forum* 25: 335–345. https://doi.org/10.1016/S0277-5395(02)00256-X.

Spade, Dean. 2009. Documenting Gender. *Dukeminier Awards - Best Sexual Orientation and Gender Identity Law Review* 8: 137–248.

———. 2015. *Normal Life: Administrative Violence, Critical Trans Politics, and the Limits of Law*. Duke University Press.

Stone, Meighan. 2018. A Place of Her Own: Women's Right to Land. *Women Around the World*.

Stryker, Susan, and Stephen Whittle. 2006. *The Transgender Studies Reader*. Lambda Literary Award Winner. Routledge.

Stupakis, Stephanie E. 2019. What the Future May Hold for Victims of Domestic and Sexual Violence without the Violence against Women Act Notes. *Hastings Women's Law Journal* 30: 261–286.

Suresh. 2015. Pendulous Penises and Couture Clitorises: What Medical Men do to Intersex Infants. In *Nothing to Fix: Medicalisation of Sexual Orientation and Gender Identity*, ed. Arvind Narrain and Vinay Chandran. Sage.

Swango-Wilson, Amy. 2008. Caregiver Perception of Sexual Behaviors of Individuals with Intellectual Disabilities. *Sexuality and Disability* 26: 75–81. https://doi.org/10.1007/s11195-008-9071-2.

Takayanagi, Mari. 2018. Women and the Vote: The Parliamentary Path to Equal Franchise, 1918–28. *Parliamentary History* 37: 168–185. https://doi.org/10.1111/1750-0206.12344.

Tavris, Carol. 1993. The Mismeasure of Woman. *Feminism & Psychology* 3: 149–168. https://doi.org/10.1177/0959353593032002.

Taylor, Maeve, Alison Spillane, and Sir Sabaratnam Arulkumaran. 2020. The Irish Journey: Removing the Shackles of Abortion Restrictions in Ireland. In *Best Practice & Research Clinical Obstetrics & Gynaecology*, vol. 62, 36–48. Abortion: Global Perspectives and Country Experiences. https://doi.org/10.1016/j.bpobgyn.2019.05.011.

Theilen, Jens T. 2018. Beyond the Gender Binary: Rethinking the Right to Legal Gender Recognition. *European Human Rights Law Review* 3: 249–257.

Tredgold, A.F. 1909. The Feeble-Minded—A Social Danger. *The Eugenics Review* 1: 97–104.

UN Women. Facts and Figures: Leadership and Political Participation. *UN Women*.

UN Women Asia Pacific. Women's Land & Property Rights. *UN Women | Asia and the Pacific*.

United Kingdom. 1882. *Married Women's Property Act 1882. 1882 CHAPTER 75*.

United Nations Free and Equal. 2015. *Transgender*. United Nations.

Victoria Office of the Public Advocate. 2017. *Annual Report 2016-2017*.

Villa, Monique. 2017. Women own less than 20% of the world's land. It's time to give them equal property rights. *World Economic Forum*.

Vogel, Ursula. 1990. Under Permanent Guardianship: Women's Condition Under Modern Civil Law. In *The Political Interests of Gender: Developing Theory and Research with a Feminist Face*, ed. Anna G. Jonasdottir and Kathleen B. Jones. Sage.

Wagner, David. 2005. *The Poorhouse: America's Forgotten Institution*. Rowman & Littlefield Publishers.

Walmsley, Jan. 2005. Institutionalisation: An Historical Perspective. In *Deinstitutionalisation and People with Intellectual Disabilities: In and Out of Institutions*, ed. Kelley Johnson and Rannveig Traustadóttir, 50–65. Jessica Kingsley Publishers.

Walsh, Oonagh. 1999. Gendering the Asylums: Ireland and Scotland, 1847–1877. In *Gendering Scottish History: an International Approach*, 199–215. Cruithne Press.

Wang, Lily C., and Dix P. Poppas. 2017. Surgical Outcomes and Complications of Reconstructive Surgery in the Female Congenital Adrenal Hyperplasia Patient: What Every Endocrinologist Should Know. *The Journal of Steroid Biochemistry and Molecular Biology* 165: 137–144. Genetic Steroid Disorders. https://doi.org/10.1016/j.jsbmb.2016.03.021.

Ward, Jennifer. 2014. *Women in Medieval Europe: 1200-1500*. Routledge. https://doi.org/10.4324/9781315842349.

Waxman, Barbara Faye. 1994. Up Against Eugenics: Disabled Women's Challenge to Receive Reproductive Health Services. *Sexuality and Disability* 12: 155–171. https://doi.org/10.1007/BF02547889.

Wilson, W. Robert. 1961. Rights of Married Women: Liabilities and Dealings with Third Persons Symposium on the Law of Domestic Relations in Oklahoma--Student Comments. *Oklahoma Law Review* 14: 317–318.

Wingfield, M., D.L. Healy, and A. Nicholson. 1994a. Gynaecological Care for Women with Intellectual Disability. *The Medical Journal of Australia* 160: 536–538.

Wingfield, M., N. McClure, P.M. Mamers, D.T. Weigall, P.J. Paterson, and D.L. Healy. 1994b. Endometrial Ablation: an Option for the Management of Menstrual Problems in the Intellectually Disabled. *The Medical Journal of Australia* 160: 533–536.

Winter, Sam, Milton Diamond, Jamison Green, Dan Karasic, Terry Reed, Stephen Whittle, and Kevan Wylie. 2016. Transgender People: Health at the Margins of Society. *The Lancet* 388: 390–400. https://doi.org/10.1016/S0140-6736(16)00683-8.

Wise, Sarah. 2013. *Inconvenient People: Lunacy, Liberty and the Mad-Doctors in Victorian England*. Vintage Books.

Wolfley, Jeanette. 1991. Jim Crow, Indian Style: The Disenfranchisement of Native Americans. *American Indian Law Review* 16: 167–202. JSTOR. https://doi.org/10.2307/20068694.

Women, Business, and the Law 2018. 2018. World Bank Group.

Wong, Sophia Isako. 2010. Duties of Justice to Citizens with Cognitive Disabilities. In *Cognitive Disability and Its Challenge to Moral Philosophy*, ed. Eva Feder Kittay and Licia Carlson, 127–146. John Wiley & Sons, Ltd. https://doi.org/10.1002/9781444322781.ch7.

Woodhouse, Jayne. 1982. Eugenics and the Feeble-Minded: The Parliamentary Debates of 1912-14. *History of Education* 11: 127–137. https://doi.org/10.1080/0046760820110205.

World Bank. 2019. *Women in Half the World Still Denied Land, Property Rights Despite Laws*. World Bank.

Zaher, Claudia. 2002. When a Woman's Marital Status Determined Her Legal Status: A Research Guide on the Common Law Doctrine of Coverture. *Law Library Journal* 94: 459–486.

Ziegler, Mary. 2020. *Abortion in America: Roe v. Wade to the Present*. Cambridge University Press.

Chapter 5
Vulnerability Created by Legal Capacity Denials

5.1 Introduction

This chapter will explore the vulnerability that is created by legal capacity denial. It will discuss the evidence that demonstrates that decision-making denial is profoundly disempowering and leaves people without tools for protecting themselves from abuse and marginalisation (Winick 1995; Ryan and Deci 2017). It will explore financial, physical and sexual abuse that can occur as a result of this vulnerability (Sobsey and Doe 1991; Acierno et al. 2010; Dunn 2010).

5.2 Vulnerability

Vulnerability is a powerful concept. When it is ascribed to an individual or to a group of people, it can transform their social world (Boyle 2003). A vulnerable person is often treated differently—they are thought to deserve higher levels of external protection, which frequently results in lower levels of autonomy and self-determination (Anderson and Honneth 2005; Anderson 2013; Rogers and Meek Lange 2013; Scully 2013). Sometimes people can benefit from being labelled as vulnerable. For example, more money may be expended by the government to provide support for groups labelled as vulnerable. However, frequently, groups labelled as vulnerable also experience significant negative repercussions of such labels. They are often inaccurately identified as weak, powerless, and ineffectual (Hollander 2002; Levine et al. 2004; Gill 2006; Scully 2013). The vulnerability that they may be experiencing is often mistakenly identified by state actors as well as others as vulnerability inherent to the individual, not vulnerability created by their social environment. In addition, these qualities are often ascribed to all individuals

Portions of this chapter are drawn from Arstein-Kerslake (2019).

A. Arstein-Kerslake, *Legal Capacity & Gender*,
https://doi.org/10.1007/978-3-030-63493-3_5

within a group labelled as vulnerable, without distinctions drawn between individuals (Luna 2009; Scully 2013). This can be profoundly disempowering, which may, in turn, beget more vulnerability.

Women, disabled women, and gender minorities are often labelled as vulnerable (Hollander 2002; Luna 2009; Chamberland and Saewyc 2011; Scully 2013; Butler 2016). They are often subjected to the externally imposed notion of the 'vulnerable female subject.' However, the realities of how these groups experience vulnerability is often much different from this externally imposed notion. In addition, this concept of the 'vulnerable female subject' can operate to reinforce marginalisation and limit an individual's choices (Lajoie 2018). This labelling is additionally complex for gender minorities. Those that are externally identified as female or as having female traits, are likely subjected to a similar imposition of the label of 'vulnerable female subject.' However, gender minorities that others do not perceive as feminine may not experience the same imposition of the label of 'vulnerable female subject.' Instead, it is possible that these individuals are also presumed by others to be vulnerable, on the basis of what some may perceive as 'otherness'. It is also possible that the history of gender minorities being ascribed with mental health issues—as discussed in Chap. 3—effectively serves to create a similar phenomenon to that experienced by people with disability—the assumption that they lack rationality and cognitive skills and that they may be assumed to be vulnerable on that basis. More research is need in this area to discover the effects of vulnerability labelling on gender minorities. For all people that experience vulnerability labelling, it creates a power dynamic which favours those who are not labelled as vulnerable. This can limit the choices and autonomy of those groups who are labelled as vulnerable (Boyle 2003).

In order for an individual to have their autonomy respected on an equal basis with others, they must have their legal capacity recognised. Legal capacity is an individual's legal personhood and legal agency. Denials of legal capacity and barriers to legal capacity—such as the imposition of guardianship, the denial of reproductive choice, and denial of decision-making in psychiatric settings—are experienced at a higher rate and in a unique manner by women, disabled women, and gender minorities. This is partially because of the label of vulnerability, which can precipitate an assumption of a need for increased protection. These denials of legal capacity and barriers to legal capacity create additional vulnerability amidst these groups due to the profoundly disempowering nature of autonomy removal that comes along with limitations on legal capacity. This Chapter explores some specific situations in which this may be occurring and why. Finally, it concludes by arguing that this connection between limitations on legal capacity and the construction of vulnerability has been overlooked in law and public policy and needs to be adequately addressed.

5.3 Vulnerability as a Social Construct

Vulnerability exists where an individual lacks control over events that may jeopardise things that are important to that individual (Anderson 2013). It is almost always used in the context of negative phenomena—an occurrence that is either undesirable to the individual or viewed as undesirable by others (Scully 2013; Pritchard-Jones 2018). It is directly contingent upon the power relations of an individual and the forces that are impacting them. If the individual gains power over those forces, vulnerability decreases. If the individual loses power over those forces, vulnerability increases (Anderson 2013).

Losses or gains of power over forces impacting an individual may occur due to losses or gains in autonomy (Anderson 2013). For example, if all funding for disability services goes directly from the government to the service provider—and the disabled person does not have autonomy to make choices regarding the distribution and use of that funding—then, the disabled person lacks control over their disability services. These services are often essential for an individual's daily activities. In this situation, the disabled person is vulnerable to the decisions of the service provider, which may or may not align with what the individual desires for themselves. If the disabled person had autonomy to make decisions regarding some or all of the funding going to the service provider—and was provided with access to appropriate support for exercising that autonomy—then, the vulnerability of the disabled person, in relation to the service provider, would decrease. As such, vulnerability is intimately tied to power relations, which are subject to change based on the relative autonomy of the parties (Anderson 2013).

Jackie Leach Scully has identified two perspectives of vulnerability. The first is when vulnerability is viewed as ontological—an inescapable aspect of all people's lives. This is vulnerability that everyone is susceptible too, such as, illness, injury, or death (Scully 2013). This perspective of vulnerability is commonly seen in legal theory and bioethical scholarship. For example, Martha Fineman has noted that vulnerability is "universal and constant, inherent in the human condition" and has used this perspective of vulnerability to reimagine the socio-legal order in a manner which accounts for vulnerability and dependence (Fineman 2004, 2008; Matambanadzo 2012; Fineman and Grear 2013; Scully 2013). This perspective of vulnerability does not ascribe vulnerability based on group membership. Instead, it discusses vulnerability as a universal trait (Matambanadzo 2012; Scully 2013; Butler et al. 2016). The downside of this perspective is that it risks overlooking the particular vulnerabilities that certain individuals face—especially those due to group marginalisation, such as is experienced by disabled people. For example, inaccessible public buildings and services, as well as overt discrimination on the basis of disability.

The second perspective of vulnerability that Leach Scully has identified is when particular groups are singled out as especially vulnerable (Scully 2013). This has also been identified as a 'status-based' approach to vulnerability (Pritchard-Jones 2018). This perspective of vulnerability is often adopted in research, medical ethics, and public health ethics. This perspective assumes that by virtue of an individual's status, or group membership, they are especially vulnerable to harm (Scully 2013; Pritchard-Jones 2018). The downside of this perspective is potentially even more dangerous than that of the first perspective—it creates a dichotomy in which the social world is divided into two groups. The first is a group that is 'normal' and invulnerable enough to have their autonomy largely respected and to be left to carry on with their lives. The other group is a 'special' group which is viewed as abnormal and particularly vulnerable to harm. This 'special' group is believed to need differential treatment in order to either restore them to normality or to limit their autonomy in the name of protection (Scully 2013). This is dangerous because the two groups are often ascribed different rights and responsibilities—the 'normal' group is granted the full gambit of rights and responsibilities, whereas the 'special' group has limited rights to autonomy and will often be deemed to not be held responsible for their actions on an equal basis with members of the 'normal' group. Disabled people are often relegated to the 'special' group and are subjected to these altered—and often disadvantageous—rights and responsibilities (Arstein-Kerslake et al. 2017). Leach Scully argues instead for an expanded view of ontological vulnerability which encompasses vulnerability created by social dependence (Scully 2013). This would allow for the acceptance of vulnerability as a universal trait, while also drawing attention to socially constructed vulnerability that could be addressed and corrected.

In addition to the two different perspectives of vulnerability, Leach Scully has also identified two different types of vulnerability in relation to disability—'inherent' and 'contingent' vulnerabilities. Inherent vulnerabilities are those which are often due to a physio-logical or biological characteristic of the individual. For example, physical weakness or chronic pain. These are vulnerabilities which the social environment may be changed to accommodate, however it would be difficult or impossible for changes in the social environment to fully negate these vulnerabilities (Scully 2013).

Conversely, contingent vulnerabilities are those that are directly created by the social environment—they are contingent on social phenomena that instigate and perpetuate situations and phenomena that create vulnerability (Scully 2013). For example, an environment, such as a public bathroom, that has not been made physically accessible for a person using a wheelchair and requires the individual to depend upon another person to utilise it. This leaves the individual using the wheelchair vulnerable to the other person because they are faced with a need to use the bathroom, but they are dependent upon the other's assistance. The other person holds power in this situation and may abuse that power. This is vulnerability that is contingent on the inaccessible environment. If the public bathroom was made accessible—with automatically opening doors, appropriate space for a wheelchair, the toilet, and other mechanisms at appropriate heights, etc.—then the individual may be able to utilise the bathroom on their own and may not need to depend on another person. The individual using the wheelchair would, therefore, not be vulnerable to the potential for the other individual to abuse their position of power and do harm to the individual using the wheelchair.

There is a misperception that inherent vulnerabilities are more common for certain groups—especially minority groups, such as women, disabled women, and gender minorities (Hollander 2002; Scully 2013). However, many vulnerabilities that are perceived to be inherent vulnerabilities, may actually be contingent vulnerabilities. For example, people with intellectual disability are often perceived as possessing the inherent vulnerability of poor decision-making skills. Poor decision-making skills are perceived as a vulnerability because they may make an individual more prone to suggestion and undue influence as well as prone to making bad decisions that may lead to harm to themselves or those around them. For many people with intellectual disability, this is simply a misperception and they, in fact, possess very good decision-making skills. For other people with intellectual disability, they may have difficulty with decision-making skills, however this may be due to being denied opportunities to develop decision-making skills, due to a lack of accessible information regarding particular decisions, due to an anxiety-producing or otherwise unfriendly environment for decision-making, or due to many other factors that are socially constructed or can be accommodated through the social environment. Where this is the case, such vulnerabilities are not inherent vulnerabilities, but are instead contingent vulnerabilities which can be lessened or eliminated through changes to the social environment.

Some may argue that women are inherently more vulnerable simply due to biological reasons, such as lesser physical strength on average than men (Hollander 2002). It is true that in some situations varying levels of physical strength alone may lead to certain individuals, with less physical strength, experiencing inherent vulnerability when physically challenged by an individual of greater strength. However, if physical strength was an indicator of social power or privilege, then physical strength would be a prominent characteristic of the extremely wealthy, law makers, CEOs, and others who experience high levels of social power and privilege. This is generally not the case. Instead, it is often those of lower social standing that develop physical strength due to work that requires high levels of manual labour and is generally poorly remunerated. Such groups of lower social standing are, in many ways, more vulnerable than those with less physical strength but high social power and privilege. For example, they generally have less monetary freedom, lower education levels, and less political decision-making power. In this way, the argument that women are inherently more vulnerable due to biological differences in physical strength is inconsistent with the wider population, in which it seems that those with the highest levels of physical strength are often in positions of less power and greater social vulnerability. As such, even physical weakness could be considered a contingent vulnerability that can be accommodated for or balanced out by social phenomena.

Perceptions of vulnerability are strongly linked to recognition of autonomy and the granting or denial of legal capacity. Women, disabled women, and gender minorities are often overly ascribed with inherent vulnerability (Hollander 2002; Scully 2013; Butler et al. 2016). As such, they are disproportionately viewed as needing a higher degree of protection than other groups. This has resulted in the denial of autonomy—including the denial of legal capacity—in various contexts, which will be explored below. These denials of autonomy lead to an increase of contingent vulnerability, which is further mistaken as inherent vulnerability. This becomes a cycle of vulnerability labelling because it then feeds back into the existing notion of women, disabled women, and gender minorities as in need of special protection and as incapable of directing their own lives or making legal decisions on an equal basis with others.

5.4 Creating Vulnerability: Gender, Legal Capacity Barriers, Autonomy, and Vulnerability

There are some tangible connections between legal capacity denial and the creation of vulnerability in women, disabled women, and gender minorities. These contingent vulnerabilities, as termed by Jackie Leach Scully, may be leaving women, disabled women, and gender minorities at greater risk of abuse (Nosek et al. 2001; Scully 2013). Other contingent vulnerability may be created by the simple existence of laws and policies that insidiously stigmatize women, disabled women, and gender minorities by either overlooking their existence completely or assuming a lack of agency and autonomy. In a vicious cycle, such laws and policy can permeate the social conscious and ripple through socio-political relationships and networks to reinforce an often-incorrect notion of inherent vulnerability of women, disabled women and gender minorities (Matambanadzo 2012). In these ways, laws and policies that deny legal capacity and remove autonomy from women, disabled women, and gender minorities may be both contributing to contingent vulnerabilities and bolstering historical and erroneous notions of inherent vulnerability.

5.4.1 Creating Vulnerability by Denying Reproductive and Sexual Choice of Women, Disabled Women, and Gender Minorities

Reproductive and sexual choice are a poignant example of laws and policies that create vulnerability by denying autonomy to women, disabled women, and gender minorities on a differential basis from men. There is a long history of denial of reproductive and sexual choice on the basis of gender. Coverture laws, described above, and other laws that prevented married women from making legal decisions without their husbands were likely applied to issues of reproductive and sexual choice (Petchesky 1990; Cheu 2012). Even legal capacity to consent to sexual acts has been removed from married women for centuries through laws that permit rape within the confines of marriage (Russell 1990; Hasday 2000). Such denial of legal capacity in the context of reproductive and sexual choices can create vulnerability via psychological disempowerment as well as due to limitations of financial resources and other situations that can lead to dependence.

In addition, rape law itself has a long history of prioritising male autonomy at the expense of female autonomy (Schulhofer 1992; Anderson 2010). For example, the concept of consent is often conceived as a female passively submitting to a male decision-maker, as opposed to an active process of negotiation and agreement between two equal parties (Anderson 2010). Rape law has also erroneously ascribed autonomy to women in order to create consistency with male choices. For example, when women's clothes and past choices are permitted to be used as evidence that she consented to a man's choices regarding sexual acts (Lennon et al. 1992; Sterling 1995; Anderson 2002). This is not a granting of autonomy, but instead a masking of the women's true choices with the effect of further entrenching the notion that a man's autonomy—his legal capacity—take precedence over a women's in the realm of sexual choice. This creates contingent vulnerability by placing the female in a position of subservience to the male—making her vulnerable to the choices of the male.

5.4.1.1 Sexual Choice and Contingent Vulnerability

Sexual choice is also frequently denied to disabled women, particularly those with cognitive disability—including mental health disability, intellectual disability, dementia and others (Waxman 1994; Arstein-Kerslake 2015). In some jurisdictions, there are laws that criminalise all sexual activity with intellectually disabled women (Kelly 2014; Arstein-Kerslake and Flynn 2016). Disabled women are often prevented from exercising legal capacity to consent to sex through policies or informal arrangements that discourage sexual relationships. For example, there is significant evidence that disabled women and girls often have limited access to sex education, which would facilitate the meaningful and informed exercise of legal capacity to consent to sex (McCarthy and Thompson 1997; Tepper 2000; Dukes and McGuire 2009; Esmail et al. 2010; Eastgate et al. 2011). In addition, there is evidence that some residential service providers for disabled people discourage romantic and sexual relationships and may even act to prevent sexual relationships (Cuskelly and Bryde 2004; Esmail et al. 2010; Kelly 2014).

This denial of the freedom to exercise legal capacity to consent to sex for disabled women creates contingent vulnerability. It often leaves disabled women without the tools necessary to exercise legal capacity to consent to sex because when they are restricted from doing so, they do not have the opportunity to develop the skills necessary for exercising choice related to sexual activity (Dukes and McGuire 2009). Decision-making is well-documented as largely a learned-skill in all people which requires education, training, and repeated experience in order to develop and grow (Byrnes 2013). This is true for all decision-making, including sexual decision-making (Juhasz 1975; Dukes and McGuire 2009). For example, when faced with a situation of sexual abuse an individual may not be able to identify or distinguish it as abuse if they were not previously exposed to sexual choices in an appropriate sexual relationship. This is a significant risk and there is a growing body of evidence to indicate that many disabled women experience this (McCarthy and Thompson 1997; Eastgate et al. 2011).

Furthermore, if legal capacity to make sexual choices is denied completely to disabled women, it is likely that safeguards and infrastructure for supporting disabled women in making such choices is not available. This creates contingent vulnerability because disabled women are left without critical support for making sexual choices and may, thereby, be left without avenues for recourse when sexual abuse occurs. There is likely multiple other ways that contingent vulnerability may be created by the denial of legal capacity to exercise sexual choice—this is merely the beginning of the discussion to highlight the multitude of opportunities for vulnerability to bubble up and the potential ineffectiveness of denying legal capacity to sexual choice as a means of protection.

5.4.1.2 Abortion and Contingent Vulnerability

Reproductive choice is also denied to women through the criminalisation of abortion. Biologically, men are not able to get pregnant and are therefore not subjected to laws that do not permit reproductive choice in the form of abortion. However, due to the historical and ongoing socio-political power that men hold, if men were able to get pregnant they may not be subjected to the denial of their autonomy—the denial of their legal capacity—to make decisions regarding reproductive choice, such as abortion (Steinem 1978; Shalev 2000; Kleinman et al. 2006; Kumar et al. 2009). This is evidenced by the long history of laws, described above, that remove autonomy from women disproportionately to that of men. This includes abortion laws which continue to restrict women's exercise of their legal capacity to make reproductive choices. For example: laws that restrict abortion to only certain circumstances, such as when the health of the mother is at risk or where there is evidence of incest or a sexual assault; policies that exclude abortion from health care insurance cover—making it prohibitively expensive and consequentially removing it as a possible choice for many women; and a lack of measures to ensure that clinics where abortions are performed are safe and accessible environments for women (Levine et al. 1996; Siegel 2007; Zampas and Gher 2008; Finer and Fine 2013; Shah et al. 2014). There is not space in this book to provide a full debate on where the right to legal capacity to reproductive choice should begin and end in the context of abortion. However, the lack of widespread availability of abortion and the on-going overbroad restrictions on abortion in law and policy likely amount, at a minimum, to denial of the right to legal capacity to reproductive choice for women.

The denial of legal capacity for reproductive choice in the context of abortion leads to contingent vulnerability in multiple ways. When a woman is faced with an unwanted pregnancy, she loses bodily autonomy which often precipitates social and psychological disempowerment (Sloane 1969; Schmiege and Russo 2005; Silverman et al. 2007). Such disempowerment can ultimately lead to vulnerability to interpersonal abuse—financial, emotional, or physical in nature (Goodwin et al.

2000; Pallitto et al. 2005; Silverman et al. 2007). Unwanted pregnancies can also often lead to an increased financial burden that arises with the care of a child or multiple children. Sometimes a woman is unable to bear this burden on her own—particularly in light of the ongoing pay gap between men and women and high unemployment rates that women experience in many countries (Blau and Kahn 2003, 2007; Azmat et al. 2006). This burden can then lead to a dependence on others, particularly men, for financial support. This dependence can also create contingent vulnerability to interpersonal abuse—financial, emotional, or physical in nature (Brandwein 1999; Kaukinen 2004; Conner 2013).

5.4.1.3 Forced Sterilisation and Contingent Vulnerability

The denial of legal capacity to choose whether to undergo sterilisation can also lead to contingent vulnerability in multiple ways. One of the most profound ways may be the loss of bodily integrity that a woman may experience when they are sterilised without their consent. This can have a significant effect on self-esteem and psycho-social perceptions of oneself (Rosenbaum and Epstein 2019). In addition, sexual abuse of disabled women and girls often occurs within the home (McFarlane et al. 2001; Mays 2006). It is also often family members that are given either formal or informal power to decide whether a disabled woman or girl will undergo sterilisation (Rosenbaum and Epstein 2019). As such, it could be an abuser who is granted the individual's legal capacity to decide to undergo sterilisation. The disabled woman or girl could then be vulnerable to new or increased sexual abuse perpetrated by the family member or others within the home with the knowledge that there will be no reproductive consequences of the sexual abuse. There are likely many other vulnerabilities created by denials of legal capacity to make sterilisation decisions. More research is needed in this area in order to fully understand all the manners in which vulnerability may be created by forced sterilisation and how to prevent and address them.

Sterilisation requirements as a prerequisite to gender recognition creates contingent vulnerability in multiple ways. First, as discussed above, the removal of legal capacity—and autonomy—for choices that are as personal and intimate as reproduction can be profoundly disempowering. In the face of the state dictating that you must undergo sterilisation in order for it to recognise the gender that you identify with, an individual can be left with a feeling of loss of control of their own body which can, in turn, have a profound effect on their self-esteem and psycho-social perception of themselves (Ramos 2011; Carastathis 2015; Winter et al. 2016). Additionally, because it is a prerequisite to gender recognition, contingent vulnerability is created in individuals who are desperate to have their gender accurately reflected in legal documents. They may be desperate for their legal documents to match their identity. They also may be desperate to protect themselves from questions arising from individuals that may cause them harm, such as those that may perpetrate hate crimes against gender minorities. As such, these individuals may also be vulnerable to doctors who are looking to make money off such procedures but may not have the best skills or the overall well-being of the individual in the forefront of their minds. This could lead to both financial abuse and bodily harm.

5.4.1.4 Conclusion

There are likely many other forms of vulnerability that are created by the denial of legal capacity to women, disabled women, and gender minorities in the context of reproductive and sexual choices. More research in this area is needed to fully understand how and where this vulnerability is being created. Such research could inform the development of law, policy, and practice that better protects the right to legal capacity to make reproductive and sexual choices and better accounts for the contingent vulnerability that is created when the right is not respected—it may even be able to eliminate such vulnerability.

5.4.2 Creating Vulnerability in Women, Disabled Women, and Gender Minorities Under Guardianship with Limited Decision-Making Control Over Their Own Lives

The loss of legal capacity under guardianship or other forms of substituted decision-making is often accompanied by loss of financial control—the substituted decision-maker can be given control over financial decisions for the individual. Loss of financial control can create contingent vulnerability because the individual loses the power and resources that accompany financial control. There is significant evidence that financial abuse under guardianship is common and often accompanied by few safeguards or avenues for recourse for the individual experiencing abuse (Wilber and Reynolds 1996; Coker and Little 1997; Bond et al. 2000; Dessin 2002). There is also evidence that women experience such financial abuse at higher rates than men (Bond et al. 2000).

Gender minorities also experience unique forms of marginalisation under guardianship regimes and are affected by contingent vulnerability created by various forms of guardianship (Holman and Goldberg 2006; Knauer 2014). More research is needed in this area however some conclusions can be drawn based on existing scholarship. Much of the difficulties faced by gender minorities, such as transgender people, under guardianship regimes are related to ongoing prejudice and lack of legal protection. There are significant gaps in non-discrimination law in some jurisdictions because it often primarily focuses on employment and education, leaving areas such as guardianship services without equality protections (Knauer 2014). In addition, there is evidence that transgender people under guardianship and in long-term care facilities are subjected to disrespect for their gender identity. Because many transgender people choose not to have ‘bottom’ surgery, they may not have genitals that conform to preconceived notions of their gender expression. As such, in long-term care facilities they are often forced to wear clothes that are gender inappropriate, they are called by incorrect names, and forced to co-habit with individuals of the opposite sex (Knauer 2014; Barrington 2015).

Gender identity is a prominent and integral aspect of an individual's personhood (Butler 2004; Spade 2015). When an individual is placed under guardianship and denied the legal capacity to choose that gender identity, it undermines that individual's personhood and may have a lasting impact on the individual's self-esteem and self-worth (Anderson and Honneth 2005; Knauer 2014). This is a form of contingent vulnerability. In addition, such denial of an individual's legal capacity to choose their gender identity creates contingent vulnerability when the individual is inappropriately forced to perform in a gender that they do not identify with. This creates vulnerability because the individual may be placed in a situation in which they are targeted for abuse due to prejudice—for example, a transgender woman (male to female) who is forced to perform as a male and to co-habit with males may be targeted for abuse. Potentially most critically, gender minorities who are denied legal capacity under guardianship and are not permitted to exercise their legal capacity to express their gender identity are forced to deny a fundamental aspect of their personality and are therefore vulnerable to all psycho-social implications of anyone who is not fully recognised as the individual who they identify as, which is true for all law and policy that has such an effect.

5.4.3 *Creating Vulnerability Through Forced Psychiatric Treatment of Women, Disabled Women, and Gender Minorities*

Forced psychiatric treatment of women has a long history tied to the concept of women as 'hysterical' and suffering from madness. While psychiatry has been deeply criticised by some of the leading scholars of our time (Erving Goffman, Michel Foucault, and others), most scholars overlooked the role that gender played in psychiatry until second-wave feminists identified it in the 1970s (Sedgwick 1982; Foucault and Howard 2001; Hubert 2002; Goffman 2017). For example, Phyllis Chesler's book *Women and Madness* and Elaine Showalter's book *The Female Malady* identified these gendered practices within psychiatry and, indeed, the gendered nature of the concept of 'madness' itself (Chesler 1974; Showalter 1987; Hubert 2002). While psychiatry has evolved significantly, woman continue to experience both internalised oppression from these early emanations of psychiatry as well as systemic and socially imposed oppression (Hubert 2002).

Rates of psychiatric disorder are virtually the same for men and women, however there are significant differences in how women are diagnosed and treated (Kessler et al. 1994). Women remain the majority of psychiatric patients (Katherine Hodges 2003). Women are more likely to be treated with psychotropic drugs and are more likely to be diagnosed with depression and anxiety (Linzer et al. 1996; Piccinelli and Gomez Homen 1997; Simoni-Wastila 2000). Stereotypically female traits are also more likely to be regarded as indications of mental health issues. For example, expression of emotions, deference to others, lack of assertiveness, and others (Russell 1987). In this way, women who are performing in accordance with gender stereotypes are at risk of being diagnosed as mentally unwell. However, women who are performing outside their gender role may also be at risk of being diagnosed as mentally unwell because they are straying from societal expectations for females (Russell 1985). As women are more likely to be involved in the psychiatric treatment systems, it follows that they are at risk for being denied legal capacity within these systems and forcibly treated or detained. A recent study has noted how little research exists in this area and how much more need to be done to accurately understand the needs of women in psychiatric care (Archer et al. 2016).

The contingent vulnerability that this produced from these gendered perspectives and practices in psychiatry is pervasive. Within the psychiatric system, there is evidence that women are vulnerable to sexual and physical abuse due to systems that are ill-suited to the needs of women (Archer et al. 2016; Mental Health Complaints Commissioner 2018). More generally, the on-going notion that women are overemotional and prone to irrationality—including extremes of panic and anxiety—undermines women as decision-makers and leaders. It may contribute to the ever-persistent pay gap between men and woman as well as the lack of women in political leadership roles which remains in most countries. Employment, financial resources, and political leadership are all areas of significant social capital that women are currently missing out on. While it is not only the psychiatric systems that may be creating and contributing to this problem, the gendered aspects of the psychiatric system—including the ever-present reality that the labelling of a psychiatric diagnosis could result in the removal of legal capacity and an experience of forced detention or treatment—are likely contributing to these negative social phenomena that women are experiencing.

5.4.4 Creating Vulnerability in Gender Minorities Through the Exclusionary Effect of Gender Binary Requirements

Some gender minorities are experiencing particular contingent vulnerabilities created by gender binary requirements (*Goodwin v. UK* 1996; Romeo 2004). While the elimination of gender binary requirements may not be enough to achieve equality for gender minorities, as discussed above, it is important to identify the vulnerabilities that are being created by such requirements in order to fully and adequately create solutions that can address these vulnerabilities. First and foremost, the denial of the legal capacity to decide on one's own gender often goes to the core of an individual's identity and self-esteem (Butler 2004; Anderson and Honneth 2005; Spade 2015). This alone can lead to significant psychological issues of disempowerment and marginalisation that create vulnerability to a range of harms—including abuse, poverty, poor health, and others (*Goodwin v. UK* 1996; Romeo 2004).

Barriers to legal documentation and identification due to gender binary requirements can lead to an individual not possessing the appropriate legal documentation and identification, which significantly hinders the individual's ability to exercise their legal capacity. This can result in the person having limited or no access to government services or benefits, which require that the individual provide legal identification (Romeo 2004). This can lead to a lack of financial resources and a consequential dependence on others. Similar to women placed in situations of financial dependence, this can lead to vulnerability to interpersonal abuse—including emotional, physical, and sexual abuse. Not having legal identification can also lead to limited access to police, courts, lawyers and justice—where identification is often a prerequisite for engagement (Romeo 2004). This can lead to a limited ability for the individual to enforce their rights—including a limited ability to seek justice or intervention when the individual is experiencing abuse. This leaves the individual vulnerable to abuse and without recourse when it occurs. There are likely a multitude of other ways in which gender binary requirements are resulting in barriers to legal capacity that create vulnerability for gender minorities. More research is needed in this area to precisely identify these barriers and create solutions accordingly.

5.5 Conclusion

Women, disabled women, and gender minorities are often inaccurately perceived as inherently vulnerable due to long histories of prejudice and marginalisation. While some women, disabled women, and gender minorities do experience some forms of inherent vulnerability due to biological factors such as physical strength or chronic pain, most of the vulnerability that they experience is contingent on social phenomena. The perception that women, disabled women, and gender minorities are inherently vulnerable can perpetuate the discrimination that these groups face by supporting the instigation of law, policy, and practice that denies autonomy to these groups either under the guise of protection or simply due to historical stigma or notions regarding the inability of these groups to possess sufficient decision-making skills.

Women, disabled women, and gender minorities face barriers to legal capacity, in part, due to their perceived inherent vulnerability. These unique legal capacity barriers that women, disabled women, and gender minorities experience further create contingent vulnerability in various ways discussed above. Law, policy, and practice has not sufficiently examined or accounted for these issues. In order to achieve equal recognition before the law for these groups, it will require more than a neo-liberal removal of barriers to legal capacity and abandonment of these individuals. Instead, it will require a reassessment of where vulnerability has been created by these legal capacity denials and what forms of support are necessary for the meaningful return of that autonomy and the successful exercise of legal capacity for members of these groups. This, in turn, will likely reduce vulnerability in these groups—at least the vulnerabilities that were contingent on the denials of autonomy that they faced.

References

Acierno, Ron, Melba A. Hernandez, Ananda B. Amstadter, Heidi S. Resnick, Kenneth Steve, Wendy Muzzy, and Dean G. Kilpatrick. 2010. Prevalence and Correlates of Emotional, Physical, Sexual, and Financial Abuse and Potential Neglect in the United States: The National Elder Mistreatment Study. *American Journal of Public Health* 100: 292–297. https://doi.org/10.2105/AJPH.2009.163089.

Anderson, Joel. 2013. Autonomy and Vulnerability Entwined. In *Vulnerability: New Essays in Ethics and Feminist Philosophy*, ed. Catriona Mackenzie, Wendy Rogers, and Susan Dodds, 134–161. Oxford University Press.

Anderson, Joel, and Axel Honneth. 2005. Autonomy, Vulnerability, Recognition, and Justice. In *In Autonomy and the Challenges to Liberalism: New Essays*, ed. John Christman and Joel Anderson. Cambridge University Press.

Anderson, Michelle J. 2002. From Chastity Requirement to Sexuality License: Sexual Consent and a New Rape Shield Law. *George Washington Law Review* 70: 51–162.

———. 2010. Sex Education and Rape Symposium: Rhetoric & Relevance: An Investigation into the Present and Future of Feminist Legal Theory. *Michigan Journal of Gender & Law* 17: 83–110.

Archer, Michaela, Yasmine Lau, and Faisil Sethi. 2016. Women in Acute Psychiatric Units, Their Characteristics and Needs: A Review. *BJPsych Bulletin* 40: 266–272. https://doi.org/10.1192/pb.bp.115.051573.

Arstein-Kerslake, Anna. 2015. Understanding Sex: The Right to Legal Capacity to Consent to Sex. *Disability & Society* 30: 1459–1473. https://doi.org/10.1080/09687599.2015.1116059.

———. 2019. Gendered Denials: Vulnerability Created by Barriers to Legal Capacity for Women and Disabled Women. *International Journal of Law and Psychiatry* 66: 101501. https://doi.org/10.1016/j.ijlp.2019.101501.

Arstein-Kerslake, Anna, and Eilionóir Flynn. 2016. Legislating Consent: Creating an Empowering Definition of Consent to Sex That Is Inclusive of People with Cognitive Disabilities. *Social & Legal Studies* 25: 225–248. https://doi.org/10.1177/0964663915599051.

Arstein-Kerslake, Anna, Piers Gooding, Louis Andrews, and Bernadette McSherry. 2017. Human Rights and Unfitness to Plead: The Demands of the Convention on the Rights of Persons with Disabilities. *Human Rights Law Review* 17: 399–419. https://doi.org/10.1093/hrlr/ngx025.

Azmat, Ghazala, Maia Güell, and Alan Manning. 2006. Gender Gaps in Unemployment Rates in OECD Countries. *Journal of Labor Economics* 24: 1. https://doi.org/10.1086/497817.

Barrington, Vanessa. 2015. *LGBT Older Adults in Long-Term Care Facilities: Stories from the Field*. Justice in Ageing.

Blau, Francine D., and Lawrence M. Kahn. 2003. Understanding International Differences in the Gender Pay Gap. *Journal of Labor Economics* 21: 106. https://doi.org/10.1086/344125.

———. 2007. The Gender Pay Gap: Have Women Gone as Far as They Can? *Academy of Management Perspectives* 21: 7.

Bond, John B., Rosemarie Cuddy, Gloria L. Dixon, Karen A. Duncan, and Doreen L. Smith. 2000. The Financial Abuse of Mentally Incompetent Older Adults: A Canadian Study. *Journal of Elder Abuse & Neglect* 11: 23–38. 21877983. https://doi.org/10.1300/J084v11n04_03.

Boyle, Mary. 2003. The Dangers of Vulnerability. *Clinical Psychology*: 27–30.

Brandwein, Ruth A. 1999. *Battered Women, Children, and Welfare Reform: The Ties That Bind*. Sage Series on Violence against Women: V. 11. Sage Publications.

Butler, Judith. 2004. *Undoing Gender*. Routledge. https://doi.org/10.4324/9780203499627.
———. 2016. Rethinking Vulnerability and Resistance. In *Vulnerability in Resistance*, ed. Judith Butler, Zeynep Gambetti, and Leticia Sabsay, 12–27. Duke University Press. https://doi.org/10.1215/9780822373490-002.
Butler, Judith, Zeynep Gambetti, and Leticia Sabsay. 2016. *Vulnerability in Resistance*. Duke University Press.
Byrnes, James P. 2013. *The Nature and Development of Decision-making: A Self-regulation Model*. Psychology Press. https://doi.org/10.4324/9780203726495.
Carastathis, Anna. 2015. Compulsory Sterilisation of Transgender People as Gendered Violence. In *(In)Fertile Citizens: Anthropological and Legal Challenges of Assisted Reproduction Technologies*, ed. Venetia Kantsa, Giulia Zanini, and Lina Papadopoulou. (In)FERCIT.
Chamberland, Line, and Elizabeth Saewyc. 2011. Stigma, Vulnerability, and Resilience: The Psychosocial Health of Sexual Minority and Gender Diverse People in Canada. *Canadian Journal of Community Mental Health* 30: 1–5. https://doi.org/10.7870/cjcmh-2011-0012.
Chesler, Phyllis. 1974. *Women and Madness*. Allen Lane.
Cheu, Maggie. 2012. Now and Then: How Coverture Ideology Informs the Rhetoric of Abortion. *Texas Journal of Women and the Law* 22: 113–130.
Coker, Johnny, and Bobby Little. 1997. Investing in the Future: Protecting the Elderly from Financial Abuse. *FBI Law Enforcement Bulletin* 1.
Conner, Dana Harrington. 2013. Financial Freedom: Women, Money, and Domestic Abuse. *William & Mary Journal of Women and the Law* 20: 339–398.
Cuskelly, Monica, and Rachel Bryde. 2004. Attitudes Towards the Sexuality of Adults with an Intellectual Disability: Parents, Support Staff, and a Community Sample. *Journal of Intellectual & Developmental Disability* 29: 255–264. https://doi.org/10.1080/13668250412331285136.
Dessin, Carolyn L. 2002. Financial Abuse of the Elderly: Is the Solution a Problem. *McGeorge Law Review* 34: 267–322.
Dukes, E., and B.E. McGuire. 2009. Enhancing Capacity to Make Sexuality-Related Decisions in People with an Intellectual Disability. *Journal of Intellectual Disability Research* 53: 727–734. https://doi.org/10.1111/j.1365-2788.2009.01186.x.
Dunn, Jennifer L. 2010. *Judging Victims: Why We Stigmatize Survivors, and How They Reclaim Respect*. Boulder, CO: Lynne Rienner Publishers.
Eastgate, Gillian, Mieke L. van Driel, Nicholas Lennox, and Elly Scheermeyer. 2011. Women with Intellectual Disabilities: A Study of Sexuality, Sexual Abuse and Protection Skills. *Australian Family Physician* 40: 226.
Esmail, Shaniff, Kim Darry, Ashlea Walter, and Heidi Knupp. 2010. Attitudes and Perceptions Towards Disability and Sexuality. *Disability and Rehabilitation* 32: 1148–1155. https://doi.org/10.3109/09638280903419277.
Fineman, Martha. 2004. *The Autonomy Myth: A Theory of Dependency*. New Press.
Fineman, Martha Albertson. 2008. The Vulnerable Subject: Anchoring Equality in the Human Condition. *Yale Journal of Law and Feminism* 20: 1–23.
Fineman, Martha, and Anna Grear. 2013. *Vulnerability: Reflections on a New Ethical Foundation for Law and Politics. Gender in Law, Culture, and Society*. Ashgate.
Finer, Louise, and Johanna B. Fine. 2013. Abortion Law Around the World: Progress and Pushback. *American Journal of Public Health* 103: 585–589. https://doi.org/10.2105/AJPH.2012.301197.
Foucault, Michel, and Richard Howard. 2001. *Madness and Civilization: A History of Insanity in the Age of Reason. Routledge Classics*. Routledge.
Gill, Carol J. 2006. Disability, Constructed Vulnerability, and Socially Conscious Palliative Care. *Journal of Palliative Care* 22: 183–189. https://doi.org/10.1177/082585970602200309.
Goffman, Erving. 2017. *Asylums: Essays on the Social Situation of Mental Patients and Other Inmates*. Routledge. https://doi.org/10.4324/9781351327763.
Goodwin, M.M., J.A. Gazmararian, C.H. Johnson, B.C. Gilbert, and L.E. Saltzman. 2000. Pregnancy Intendedness and Physical Abuse Around the Time of Pregnancy: Findings from the

Pregnancy Risk Assessment Monitoring System, 1996-1997. *Maternal & Child Health Journal* 4: 85–92.

Goodwin v. UK. 1996. European Court of Human Rights.

Hasday, Jill Elaine. 2000. Contest and Consent: A Legal History of Marital Rape. *California Law Review* 88: 1373–1506.

Hodges, Katherine. 2003. The Invisible Crisis: Women and Psychiatric Oppression. *Off Our Backs* 33: 12.

Hollander, Jocelyn A. 2002. Resisting Vulnerability: The Social Reconstruction of Gender in Interaction. *Social Problems* 49: 474–496. https://doi.org/10.1525/sp.2002.49.4.474.

Holman, Catherine White, and Joshua M. Goldberg. 2006. Social and Medical Transgender Case Advocacy. *International Journal of Transgenderism* 9: 197–217. https://doi.org/10.1300/J485v09n03_09.

Hubert, Susan J. 2002. *Questions of Power: The Politics of Women's Madness Narratives*. University of Delaware Press.

Juhasz, Anne McCreary. 1975. A Chain of Sexual Decision-Making. *The Family Coordinator* 24: 43–49. JSTOR. https://doi.org/10.2307/583049.

Kaukinen, Catherine. 2004. Status Compatibility, Physical Violence, and Emotional Abuse in Intimate Relationships. *Journal of Marriage and Family* 66: 452–471. https://doi.org/10.1111/j.1741-3737.2004.00031.x.

Kelly, Brendan D. 2014. Dignity, Human Rights and the Limits of Mental Health Legislation. *Irish Journal of Psychological Medicine* 31: 75–81. https://doi.org/10.1017/ipm.2014.22.

Kessler, Ronald C., Katherine A. McGonagle, Shanyang Zhao, Christopher B. Nelson, Michael Hughes, Suzann Eshleman, Hans-Ulrich Wittchen, and Kenneth S. Kendler. 1994. Lifetime and 12-Month Prevalence of DSM-III-R Psychiatric Disorders in the United States: Results from the National Comorbidity Survey. *Archives of General Psychiatry* 51: 8–19. https://doi.org/10.1001/archpsyc.1994.03950010008002.

Kleinman, Sherryl, Martha Copp, and Kent Sandstrom. 2006. Making Sexism Visible: Birdcages, Martians, and Pregnant Men. *Teaching Sociology* 34: 126–142. https://doi.org/10.1177/0092055X0603400203.

Knauer, Nancy J. 2014. LGBT Issues and Adult Guardianship: A Comparative Perspective. In *Comparative Perspectives on Adult Guardianship*, ed. A. Kimberley Dayton. Carolina Academic Press.

Kumar, Anuradha, Leila Hessini, and Ellen M.H. Mitchell. 2009. Conceptualising Abortion Stigma. *Culture, Health & Sexuality* 11: 625–639. https://doi.org/10.1080/13691050902842741.

Lajoie, Amie. 2018. *Challenging Assumptions of Vulnerability: The Significance of Gender in the Work, Lives and Identities of Women Human Rights Defenders*. National University of Ireland Galway.

Lennon, Theresa L., Sharron J. Lennon, and Kim K.P. Johnson. 1992. Is Clothing Probative of Attitude or Intent - Implications for Rape and Sexual Harassment Cases. *Law and Inequality: A Journal of Theory and Practice* 11: 391–416.

Levine, Carol, Ruth Faden, Christine Grady, Dale Hammerschmidt, Lisa Eckenwiler, and Jeremy Sugarman. 2004. The Limitations of "Vulnerability" as a Protection for Human Research Participants. *The American Journal of Bioethics: AJOB* 4: 44–49. 16192138.

Levine, Phillip B., Amy B. Trainor, and David J. Zimmerman. 1996. The Effect of Medicaid Abortion Funding Restrictions on Abortions, Pregnancies and Births. *Journal of Health Economics* 15: 555–578. https://doi.org/10.1016/S0167-6296(96)00495-X.

Linzer, Mark, Robert Spitzer, Kurt Kroenke, Janet B. Williams, Steven Hahn, David Brody, and Frank de Gruy. 1996. Gender, Quality of Life, and Mental Disorders in Primary Care: Results from the PRIME-MD 1000 Study. *The American Journal of Medicine* 101: 526–533. https://doi.org/10.1016/S0002-9343(96)00275-6.

Luna, Florencia. 2009. Elucidating the Concept of Vulnerability: Layers Not Labels. *International Journal of Feminist Approaches to Bioethics* 2: 121–139. JSTOR.

Matambanadzo, Saru M. 2012. Embodying Vulnerability: A Feminist Theory of the Person. *Duke Journal of Gender Law & Policy* 20: 39.

Mays, Jennifer M. 2006. Feminist Disability Theory: Domestic Violence Against Women with a Disability. *Disability & Society* 21: 147–158. https://doi.org/10.1080/09687590500498077.

McCarthy, Michelle, and David Thompson. 1997. A Prevalence Study of Sexual Abuse of Adults with Intellectual Disabilities Referred for Sex Education. *Journal of Applied Research in Intellectual Disabilities* 10: 105–124. https://doi.org/10.1111/j.1468-3148.1997.tb00012.x.

McFarlane, Judith, Rosemary B. Hughes, Maraget A. Nosek, Janet Y. Groff, Nancy Swedlend, and Patricia Dolan Mullen. 2001. Abuse Assessment Screen-Disability (AAS-D): Measuring Frequency, Type, and Perpetrator of Abuse Toward Women with Physical Disabilities. *Journal of Women's Health & Gender-Based Medicine* 10: 861–866. https://doi.org/10.1089/152460901753285750.

Mental Health Complaints Commissioner. 2018. *The Right to be Safe: Ensuring Sexual Safety in Acute Mental Health Inpatient Units*. Victorian Government.

Nosek, Margaret A., Catherine Clubb Foley, Rosemary B. Hughes, and Carol A. Howland. 2001. Vulnerabilities for Abuse Among Women with Disabilities. *Sexuality & Disability* 19: 177–189.

Pallitto, Christina C., Jacquelyn C. Campbell, and Patricia O'Campo. 2005. Is Intimate Partner Violence Associated with Unintended Pregnancy? A Review of the Literature. *Trauma, Violence, & Abuse* 6: 217–235. https://doi.org/10.1177/1524838005277441.

Petchesky, Rosalind P. 1990. *Abortion and Woman's Choice: The State, Sexuality, and Reproductive Freedom*. Rev. ed. Northeastern Series in Feminist Theory. Northeastern University Press.

Piccinelli, M., and F. Gomez Homen. 1997. *Gender Differences in the Epidemiology of Affective Disorders and Schizophrenia*. World Health Organisation.

Pritchard-Jones, Laura. 2018. "Adults at Risk": "Vulnerability" by Any Other Name? *The Journal of Adult Protection; Brighton* 20: 47–58.

Ramos, Marta: Pallos de Azevedo Pascoal. 2011. Transgender persons and family life: the issues of sterilisation and loss of child custody rights. Thesis.

Rogers, Wendy, and Margaret Meek Lange. 2013. Rethinking the Vulnerability of Minority Populations in Research. *American Journal of Public Health* 103: 2141–2146. https://doi.org/10.2105/AJPH.2012.301200.

Romeo, Franklin H. 2004. Beyond a Medical Model: Advocating for a New Conception of Gender Identity in the Law Note. *Columbia Human Rights Law Review* 36: 713–754.

Rosenbaum, Stephen A., and Julia Epstein. 2019. Revisiting Ashley X: An Essay on Disabled Bodily Integrity, Sexuality, Dignity, and Family Caregiving. *Touro Law Review* 35: 101–138.

Russell, Denise. 1985. Psychiatric Diagnosis and the Oppression of Women. *International Journal of Social Psychiatry* 31: 298–305. https://doi.org/10.1177/002076408503100408.

———. 1987. Psychiatric Diagnosis and the Oppression of Women. *Women & Therapy* 5: 83–98. https://doi.org/10.1300/J015V05N04_09.

Russell, Diana E.H. 1990. *Rape in Marriage. Expanded and rev. ed., with a new introd.* Indiana University Press.

Ryan, Richard M., and Edward L. Deci. 2017. *Self-Determination Theory: Basic Psychological Needs in Motivation, Development, and Wellness*. Guilford Publications.

Schmiege, Sarah, and Nancy Felipe Russo. 2005. Depression and Unwanted First Pregnancy: Longitudinal Cohort Study. *BMJ* 331: 1303. https://doi.org/10.1136/bmj.38623.532384.55.

Schulhofer, Stephen J. 1992. Taking Sexual Autonomy Seriously: Rape Law and Beyond. *Law and Philosophy* 11: 35–94. JSTOR. https://doi.org/10.2307/3504904.

Scully, Jackie Leach. 2013. Disability and Vulnerability: On Bodies, Dependence, and Power. In *Vulnerability: New Essays in Ethics and Feminist Philosophy*, ed. Catriona Mackenzie, Wendy Rogers, and Susan Dodds, 204–221. Oxford University Press.

Sedgwick, Peter R. 1982. *Psycho Politics: Laing, Foucault, Goffman, Szasz, and the Future of Mass Psychiatry*. 1st Harper & Row ed. Harper & Row.

Shah, Iqbal H., Elisabeth Åhman, and Nuriye Ortayli. 2014. Access to Safe Abortion: Progress and Challenges Since the 1994 International Conference on Population and Development (ICPD). *Contraception* 90: S39–S48. https://doi.org/10.1016/j.contraception.2014.04.004.

Shalev, Carmel. 2000. Rights to Sexual and Reproductive Health: The ICPD and the Convention on the Elimination of All Forms of Discrimination Against Women. *Health and Human Rights* 4: 38–66. JSTOR. https://doi.org/10.2307/4065196.

Showalter, Elaine. 1987. *The Female Malady: Women, Madness and English Culture 1830-1980*. Virago.

Siegel, Reva B. 2007. Dignity and the Politics of Protection: Abortion Restrictions under Casey/Carhart Feature. *Yale Law Journal* 117: 1694–1801.

Silverman, J.G., J. Gupta, M.R. Decker, N. Kapur, and A. Raj. 2007. Intimate Partner Violence and Unwanted Pregnancy, Miscarriage, Induced Abortion, and Stillbirth Among a National Sample of Bangladeshi Women. *BJOG: An International Journal of Obstetrics & Gynaecology* 114: 1246–1252. https://doi.org/10.1111/j.1471-0528.2007.01481.x.

Simoni-Wastila, Linda. 2000. The Use of Abusable Prescription Drugs: The Role of Gender. *Journal of Women's Health & Gender-Based Medicine* 9: 289–297.

Sloane, R. Bruce. 1969. The Unwanted Pregnancy. *New England Journal of Medicine* 280: 1206–1213. https://doi.org/10.1056/NEJM196905292802205.

Sobsey, Dick, and Tanis Doe. 1991. Patterns of Sexual Abuse and Assault. *Sexuality and Disability* 9: 243–259. https://doi.org/10.1007/BF01102395.

Spade, Dean. 2015. *Normal Life: Administrative Violence, Critical Trans Politics, and the Limits of Law*. Duke University Press.

Steinem, Gloria. 1978. If Men Could Menstruate. *Ms. Magazine*, October.

Sterling, Alinor C. 1995. Undressing the Victim: The Intersection of Evidentiary and Semiotic Meanings of Women's Clothing in Rape Trials. *Yale Journal of Law and Feminism* 7: 87–132.

Tepper, Mitchell S. 2000. Sexuality and Disability: The Missing Discourse of Pleasure. *Sexuality and Disability* 18: 283–290. https://doi.org/10.1023/A:1005698311392.

Waxman, Barbara Faye. 1994. Up Against Eugenics: Disabled Women's Challenge to Receive Reproductive Health Services. *Sexuality and Disability* 12: 155–171. https://doi.org/10.1007/BF02547889.

Wilber, Kathleen H., and Sandra L. Reynolds. 1996. Introducing a Framework for Defining Financial Abuse of the Elderly. *Journal of Elder Abuse & Neglect; London* 8: 61–80.

Winick, Bruce J. 1995. The Side Effects of Incompetency Labeling and the Implications for Mental Health Law. *Psychology, Public Policy, and Law* 1: 6–42. https://doi.org/10.1037/1076-8971.1.1.6.

Winter, Sam, Milton Diamond, Jamison Green, Dan Karasic, Terry Reed, Stephen Whittle, and Kevan Wylie. 2016. Transgender People: Health at the Margins of Society. *The Lancet* 388: 390–400. https://doi.org/10.1016/S0140-6736(16)00683-8.

Zampas, Christina, and Jaime M. Gher. 2008. Abortion as a Human Right—International and Regional Standards. *Human Rights Law Review* 8: 249–294. https://doi.org/10.1093/hrlr/ngn008.

Chapter 6
Creating Change: Examples of Modern Reform and Recommendations

6.1 Introduction

This final chapter will use case studies to highlight reform processes around the world that can be drawn on to learn how to better protect the right to legal capacity of women, disabled women, and gender minorities. It will discuss the abolition of guardianship in Peru in 2018; the reform of capacity to consent to sex laws in Ireland in 2017; and Malta's 2015 *Gender Identity, Gender Expression and Sex Characteristics Act*. To conclude, it will present reform recommendations. These recommendations include a four-part process for bringing law, policy and practice into compliance with the right to legal capacity on an equal basis for women, disabled women, and gender minorities.

6.2 Case Studies: Examples to Learn From

In Chap. 4, I identified modern and historical denials of the right to legal capacity on the basis of gender—specifically looking at how women, disabled women, and gender minorities have been affected by these denials. The historical denials that I identified included: denials of the right to legal capacity of married women; denials of the right to legal capacity of women to vote and enter into contracts; denials of the right to legal capacity via the institutionalisation of disabled women; denials of the right to legal capacity for reproductive choice of disabled women precipitated by the eugenics movement; the denial of the right to legal capacity to consent to medical treatment of gender minorities; as well as the denial of the right to legal capacity to sexual choice and gender expression via the criminalisation of various aspects of the lives of gender minorities. Not all of these denials of the right to legal capacity have been rectified—many of them persist today. However, there have been successful reform efforts in some areas and, in Chaps. 3 and 4, I identified some reforms that

A. Arstein-Kerslake, *Legal Capacity & Gender*,
https://doi.org/10.1007/978-3-030-63493-3_6

have occurred that have reduced or virtually eliminated these legal capacity denials—such as, reforms to coverture laws that have ensured that married women have their right to legal capacity protected in many countries around the world.

In this chapter, I'm examining examples of reform efforts for ameliorating modern denials of the right to legal capacity. I've chosen to focus on reform efforts of modern denials of the right to legal capacity, as opposed to historical denials of the right to legal capacity, because I believe successful modern reform efforts may be more relevant to the contemporary situation and may provide greater guidance for ongoing and future reform efforts aimed at securing the right to legal capacity for women, disabled women, and gender minorities. The modern denials of the right to legal capacity that I identified in Chap. 4, include: denials of the right to legal capacity of women in modern immigration law, inheritance rights, contracting, reproductive choice, and consent to sex; denials of the right to legal capacity of disabled women under guardianship, subjected to forced sterilisation, and restricted from consenting to sex; and denials of the right to legal capacity of gender minorities under restrictive gender recognition laws, or in jurisdictions where there is no means to have the gender they identify with be accurately represented on legal documents. This is by no means an exhaustive list of the many ways in which women, disabled women, and gender minorities have their right to legal capacity denied in the modern world. It is only a snapshot, intended to shed light on the right to legal capacity of these groups and to begin a conversation about the many ways in which it is denied and how this can be rectified. In the following section, I will examine a selection of reform efforts in relation to a few of these denials of legal capacity in an effort to provide examples of how the right to legal capacity can be protected for these groups.

6.2.1 Peru: Guardianship Abolished

In 2018, legislation was enacted in Peru that goes farther to implement Article 12 of the CRPD than any previous legislation. The Peruvian legislation is notable because: there is no restriction of legal capacity on the basis of disability; the guarantee of the right to legal capacity extends across the entire Civil Code, not merely guardianship laws or any other specific area; it outlines a flexible model of support for the exercise of legal capacity; and the will and preference of the individual is the guiding paradigm (Glen 2019, pp. 37–38; Martinez-Pujalte 2019, pp. 16–17). While this new Peruvian legislation pertains to all people and is not gender specific, it is particularly important for women, disabled women, and gender minorities because of the many violations of the right to legal capacity that they experience, as is described in Chap. 4.

This 2018 legislation was preceded by the *General Act on Persons with Disabilities*, which was enacted on 13 December 2012. That Act stated, "persons with disabilities have legal capacity in all aspects of life on an equal basis with others. The Civil Code regulates the support systems and reasonable accommodations that they require for decision-making." However, at that time, the Civil Code had not yet been reformed to include these principles. The Act established a Special Committee, made up of representatives of disabled people's organisations (DPOS) and others, to develop draft legislation for the inclusion of these principles into the Civil Code. The draft was presented to the parliament in 2015, which led to the reform that was enacted in 2018 (Martinez-Pujalte 2019, pp. 15–16; Caycho 2020, pp. 158–159).

In line with Article 12 of the CRPD, Article 42 of the reformed Civil Code specifically states that all disabled people have full capacity to exercise their rights on an equal basis with others and in all aspects of life. This reaffirmed the statement in the 2012 *General Act on Persons with Disabilities*, which made it clear that disabled people have an equal right to both legal personhood and legal agency—they have an equal right to be holders of rights as well as actors before the law. In the new Civil Code, according to Article 44.9, the law can only restrict the legal capacity of people in a coma who did not previously designated a support mechanism (Glen 2019, p. 78; Martinez-Pujalte 2019, p. 16).

This reform of the Civil Code in Peru appears to nearly completely abolish guardianship (Glen 2019, p. 37). This is important for women, disabled women, and gender minorities, in particular, because of the unique and strong impact of guardianship laws on these groups. As discussed in Sect. 4.3.3. in Chap. 4, there is evidence that women and disabled women are disproportionately placed under guardianship (Tavris 1993; Rosenberg 2009; Prokhovnik 2012; Victoria Office of the Public Advocate 2017). There is also evidence that there are issues that are unique to women, disabled women, and gender minorities that are frequently not appropriately dealt with under guardianship laws. For example, issues of reproductive choice, sexual expression, and sexual identity, as also described in Sect. 4.3.3 (Wingfield et al. 1994; Grover 2002; Atkinson et al. 2003; Lin et al. 2011). Legislation such as the new Civil Code in Peru, which appears to abolish guardianship, has the potential to significantly ameliorate these problems and many of the other denials discussed in Chap. 4. Although the reform maintains narrow circumstances in which guardianship may remain—which may be inconsistent with the demands of Article 12—the reform in Peru can be drawn on as a good example of law reform that significantly improves the realisation of the right to equal recognition before the law of all people (Caycho 2020). It may particularly benefit women, disabled women, and gender minorities because of the rate and severity of denials of the right that they are currently facing.

Another significant aspect of the Peruvian reforms is the degree to which civil society—and disabled people and their representative organisations, in particular—were involved with the development of both the *General Act on Persons with Disabilities* and the reform of the Civil Code. There was consultation with and leadership from disabled people and their representative organisations for over a decade while the laws were being drafted and going through the parliament (Glen 2019, pp. 37, 76–77). It is likely that it was this robust involvement of disabled people and their representative groups that led to the strength and effectiveness of the reform. It is the first reform of legal capacity laws in the world to go as far as they have in protecting the right to legal capacity (Glen 2019, p. 37).

6.2.2 Ireland: Capacity to Consent to Sex[1]

The previous sexual offenses law in Ireland provides an example of a modern status-based denial of legal capacity to consent to sex. It was the remnant of a time when differential treatment on the basis of disability was accepted (Irish Law Reform Commission 2011, sec. 1.03). It is also a good example for analysis because the legislation has been recently reformed in an attempt to better protect the sexual agency of disabled people (Irish Law Reform Commission 2013, sec. 1.01–1.11 and 6.01–6.29).

Section 5 of the 1993 Irish Criminal Law (Sexual Offenses) Act made it illegal to engage in sexual activity with an individual who is 'mentally impaired.' The law stated:

> 5.—(1) A person who—
>
> (a) has or attempts to have sexual intercourse, or
>
> (b) commits or attempts to commit an act of buggery,
>
> with a person who is mentally impaired (other than a person to whom he is married or to whom he believes with reasonable cause he is married) shall be guilty of an offence…
>
> (5) In this section "mentally impaired" means suffering from a disorder of the mind, whether through mental handicap or mental illness, which is of such a nature or degree as to render a person incapable of living an independent life or of guarding against serious exploitation.

The language of this statue explicitly treated individuals with intellectual disability differently and restricted their right to legal capacity. This is not compliant with Article 12, which calls for the right to legal capacity on an equal basis. This status-based approach denies legal capacity to consent to sex on the basis of disability.

This law has had a negative effect on the sexual rights of people with intellectual disabilities in Ireland. The law made most sexual activity involving a person with a mental impairment illegal and punishable by criminal law (Finlay 2013). Some of the individuals most adversely affected by this law may have been individuals living in institutional settings as well as other restrictive settings, such as group homes. Individuals in these settings are often dependent upon the staff members to facilitate their sexual relationships (Carson and Docherty 2002). This is because the staff controls the residents' time and physical environment. In order to find a physical space for engaging in intimate encounters and to have the time to do so, the staff must permit it and organize it. The criminalization of sexual activity with a person with mental impairment in Ireland made it difficult for staff and service providers to permit or facilitate romantic relationships for people with intellectual disabilities living in these settings (O'Reilly 2012; Rodgers 2014). This created settings where individuals are living depersonalized lives in which they are not allowed to make one of the most basic and highly valued decisions: the choice to engage in intimate relationships.

[1]Portions of this section are drawn from (Arstein-Kerslake 2015).

Two documents were published by the Irish Law Reform Commission (ILRC)—providing an analysis of the issues, the history of the law in Ireland, and a comparative look at the laws of other jurisdictions. In 2011, the ILRC published the first document, a consultation paper on sexual offenses and capacity to consent. The consultation paper was intended to open up the discussion in Ireland and to call for submissions from civil society and other groups on the issue. The submissions were to inform the ILRC in their efforts to assemble a full report analysing the law on capacity to consent to sex in Ireland and providing recommendations for reform. The consultation paper professed to have a general approach of 'empowerment and protection.' It aimed to respect the right of people with intellectual disabilities to express their sexuality, but also strove to provide for the protection of people with intellectual disabilities from what it perceived to be a greater risk of sexual exploitation and abuse (Irish Law Reform Commission 2011, pp. 2–3).

The consultation paper barely touches on the issue of equality before the law (Irish Law Reform Commission 2011, sec. 1.86–1.88). Had it done so, it might have found a different solution to the problem of the status based test that existed. Instead, the paper advocates for the elimination of the status based test that exited and its replacement with a functional test of capacity to consent to sex (Irish Law Reform Commission 2011, sec. 2.42–2.44). For the reasons discussed above, such functional tests are frequently contrary to Article 12. The ILCR was on the right track to human rights compliant legislation, but it failed to sufficiently consider and protect the right to equality before the law by ensuring that any denial of legal capacity applies on an equal basis to people with and without intellectual disabilities.

In 2013, the ILRC published their second document on sexual offenses and capacity to consent. It is a report that includes a new analysis based partially on the submissions received in response to the 2011 consultation paper. It makes new recommendations accordingly. The report includes positive language about coordinating and strengthening sexual education across services. It also includes an understanding of the violation that the status based test infringed on the right of individuals with intellectual disabilities to sexual expression. However, similar to the consultation paper, it lacks a thorough analysis and understanding of the right to equal recognition before the law and the accompanying right to legal capacity to consent to sex on an equal basis with others. It again recommends a functional test of capacity and proclaims that it is in line with the CRPD (Irish Law Reform Commission 2013, sec. 6.06–6.11). It recommends that a relevant person's lack of capacity to consent may arise because of (a) a disability, (b) ill health or (c) any other reason. However, this places disabled people into a category of people that are presumed to potentially lack mental capacity to consent to sex and are, therefore, subjected to the functional test (Irish Law Reform Commission 2013, sec. 6.02).

The functional test, at first blush, seems to be a solution to the blatant discrimination in the status based denials. However, upon a closer look and a step back to look at the societal structures of oppression that are active in denying the rights of persons with intellectual disabilities, it seems that there is a need for something more in order for the right to equal recognition before the law to truly be respected. There is a need to remove presumptions that people with intellectual disabilities are inherently vulnerable (Hough 2012, p. 132). There is also a need to remove presumptions that people with intellectual disabilities cannot decide to enter into sexual relationships. People with intellectual disabilities are not a different category of people that must be regulated differently than people without intellectual disabilities. The reality is that all people are vulnerable at different points and need state intervention for protection in certain situations, but not a higher level of intervention based on a diagnosis of intellectual disability. Everyone can benefit from sexual education before entering into a sexual relationship or engaging in sexual acts. Every person has a right to be free to engage in sexual acts on an equal basis. If it is the state's role to infringe on an individual's right to legal capacity to consent to sex, then—in accordance with Article 12—individuals with and without intellectual disabilities must be respected as equal before the law. As such, people with intellectual disabilities can only be denied the right to legal capacity to consent to sex if it is done on a truly equal basis for all.

6.2.2.1 Learning from England and Wales' Functional Approach to Denials of Legal Capacity to Consent to Sex

England and Wales use functional approaches for the denial of legal capacity to consent to sex. They are found in two different laws: the Sexual Offenses Act (SOA) 2003, section 30–33; and the Mental Capacity Act (MCA) 2005 (Series 2015, p. 149). The applicability of the SOA is consistent with the goals of criminal law. It is to retrospectively convict those who have engaged in sexual acts with individuals who the SOA deems to lack the capacity to consent. The MCA exists in the civil law context. When applied to sexual consent, the MCA is generally used to make a determination of an individual's potential to consent to sex (Herring and Wall 2014, pp. 623–624). Both the SOA and the MCA have aspects that could be interpreted to run afoul of Article 12.

The SOA criminalizes 'sexual activity' and the 'incitation of sexual activity' with a person with a 'mental disorder impeding choice.' It criminalizes the activity if the individual with mental disorder is 'unable to refuse.' The law defines unable to refuse as:

> (2) B is unable to refuse if—
>
> (a) he lacks the capacity to choose whether to agree to engaging in the activity caused or incited (whether because he lacks sufficient understanding of the nature or reasonably foreseeable consequences of the activity, or for any other reason), or
>
> (b) he is unable to communicate such a choice to A.
>
> (England and Wales Sexual Offenses Act 2003, section 30)

Here, there is a differential treatment of disabled people. The law only applies to a person with a 'mental disorder.' If the individual in question has a mental disorder, then the sexual act may be criminalized if the individual does not pass the functional test, which requires an understanding of the nature or reasonably foreseeable consequences of the activity. This differential treatment, then, is the basis for denying the right to legal capacity to consent to sex. This contradicts the Article 12 requirement that disabled people have the right to legal capacity on an equal basis.

The MCA applies broadly to decision-making (MCA Sec. 1 & 27–29). In an ever-expanding series of cases, it has been applied to sexual decision-making of people with intellectual disabilities (Curtice et al. 2013; Herring and Wall 2014). The MCA has a functional test of decision-making that can be applied only to people with 'an impairment of, or a disturbance in the functioning of, the mind or brain' (MCA Sec. 2(1)). For this group of people, their legal capacity is denied if,

> he is unable—
>
> (a) to understand the information relevant to the decision,
>
> (b) to retain that information,
>
> (c) to use or weigh that information as part of the process of making the decision, or
>
> (d) to communicate his decision (whether by talking, using sign language or any other means).
>
> (England and Wales Mental Capacity Act, section 3(1))

Again, there is a differential treatment of disabled people. It is only people with 'an impairment of, or a disturbance in the functioning of, the mind or brain' who are held to this functional test of decision-making. If you are an individual who is not seen has having an impairment or disturbance, you never have to pass this functional test. It could be argued that the language in the MCA can be interpreted to include individuals without disabilities who have a 'disturbance in the functioning of' the mind or brain. However, the Act has been largely applied to disabled people and, therefore, provided significant opportunity to legally deny the decision-making of people with intellectual disabilities (Series 2013). Ironically, the MCA has been particularly praised as legislation that expands autonomy generally (Jones 2005; Herring and Wall 2014, p. 625). However, if the MCA is to provide an equal right to decision-making for disabled people, the language should more clearly apply beyond disabled people and a specific intention of this should be included in the legislation. In addition, the implementation of the legislation must be done on a disability neutral basis.

The SOA and the MCA have largely only denied legal capacity to consent to sex to people who have a mental disorder—the SOA explicitly only denies legal capacity to this group. Both were created with the intention of providing protection for people with mental disorder, including people with intellectual disabilities (Jones 2005, p. 423). This is a laudable and important goal. However, Article 12 demands that this be achieved through legislation that does not deny legal capacity on the basis of disability, which both of these pieces of legislation, arguably, do.

The functional approaches in the SOA and MCA may not be the best way to provide protection against abuse for people with intellectual disabilities. While it does criminalize abuse of an individual with intellectual disabilities that is unable to understand a sexual activity and therefore unable to agree to it, it also forces the courts to treat that individual differently than it would treat an individual that does not have the label of disability. It places the individual with an intellectual disability in a separate category of 'person' where the law does not apply to her in the same way as it does to others. It has the court examine whether it will recognize her as a decision-making agent. In order to respect the right to legal capacity of the individual on an equal basis with those without intellectual disabilities, the law must not create a separate category of law that only applies to people with intellectual disabilities and places them at a higher risk of having autonomy denied than it does for people without intellectual disabilities.

6.2.2.2 Case Law in England and Wales

The courts have had difficulty in applying the two different capacity to consent to sex laws in England and Wales (Herring and Wall 2014, p. 620). Prior to the MCA, the SOA was the primarily legislation relevant in instances where there was a question around the decision-making abilities of a person with mental impairment with regard to sex. However, since the enactment of the MCA, courts have also relied on it for such determinations (Series 2015).

In 2014, the Court of Appeals provided some clarity on the application of both laws. In *IM v LM*, the issue before the court was whether LM could consent to sexual relationships. The Court ultimately held that the court of first instance was correct in recognizing LM's legal capacity to consent to sex and in denying LM legal capacity to make decisions about where to live, how her care should be provided, or how much time she should spend with others. The court found that in a criminal case, a person-specific test of capacity to consent should be used. This would ask whether a person can consent to sex with a particular person at a particular point in time. Where the court is being asked to determine whether an individual could ever be capable of consenting to sex, an issue-specific test should be used. This would ask whether the individual has the general ability to give consent (Herring and Wall 2014, p. 623). Although not within the scope of this book, it is worth questioning whether the court is an appropriate venue for making such broad determinations about an individual's private life—particularly when they are being made outside the scope of the criminal law and prior to any potentially criminal act occurring. It is also worth noting that people with intellectual disability are at a much higher risk of court intervention of this kind.

IM v LM does not address the international human rights implications of functional tests of capacity to consent to sex. However, it does provide new insights into the state's obligations to protect against sexual abuse of people with intellectual disabilities. It articulates that it may not be practicable or desirable for the state to assess all potential instances of difficulties in capacity to consent to sex (Series 2014, p. 319). This suggests that there may be a limit on state intervention into the sexual lives of people with intellectual disabilities where that would constitute a significant invasion into private lives or a denial of the right to enjoy sexual autonomy and sexual relationships on an equal basis with others (Series 2014, p. 319).

6.2.2.3 Reconceptualizing Capacity to Consent to Sex to Conform to Human Rights Law

Capacity to consent to sex law reaches into the intensely private sphere of sexual intimacy. While it professes to provide protection against sexual abuse of people with intellectual disabilities, as described above, the removal of agency that it embodies may actually be causing more disempowerment and vulnerability than protection, as discussed in Chap. 5 (Raybeck 1988; Winick 1992). It has the power to further stigmatize by holding people with intellectual disabilities to a different standard of sexual decision-making than people without intellectual disabilities. Article 12 has shined a new light on this issue and provided an opportunity to re-evaluate how to end such unequal treatment.

The primary focus of this section is the reform of sexual offenses law, which retrospectively applies to certain acts. Other laws, such as the *England and Wales Mental Capacity Act (MCA),* which have the power to deem that an individual with intellectual disabilities is denied legal capacity to consent to sex into the future, raise distinct issues. Broadly, such laws seem overly invasive and may raise other human rights concerns, such as the right to privacy, but there is not room to discuss that fully in this book.

It is, of course, important to ensure that all parties in any sexual activity are agreeing to that sexual activity. That agreement cannot exist without the parties having the decision-making skills necessary to understand, to some extent, what the nature of the sexual activity is. However, there may be a way to discover the existence of this agreement without denying the agency of either party or creating a system where legal capacity to agree to sex can be denied on the basis of disability. Anderson has discussed a 'negotiation model'. Her model requires consultation and an exchange of views before the initiation of sexual penetration (Anderson 2004, p. 1421). This book proposes an agreement model that builds on Anderson's negotiation model. This agreement model requires two elements: agreement and understanding.

Agreement would need to be defined very carefully. Anderson's negotiation model requires that the parties have a verbal agreement unless there is an established context in which the parties would be able to assess non-verbal communication (Anderson 2004, p. 1407). However, non-traditional communication methods would also need to be taken into account, in order to be inclusive of people with intellectual disabilities who may use assistive communication devices or may have other unique forms of communication. The evidence for determining agreement would have to come from a holistic examination of the interaction between the two individuals.

An agreement requires evidence of some level of understanding (Leonhard 2012, p. 89). The specific level of understanding must realistically reflect sexual decision-making, which is generally quite basic (Ariely and Loewenstein 2006). This could be merely an understanding of the physiological elements of a particular sexual encounter. The element of understanding must be present in all sexual encounters, not only those of persons with intellectual disabilities. This disability neutral approach to sexual offenses law may provide a more robust definition of sexual offenses generally. It is compliant with Article 12 and distinct from 'capacity to consent' law because it is applicable in all sexual situations and holds everyone to the same level of understanding. It is also preferable because it examines the acts taken to secure agreement and understanding as opposed to merely attempting to identify decision-making deficits in an individual.

A possible concern is that people with intellectual disabilities are at higher risk of being sexually taken advantage of by carers or authority figures. The reality is that the lives of disabled people have been highly regulated and controlled by services for decades (Barnes and Mercer 2006, pp. 11–15, 16–28). While the movement is underway to place the power back in the hands of disabled people, much work remains to be done. People with intellectual disabilities, in particular, continue to face high rates of institutionalization and are subjected to services that create vulnerability through disempowerment (McCarthy and Thompson 1996; Hollomotz 2011). This occurs in settings such as group homes, but also in familial settings (Winik et al. 1985, pp. 414–419; Walmsley 1996, pp. 333–339; Jingree et al. 2006; Series 2015). As a result of this societal deficiency that is in desperate need of reformation, there is a need to ensure that people with intellectual disabilities who are dependent on others are not being taken advantage of sexually, or otherwise, by those wielding power over them.

There may also be a need for a system of ensuring that people who are in positions of power are not abusing their power as carers, assistants, teachers and others. Many jurisdictions already have provisions that criminalize such abuses of power; for example, the Kenyan Sexual Offenses Act creates an offense for the abuse of a position of trust that is disability neutral (The Kenyan Sexual Offenses Act 2006, Section 24(5)) and the Norwegian Penal Code creates an offense of abuse of power, however it is not disability neutral, as would be required for CRPD compliance (Norwegian General Civil Penal Code 2005, Chapter 19, Section 193). In order to respect the right to equal recognition before the law, these laws must be disability neutral and apply to specific relationships and specific circumstances as opposed to people with specific disabilities.

6.2.2.4 A Note on State Intervention in Abusive Relationships

There is debate about when the state should intervene in abusive familial and intimate relationships. When there is sufficient evidence of criminal offenses the law steps in. The issue is whether the state has an obligation to intervene before this point. There is not room in this book for a full discussion on when exactly state intervention should or should not be permitted. In most jurisdictions, people of majority age are permitted to make their own choices with regard to the relationships they choose to enter into, whether or not their partner is abusive. Because of a perception that people with intellectual disabilities need more protection than others, there may be a particular inclination to create mechanisms for early state intervention into relationships that involve a person with an intellectual disability. This book argues that greater intervention in the lives of persons with intellectual disabilities is inappropriate and may violate the right to equal recognition before the law and legal capacity on an equal basis.

Meaningful choice and decreased dependence can be helpful in providing individuals the tools to leave abusive relationships, as discussed in Chap. 5 (Wuest and Merritt-Gray 1999; Anderson and Saunders 2003). Meaningful choice for people with intellectual disabilities requires support for independent living options and opportunities for building social relationships outside services and family (Walter-Brice et al. 2012). This can decrease dependency on family and allow opportunities for increasing social experience and knowledge of intimate relationships. Education is also a key element of decreasing dependency (Hough 2012, p. 133). Sexual education as well as education on relationships is key for providing tools for understanding what an individual wants and doesn't want out of an intimate relationship (Priestley 2003, p. 98; Hollomotz 2011). This book therefore recommends increased resources for sexual education, programs supporting healthy relationships, as well as services that allow independence where desired by an individual with disabilities.

6.2.2.5 Current Sexual Offenses Law in Ireland and Impact on Women, Disabled Women, and Gender Minorities

It is important to note that the laws discussed above were recently reformed in Ireland. The *Criminal Law (Sexual Offenses) Act 2017* reformed the law so that sexual activity with a person with a "mental impairment" is no longer a criminal offense. Instead, the law addresses "sexual acts with protected person[s]." Protected persons, in the Act, are considered to be individuals with 'a mental or intellectual disability or a mental illness,' and who are considered to be incapable of:

> (a) understanding the nature, or the reasonably foreseeable consequences, of that act,
>
> (b) evaluating relevant information for the purposes of deciding whether or not to engage in that act, or
>
> (c) communicating his or her consent to that act by speech, sign language or otherwise... (Criminal Law (Sexual Offenses) Act 2017 [Ireland] 2020, vol. Number 2 of 2017, sec. 21(7 (a-c)))

This new law, unfortunately, looks very similar to the functional approach taken in England and Wales, discussed above in Sect. 6.2.2.1. For the many reasons discussed above, this is likely not complaint with Article 12 of the CRPD. However, it has removed the prior wholly status-based approach that criminalised all sexual activity with anyone with "mental impairment". While this reform is far from the human rights compliant possibilities that are discussed above, it has—at least—signalled to the community that it is not appropriate to completely remove a person's right to sexual agency (their legal capacity to consent to sex) simply on the basis of disability.

I cannot hold this reform up as good practice itself. However, I do think that there are many important lessons that can be learned from the reform process. There was an impressive coalition of civil society stakeholders, including disabled people and their representative organisations, that formed and fought consistently to have their voices heard (Arstein-Kerslake and Flynn 2016). Unfortunately, the government does not appear to have let those voices lead the reform efforts. The reason that I have chosen to include this example of reform in this chapter is not the actions taken on the part of the government or the reform that was enacted. Instead, I have highlighted this reform as an opportunity to understand the issues of capacity to consent to sex legislation that deny sexual autonomy to disabled people either on the basis of their disability or through a functional test of their ability to consent that will only apply to disabled people and is often not reflective of how almost anyone actually makes sexual decisions.

This is particularly important for disabled women, because they are often perceived as incapable of consenting to sex and are denied their right to legal capacity to consent to sex, as discussed in Sect. 4.3.2.2 in Chap. 4. Getting sexual offenses legislation right—making sure that it complies with Article 12 and secures the right to legal capacity on an equal basis for all—is essential for disabled women to be able to be respected as equal decision-makers in sexual relationships and to be empowered to understand abuse when it is occurring and to seek help, as discussed in Chap. 5.

6.2.3 Malta: Gender Recognition

As discussed in Chaps. 3, 4 and 5, the lack of laws that permit gender minorities to freely and legally change their gender to accurately reflect their gender identity can lead to a denial of the right to legal capacity in multiple ways. For example, it may prevent the individual from having legal identification that is often required for exercising legal capacity. As also discussed, the right to legal capacity is also denied by laws that permit a legal gender change, but require sterilisation, certification by medical professionals, divorce, or other intrusive practices. These requirements deny the individual the right to legal capacity to exercise choice in their legal gender as well as in the areas that they are required to change in order to have their legal gender changed. As discussed in Chap. 5, these laws lead not only to denials of the right to legal capacity but also to the potential for considerable damage to the individual's safety, self-image, and mental health, among others.

Scholars and activists alike have argued for gender recognition laws that allow individuals the ability to change their legal gender based on self-determination, rather than determinations by medical professionals or in other ways (Transgender Europe (TGEU) 2017, pp. 28–29; Cannoot 2019b). They also argue for the removal of barriers to legal gender recognition that intrude on other rights of the individual—

such as the right to reproductive choice and the right to marriage (Carastathis 2015; Transgender Europe (TGEU) 2017, pp. 32–36; Cannoot 2019a, b). The removal of such barriers and the development of gender recognition laws that allow gender change based on self-determination are also required for the realisation of the right to legal capacity for gender minorities.

To address the many human rights issues, such as those discussed above, a group of international human rights experts met in Yogyakarta, Indonesia in 2006 and developed a set of principles relating to sexual orientation and gender identity. Principle 3 is 'The right to Recognition Before the Law,' it states:

> Everyone has the right to recognition everywhere as a person before the law. Persons of diverse sexual orientations and gender identities shall enjoy legal capacity in all aspects of life. Each person's self-defined sexual orientation and gender identity is integral to their personality and is one of the most basic aspects of self-determination, dignity and freedom. No one shall be forced to undergo medical procedures, including sex reassignment surgery, sterilisation or hormonal therapy, as a requirement for legal recognition of their gender identity. No status, such as marriage or parenthood, may be invoked as such to prevent the legal recognition of a person's gender identity. No one shall be subjected to pressure to conceal, suppress or deny their sexual orientation or gender identity.

It also identifies that in order to implement this principle, States shall:

A. Ensure that all persons are accorded legal capacity in civil matters, without discrimination on the basis of sexual orientation or gender identity, and the opportunity to exercise that capacity, including equal rights to conclude contracts, and to administer, own, acquire (including through inheritance), manage, enjoy and dispose of property;
B. Take all necessary legislative, administrative and other measures to fully respect and legally recognise each person's self-defined gender identity;
C. Take all necessary legislative, administrative and other measures to ensure that procedures exist whereby all State-issued identity papers which indicate a person's gender/sex — including birth certificates, passports, electoral records and other documents — reflect the person's profound self-defined gender identity;
D. Ensure that such procedures are efficient, fair and non-discriminatory, and respect the dignity and privacy of the person concerned;
E. Ensure that changes to identity documents will be recognised in all contexts where the identification or disaggregation of persons by gender is required by law or policy;
F. Undertake targeted programmes to provide social support for all persons experiencing gender transitioning or reassignment.

Due to ongoing violations, as well as developments in international law, in 2017, there were an additional 10 principles developed. Within those new principles, number 31 outlines the right to legal recognition. It states:

> Everyone has the right to legal recognition without reference to, or requiring assignment or disclosure of, sex, gender, sexual orientation, gender identity, gender expression or sex characteristics. Everyone has the right to obtain identity documents, including birth certificates, regardless of sexual orientation, gender identity, gender expression or sex characteristics. Everyone has the right to change gendered information in such documents while gendered information is included in them.

There is also an accompanying list of obligations that states must undertake to realise the right. These principles and their accompanying states obligations mirror the requirement of Article 12 of the CRPD and reflect the rights issues raised throughout this book in relation to gender minorities.

Similarly, in Europe, Mr Thomas Hammarberg, Council of Europe Human Rights Commissioner, developed an Issue Paper in 2009, *Human Rights and Gender Identity*. In the paper, he supports the Yogyakarta Principles, and also develops his own 12 recommendations for the member states of the council of Europe in order for them to protect the human rights of gender minorities. These recommendations include:

> 3. Develop expeditious and transparent procedures for changing the name and sex of a transgender person on birth certificates, identity cards, passports, educational certificates and other similar documents;
>
> 4. Abolish sterilisation and other compulsory medical treatment as a necessary legal requirement to recognise a person's gender identity in laws regulating the process for name and sex change; . . .
>
> [and]
>
> 6. Remove any restrictions on the right of transgender persons to remain in an existing marriage following a recognised change of gender;. . .

I've included the text of these principles and recommendations here because they are one of very few specific guidelines that are available regarding how the law can be reformed to protect the human right to legal capacity of women, disabled women, and gender minorities. Although relatively little scholarship has focused on the right to legal capacity of gender minorities, these principles and recommendations provide very sophisticated direction for law and policy makers regarding how to protect the right (Cannoot 2019a, b).

In addition, to these principles and recommendations, we can turn to legislation in Malta to examine an example of legislation that embraces the principles and recommendations discussed above and, arguably, goes farther than any other legislation in securing the right to legal capacity of gender minorities. The 2015 Maltese *Gender Identity, Gender Expression and Sex Characteristics Act* secures the right of every citizen to have their gender identity legally recognised and to be able to gain the necessary documents that will reflect their gender identity. Psychological or medical proof is not needed. It criminalises unnecessary medical interventions or treatment on the sex characteristics of an individual without their consent. It bans sex-assignment surgery on intersex children—recognising that such surgery must only be done upon consent of the individual. It also allows the parents or guardians of intersex newborns to delay their registration of the gender marker on their birth certificate (Transgender Europe (TGEU) 2017, p. 28).

Although the Maltese legislation does not explicitly refer to the right to legal capacity of gender minorities, the provisions of the legislation secure the right to legal capacity in an unprecedented manner (Transgender Europe (TGEU) 2017, p. 28). They respect gender minorities as persons before the law and they seek to secure their recognition as persons before the law as well as to protect their ability to exercise legal agency in all areas of their lives on an equal basis with others.

6.3 Conclusion

These three examples are only a sample of some of the reform movements that are taking place across the world (Arbour 2013; Martinez-Pujalte 2019; Caycho 2020). There is increasing attention being given to the right to equal recognition before the law—and the right to legal capacity, as a subsidiary of the right to equal recognition before the law (Arstein-Kerslake 2017; Flynn et al. 2018; Cannoot 2019b). However, most reform efforts, activists, and scholars have not framed their struggle as one for the realisation of the right to equal recognition. I believe that there are several possible reasons for this—the right to equal recognition before the law may feel like an abstract concept that is not relevant on-the-ground in reform efforts. There is also a relative lack of information regarding the right—other than the United Nations (UN) Committee on the Rights of Persons with Disabilities, there has not been significant engagement with the right from UN bodies. It may also be the case, in some specific reform efforts, that framing them in the context of the right to equal recognition or the right to legal capacity is not perceived to be the best strategy for achieving the desired reform. However, I believe that there is significant power in framing an overall social justice agenda for equality for women, disabled women, and gender minorities using the right to equal recognition before the law.

The power of the right to equal recognition before the law is its simplicity. To most, it feels self-evident that all people have a right to equal recognition before the law. It is only when you begin examining all the various ways that recognition before the law is denied to particular groups that you begin to see that although it feels self-evident that everyone should have this right, it is pervasively denied to many. I believe that this simplicity and the accompanying paradox of the elusiveness of the right are what give it the potential to be so powerful.

6.4 Reform Recommendations

This book has examined the theoretical foundations of the denial of legal capacity to women, disabled women, and gender minorities—including an exploration of personhood and an analysis via critical feminist, disability, and queer theory. It has explored historical and modern denials of legal capacity to these groups. It has also discussed the vulnerability that is created by such denials. In this last chapter, I have discussed examples of reform towards the protection of the right to legal capacity for women, disabled women, and gender minorities. In this last section of the book, I would like to discuss recommendations for future reforms. In the first instance, some reforms can draw on the examples described in the beginning of this chapter. However, for general guidance regarding law reform to protect the rights to equal recognition before the law and legal capacity for women, disabled women, and gender minorities, I would like to recommend a four-part process for government and other actors seeking and orchestrating law, policy, and practice reform:

1. **Leadership from women, disabled women, and gender minorities** and/or their representative groups. In order for any reform efforts to accurately reflect the needs of women, disabled women, and gender minorities and for those reform efforts to be effective in protecting the rights of these groups, there must be leadership from individuals in these groups. This may come in many different forms, including: the hiring of members of these groups by government departments or ministries to lead reform efforts; the establishment of advisory bodies made up of representatives from these groups that will have the power to lead reform efforts; or reform efforts that originate and are driven by members of these group and their representative organisations; among others.
2. **An analysis of current law, policy, and practice** in light of the definition of the right to legal capacity as interpreted by the Committee on the Rights of Persons with Disabilities in their General Comment No.1—and as described in Chap. 1 of this book—and with a focus on where current law, policy, and practice may be denying or jeopardising the right to legal capacity for women, disabled women, and gender minorities.
3. A **consultation with representative groups** of women, disabled women, and gender minorities. Where there are no existing representative groups—the creation of such groups can be facilitated, or a larger consultation can be done seeking input from a statistically significant number of individuals from the various groups. The consultations should focus on the laws, policies, and practices that have been identified as potentially violating the right to equal recognition before the law and legal capacity for women, disabled women, and gender minorities. It should seek to discover whether there are areas that have not yet been identified but are areas in which women, disabled women, and gender minorities are experiencing barriers to or violations of these rights. Finally, the consultation should seek guidance regarding how best to ameliorate these barriers to or violations of these rights. Sufficient consultation will require an ongoing relationship of consultation—not a one-off event. Leadership from women, disabled women, and gender minorities (as outlined in point 1, above), combined with on-going consultation with these groups provides multiple entry points for the voices of these groups in the reform process. The multiple points of entry for these voices will facilitate a reform process that is reflective of needs on-the-ground and has the highest potential to create real and lasting change towards social justice and equality.
4. **Reform of relevant law, policy and practice** in line with the voices of women, disabled women, and gender minorities gathered in the consultations discussed above. This will require targeted reform efforts in multiple areas of the law. It is critical that these reform efforts are in line with the appropriate solutions to rights violations that women, disabled women, and gender minorities and their representative organisations identified in the consultations described above. In order to ensure that the reform effort remains consistent with those identified solutions, the consultations must continue during and after all reform efforts. Women, disabled women, and gender minorities must be meaningfully involved in the inevitable negotiations and compromises that occur during reform efforts. They

must also be involved in the assessment of the effectiveness of reform efforts once they are implemented.

The realisation of the right to legal capacity will not be enough to achieve full equality for women, disabled women, or gender minorities. The history of oppression, the ongoing marginalisation, and the existing structures that are maintaining the status quo of social hierarchies cannot be overcome by the realisation of the right to legal capacity alone. Equality is a long road—and it is yet to be seen whether it is actually an achievable goal. However, while history has shown us the perils of discrimination and marginalisation of minority groups—it has also show us the power of social justice movements to achieve change—including greater equality. The realisation of the right to legal capacity for all may provide one avenue for the continued struggle toward equality for all. It may provide increased power and privilege for marginalised groups, which may allow them to interact in socio-legal systems in such a way that equality with dominant groups—such as white, able-bodied, cisgender males—is much more achievable.

The realisation of the right to legal capacity won't overthrow the patriarchal legal system or undo centuries of oppression against women, disabled women, and gender minorities. However, it can be one tool in the struggle for social justice and equality for these groups—and, potentially, other marginalised groups.

References

Anderson, Deborah K., and Daniel G. Saunders. 2003. Leaving An Abusive Partner: An Empirical Review of Predictors, the Process of Leaving, and Psychological Well-Being. *Trauma, Violence, & Abuse* 4: 163–191. SAGE Publications. https://doi.org/10.1177/1524838002250769.

Anderson, Michelle J. 2004. Negotiating Sex. *Southern California Law Review* 78: 1401.

Arbour, Louise. 2013. Women's Rights: Does the Law Matter? presented at the International Conference: Women, Power and Politics – The Road to Sustainable Democracy, November 14.

Ariely, Dan, and George Loewenstein. 2006. The Heat of the Moment: The Effect of Sexual Arousal on Sexual Decision Making. *Journal of Behavioral Decision Making* 19: 87–98. https://doi.org/10.1002/bdm.501.

Arstein-Kerslake, Anna. 2015. Understanding Sex: The Right to Legal Capacity to Consent to Sex. *Disability & Society* 30: 1459–1473. https://doi.org/10.1080/09687599.2015.1116059.

———. 2017. *Restoring Voice to People with Cognitive Disabilities*. Cambridge University Press.

Arstein-Kerslake, Anna, and Eilionóir Flynn. 2016. Legislating Consent: Creating an Empowering Definition of Consent to Sex That Is Inclusive of People With Cognitive Disabilities. *Social & Legal Studies* 25: 225–248. https://doi.org/10.1177/0964663915599051.

Atkinson, Eleanor, Michael J. Bennett, Jan Dudley, Sonia Grover, Kim Matthews, Paddy Moore, Julie Quinlivan, and Tamara Walters. 2003. Consensus Statement: Menstrual and Contraceptive Management in Women with an Intellectual Disability. *Australian and New Zealand Journal of Obstetrics and Gynaecology* 43: 109–110. https://doi.org/10.1046/j.0004-8666.2003.00046.x.

Barnes, Colin, and Geof Mercer. 2006. Independent Futures. Creating User-led Disability Services in a Disabling Society. *Scandinavian Journal of Disability Research* 8: 317–320. Taylor & Francis. https://doi.org/10.1080/15017410600973523.

Cannoot, Pieter. 2019a. The Pathologisation of Trans* Persons in the ECtHR's Case Law on Legal Gender Recognition. *Netherlands Quarterly of Human Rights* 37: 14–35. https://doi.org/10.1177/0924051918820984.

———. 2019b. '#WontBeErased': The Effects of (De)pathologisation and (De)medicalisation on the Legal Capacity of Trans* Persons. *International Journal of Law and Psychiatry* 66: 101478. https://doi.org/10.1016/j.ijlp.2019.101478.

Carastathis, Anna. 2015. Compulsory Sterilisation of Transgender People as Gendered Violence. In *(In)Fertile Citizens: Anthropological and Legal Challenges of Assisted Reproduction Technologies*, ed. Venetia Kantsa, Giulia Zanini, and Lina Papadopoulou. (In)FERCIT.

Carson, Iain, and Daniel Docherty. 2002. Friendships, Relationships, and Issues of Sexuality. In *Learning Disability – A Social Approach*, ed. David Race. Routledge.

Caycho, Renato Antonio Constantino. 2020. The Flag of Imagination: Peru's New Reform on Legal Capacity for Persons with Intellectual and Psychosocial Disabilities and the Need for New Understandings in Private Law. *The Age of Human Rights Journal*: 155–180. https://doi.org/10.17561/tahrj.v14.5482.

Criminal Law (Sexual Offenses) Act 2017 [Ireland]. 2020. Vol. Number 2 of 2017. Office of the Attorney General. http://www.irishstatutebook.ie/eli/2017/act/2/section/21/enacted/en/html. Accessed September 15.

Curtice, Martin, Jonathan Mayo, and Juli Crocombe. 2013. Consent and Sex in Vulnerable Adults: A Review of Case Law. *British Journal of Learning Disabilities* 41: 280–287. https://doi.org/10.1111/j.1468-3156.2012.00753.x.

Finlay, Fergus. 2013. Consensual Sex Between Adults is Illegal If They Have an Intellectual Disability. *Irish Examiner*, November 12, sec. IE-Opinion/COLUMNISTS.

Flynn, Eilionoir, Anna Arstein-Kerslake, Clíona de Bhailís, and Maria Laura Serra. 2018. *Global Perspectives on Legal Capacity Reform: Our Voices, Our Stories*. Routledge.

Glen, Kristin Booth. 2019. Not Just Guardianship: Uncovering the Invisible Taxonomy of Laws, Regulations and Decisions That Limit or Deny the Right of Legal Capacity for Persons with Intellectual and Developmental Disabilities Selected Works regarding Government Law. *Albany Government Law Review* 13: 25–93.

Grover, Sonia R. 2002. Menstrual and Contraceptive Management in Women with an Intellectual Disability. *Medical Journal of Australia* 176: 108–110. https://doi.org/10.5694/j.1326-5377.2002.tb04315.x.

Herring, Jonathan, and Jesse Wall. 2014. Capacity to Consent to Sex. *Medical Law Review* 22: 620–630. Oxford Academic. https://doi.org/10.1093/medlaw/fwu019.

Hollomotz, Andrea. 2011. *Learning Difficulties and Sexual Vulnerability: A Social Approach*. Jessica Kingsley Publishers.

Hough, Rebecca Emily. 2012. Adult Protection and 'Intimate Citizenship' for People with Learning Difficulties: Empowering and Protecting in Light of the No Secrets Review. *Disability & Society* 27: 131–144. https://doi.org/10.1080/09687599.2012.631802.

Irish Law Reform Commission. 2011. *Consultation Paper on Sexual offences and capacity to consent*. Law Reform Commission.

———. 2013. *Report on Sexual Offences and Capacity to Consent*.

Jingree, T., W.M.L. Finlay, and C. Antaki. 2006. Empowering Words, Disempowering Actions: An Analysis of Interactions Between Staff Members and People with Learning Disabilities in Residents' Meetings. *Journal of Intellectual Disability Research* 50: 212–226. https://doi.org/10.1111/j.1365-2788.2005.00771.x.

Jones, Rowena. 2005. Review of the Mental Capacity Act 2005. *Psychiatric Bulletin* 29: 423–427. Cambridge University Press. https://doi.org/10.1192/pb.29.11.423.

Leonhard, Chunlin. 2012. The Unbearable Lightness of Consent in Contract Law. *Case Western Reserve Law Review* 63: 57.

Lin, Lan-Ping, Jin-Ding Lin, Cordia M. Chu, and Li-Mei Chen. 2011. Caregiver Attitudes to Gynaecological Health of Women with Intellectual Disability. *Journal of Intellectual & Developmental Disability* 36: 149–155. https://doi.org/10.3109/13668250.2011.599316.

Martinez-Pujalte, Antonio. 2019. Legal Capacity and Supported Decision-Making: Lessons from Some Recent Legal Reforms. *Laws* 8: 4. https://doi.org/10.3390/laws8010004.

McCarthy, Michelle, and David Thompson. 1996. Sexual Abuse by Design: An Examination of the Issues in Learning Disability Services. *Disability & Society* 11. 205–218. Routledge. https://doi.org/10.1080/09687599650023236.

O'Reilly, Christian. 2012. *Sanctuary*. Play. Galway Arts Festival.

Priestley, Mark. 2003. *Disability: A Life Course Approach*. Wiley.

Prokhovnik, Raia. 2012. *Rational Woman: A Feminist Critique of Dichotomy*. Routledge. https://doi.org/10.4324/9780203024485.

Raybeck, Douglas. 1988. Anthropology and Labeling Theory: A Constructive Critique. *Ethos* 16: 371–397. JSTOR. [American Anthropological Association, Wiley].

Rodgers, Anna. 2014. *Somebody to Love*. Documentary. RTE.

Rosenberg, Joseph A. 2009. Poverty, Guardianship, and the Vulnerable Elderly: Human Narrative and Statistical Patterns in a Snapshot of Adult Guardianship Cases in New York City. *Georgetown Journal on Poverty Law & Policy* 16: 315–344.

Series, Lucy. 2013. *The Mental Capacity Act 2005 and the Institutional Domination of People with Learning Disabilities*. University of Exeter.

———. 2014. Sex, capacity and forensic cotton wool: IM v LM [2014] EWCA Civ 37. *Journal of Social Welfare and Family Law*: 36:317–319. Routledge. https://doi.org/10.1080/09649069.2014.933594.

———. 2015. Mental Capacity and the Control of Sexuality of People with Intellectual Disabilities in England and Wales. In *Disability Research Today: International Perspectives*, ed. Tom Shakespeare. Routledge.

Tavris, Carol. 1993. The Mismeasure of Woman. *Feminism & Psychology* 3: 149–168. https://doi.org/10.1177/0959353593032002.

Transgender Europe (TGEU). 2017. *Human Rights & Gender Identity: Best Practice Catalogue*.

Victoria Office of the Public Advocate. 2017. *Annual Report 2016-2017*.

Walmsley, Jan. 1996. Doing What Mum Wants Me To Do: Looking at Family Relationships from the Point of View of People with Intellectual Disabilities. *Journal of Applied Research in Intellectual Disabilities* 9: 324–341. https://doi.org/10.1111/j.1468-3148.1996.tb00118.x.

Walter-Brice, Alison, Rachel Cox, Helena Priest, and Fiona Thompson. 2012. What do Women with Learning Disabilities Say About Their Experiences of Domestic Abuse Within the Context of Their Intimate Partner Relationships? *Disability & Society* 27: 503–517. Routledge. https://doi.org/10.1080/09687599.2012.659460.

Wingfield, M., D.L. Healy, and A. Nicholson. 1994. Gynaecological Care for Women with Intellectual Disability. *The Medical Journal of Australia* 160: 536–538.

Winick, Bruce J. 1992. On Autonomy: Legal and Psychological Perspectives Symposium - Integrating Legal and Psychological Perspectives. *Villanova Law Review* 37: 1705–1778.

Winik, Lesley, Andrea G. Zetlin, and Sandra Z. Kaufman. 1985. Adult Mildly Retarded Persons and Their Parents: The Relationship Between Involvement and Adjustment. *Applied Research in Mental Retardation* 6: 409–419. https://doi.org/10.1016/0270-3092(85)90017-7.

Wuest, Judith, and Marilyn Merritt-Gray. 1999. Not Going Back: Sustaining the Separation in the Process of Leaving Abusive Relationships. *Violence Against Women* 5: 110–133. SAGE Publications Inc. https://doi.org/10.1177/1077801299005002002.